Movie-Made Jews

Movie-Made Jews

• •

An American Tradition

HELENE MEYERS

Rutgers University Press

New Brunswick, Camden, and Newark, New Jersey, and London

Library of Congress Cataloging-in-Publication Data

Names: Meyers, Helene, author.
Title: Movie-made Jews : an American tradition / Helene Meyers.
Description: New Brunswick : Rutgers University Press, c2021. | Includes bibliographical
references and index.
Identifiers: LCCN 2020050960 | ISBN 9781978821880 (paperback) |
ISBN 9781978821897 (hardcover) | ISBN 9781978821903 (epub) |
ISBN 9781978821910 (mobi) | ISBN 9781978821927 (pdf)
Subjects: LCSH: Jews in the motion picture industry. | Jews in motion pictures. |
Motion pictures—United States—History—20th century. | Motion pictures—
United States—History—21st century. | Jews—United States—Identity.
Classification: LCC PN1995.9.J46 M49 2021 | DDC 791.43/6529924—dc23
LC record available at https://lccn.loc.gov/2020050960

A British Cataloging-in-Publication record for this book is available from the British Library.

♾ The paper used in this publication meets the requirements of the American National
Standard for Information Sciences—Permanence of Paper for Printed Library Materials,
ANSI Z39.48-1992.

www.rutgersuniversitypress.org

Manufactured in the United States of America

To Klal Yisrael, in all its diversity
and
to those who know that it's never only a movie

Contents

Movie-Made Jews

1

Introduction

• •

Making Jews Onscreen
and Off

In *The Hebrew Hammer* (2003), the threat to Jewish children, Hanukkah, and Jewish continuity arrives in the form of a movie: bootleg versions of *It's a Wonderful Life* are peddled on the streets by an evil Tiny Tim and an "antisemitic psycho Santa." Responding as expected to the "most addictive, Jewish pride–weakening substance known to man," Jewishly observant youth are suddenly seized with the need to decorate Christmas trees, to sing "Silent Night, Holy Night" in the streets, and to robotically repeat "Mommy says, every time you hear a bell ringing, an angel gets its wings." The Hebrew Hammer (played by Adam Goldberg), aka Mordechai Jefferson Carver, "a certified, circumcised dick," recognizes that "people can get hurt watching this shit." In order to deal with this epidemic of assimilation caused by cinematic crack, he asks the Jewish Defense League to contact the Jewish Worldwide Media Conspiracy and have them "mass-produce every Hollywood movie ever made featuring a positive Jewish protagonist as its lead." Chief Bloomenbergensteinenthal understands this request to mean "copies of *Yentl* and *Fiddler on the Roof* and Chaim Potok's *The Chosen*," the same trinity of films that Mordechai keeps in the trunk of his jazzy Jewmobile.

The Hebrew Hammer is a profoundly crude but also hilariously smart parody and Jewish revision of the blaxploitation films that both traffic in stereotypes and resist dominant white culture's ways of seeing. The scene just

1

FIG. 1.1 The usual suspects in *The Hebrew Hammer* (2003)

described, occurring midway through the film, implicitly tells a story about American Jewish movies that *Movie-Made Jews* confirms, complicates, and challenges. While it's a truism that Jews make movies, this book brings into focus the diverse ways movies make Jews.

At its most basic, this scene suggests that we are what we watch and that Jews can be made, unmade, and remade by and through movies. *Movie-Made Jews* focuses on a rich, usable American Jewish cinematic tradition that extends well beyond *Fiddler*, *Yentl*, and *The Chosen* and that is too often overlooked. It includes feature fiction films and documentaries primarily from the 1970s to the present that, taken together, represent a pluralistic Jewish gaze. Obviously, this cinematic construction work happens onscreen, but it also happens behind the scenes and in the conversations that these films incite. As Laura Mulvey points out in "Visual Pleasure and Narrative Cinema," an essay that centered the idea of the gaze in film studies generally and in feminist film theory in particular, the power and politics of looking resides not only between characters but also behind the camera and in the audience.[1] That's why *Movie-Made Jews* pays close attention to the production and reception histories of these diverse films as it charts continuity and change within the American Jewish movie scene.

Those schooled in film studies will recognize that my title recalls that of Robert Sklar's classic text *Movie-Made America* and that I am particularizing his overarching argument that "the content and control" of movies "helps to shape the character and direction of American culture as a whole."[2] Sklar usefully reminds us that "we need to be wary of postulating a direct correspondence between society and cinema or condemning its absence."[3] Although no one should assume that there's a simple one-to-one correspondence between what appears onscreen and what happens offscreen, most critics agree that movies matter because representation matters. Put another way, what we watch helps to form our images of ourselves, others, and the world. But that doesn't mean that what we watch inevitably determines who we are or how we see the world or what kind of Jew we become.

To be sure, being moved by a film can result in life imitating art. After watching *Hineini: Coming Out in a Jewish High School* (2005), a documentary about a religiously pluralistic school challenged by a student who demanded to be seen as a queer Jew, one teacher responded to a student who came out to her with a hearty "Mazel tov."[4] What appeared onscreen served as the catalyst for that teacher's congratulatory response. Some Jews worried that *Gentleman's Agreement*, a 1947 film critical of the not so genteel forms of antisemitism rampant in the United States even as Americans fought Nazism abroad, would increase intolerance toward Jews. However, studies showed that it actually diminished anti-Jewish prejudice (though, as I argue in chapter 2, "Looking at Antisemites and Jews," it did so by representing Jews in name only, in sharp contrast to *School Ties* [1992], what some consider a 1990s version of *Gentleman's Agreement*).[5]

Sometimes the impact of a movie occurs through talking back to it, that is, not accepting or not wholly accepting the worldview presented onscreen. Talking back in and to movies also makes Jews. For example, as a child, Letty Cottin Pogrebin, a prominent Jewish feminist, "went to the movies almost every Saturday after shul." After experiencing a "religion rebellion," she found her way back to Jewishness through the movies.[6] Such cinematically induced teshuvah (affirmed by and in *The Hebrew Hammer*) led her to "the open field of cultural Judaism where [she] found something of an alternative identity."[7] However, the stereotypical representations of Jewish women that she found at the movies "helped [her] to define the Jewish women [she] did *not* want to be."[8] According to her own account, the movies helped Pogrebin remake herself as a Jewish feminist, though not in the image of many Jewish women onscreen. Ultimately, she did find cinematic resources in the Jewish Big Mouth type, aptly represented by Katie Morosky in *The Way We Were* (1973), a film I discuss in chapter 4, "Focusing on Assimilation and Its Discontents." As Pogrebin's discussion of her deep relationship with film makes clear, a movie and its politics need not be pure or perfect to be usable in the making of Jews.

The making of Jews through film also happens through watching and talking with other Jews. In an essay titled "I Found It at the Movies," Ilan Stavans movingly writes about watching films with his father, an activity that "defined" his identity as well as his sense of a diverse diaspora Jewry.[9] Such cinematic Jewish identity formation continues with his own son as they "watch movies frequently, especially Jewish ones." Stavans recounts a viewing of Paul Mazursky's *Enemies, A Love Story* (1989), a film discussed in chapter 3: "The discussion that ensued was invigorating. Our opinions were different, as befits our generation gap, I suppose. But I see myself as a replica of my father, allowing the moving image to educate him subtly and decisively. . . . And if my father is around to watch movies with us, sitting side by side, the experience is transcendental—and unreservedly Jewish."[10] Such "invigorating" discussions across generations remind us that it is important to chart cinematic traditions and to make Jewish film new, that is, to embrace the continued relevance of films at different historical moments.

Jewhooing, defined by David Kaufman as "the naming and claiming of famous 'members of the tribe'—and the consequent projection of group identity onto them," is a particular form of reception that makes Jews.[11] According to Kaufman, "The main motive of Jewhooing today remains the construction of Jewish identity and the related countering of assimilation—an unconscious attempt to reverse the very processes of social integration and de-Judaization that touch most every Jew in the modern world."[12] At first glance and based on what appears onscreen, *RBG* (2018) and *Milk* (2008) might not be considered significant Jewish movies. However, the communal Jewhooing of Ruth Bader Ginsburg by the Jewish press and Jewish film festivals—not to mention by Julie Cohen, codirector of *RBG*—indicates that this film is a Jewish experience for many viewers and a Jewish feminist event for some. Similarly, *Milk* became an occasion for specifically queer Jewhooing—what I term "Jewqhooing"—a process that affirms and simultaneously constructs queer Jewishness. In these pages, *RBG* and *Milk* are limit cases for defining a Jewish movie and for including reception to construct a usable American Jewish film tradition.

To some, the notion of a tradition of Jewish film in general and American Jewish film in particular may seem nonsensical. Even as *The Hebrew Hammer* intimates that we are what we watch, it also suggests that very few films productively make Jews (notwithstanding conspiracy theories about Jews having ironclad control over Hollywood). To be sure, this supposed lack of an American Jewish tradition owes much to early Hollywood history. In the classic study *An Empire of Their Own: How the Jews Invented Hollywood*, Neal Gabler compellingly charts the tradition of Jews making movies.[13] As Deborah Kaufman puts it, Gabler "completely outed Jews in Hollywood."[14] However, even as most of the studio heads were Jewish, they tended toward assimilationism in both life and art. According to this story, even that rare classic film with explicit Jewish content, *The Jazz Singer* (1927), initiated the transition not only from silent to sound film but also from the Old World to the New: a stereotypical stiff-necked patriarchal cantor falls and his son rises to whiteness by singing "Mammy" in blackface and by courting not only his Yiddishe mama but also his Gentile love object, Mary Dale.[15] The numerous Jewish actors who Americanized their names (i.e., made them less Jewish-sounding) provide more evidence for this assimilation narrative, as do the studio heads who, out of fear or greed, soft-pedaled a critique of Nazism in the years preceding World War II.

This assimilation narrative has been tempered in recent years by scholars such as Henry Bial, who argues that Jewishness was not erased but rather was coded, discernible to Jewishly literate spectators.[16] Whether the Jewish studio heads were complicit with Nazism or were engaged in largely behind-the-scenes efforts to aid European Jewish communities, to expose and immobilize fascists at home, and to use their cultural and economic capital to mobilize a Jewishly interested form of American patriotism is also the subject of renewed debate.[17] And although scholars such as Bial and Nathan Abrams disagree about whether the normalization of Jewishness in film should be keyed to the 1960s or the 1990s, they view cinematic Jews as coming out of the ethnoreligious closet and becoming sexy or just everyday folk, with both positive and negative characteristics.[18] According to Abrams, in the post-1990 period, the film industry has become "more willing to put Jews onscreen regardless of plot imperative and without feeling the need to either explain or explain away their presence/absence"; this has led to "an unselfconscious, normalised, 'casual' or 'matter of fact' Jewishness that has become ordinary or quotidien." For Abrams, the "in-joke" is also part of normalization; "the New Jews neither know nor care if their Gentile audiences can share the laugh with them."[19] This is a progressive narrative of American Jewish film history—first the Jews hid, though perhaps they could be plainly seen by those in the know, but then we came out and diversely reproduced ourselves with Jew sightings for all to see—or not.

Although such a progressive narrative of American Jewish film history is compelling and appealing, it nonetheless has some serious limitations. If we accept Abrams's premise that 1990 starts the age of the New Jew, we risk losing renewed Jewish conversations around such New Hollywood films as Paul Mazursky's *Next Stop, Greenwich Village* (1976), Sydney Pollack's *The Way We Were* (1973), and Sidney Lumet's *The Pawnbroker* (1964), not to mention such late 1980s gems as Mazursky's *Enemies, A Love Story*, Joan Micklin Silver's *Crossing Delancey* (1988) and Woody Allen's *Crimes and Misdemeanors* (1989). This progressive narrative also emphasizes what's onscreen and potentially leaves behind Jewish stories of film production and reception, which I argue remain central to an American Jewish cinematic history of continuity and change. We should not underestimate the extent to which the Jewishness of films such as *Milk* and *RBG* resides in reception by a select audience. And we should not gloss over another, troubling reception issue—that what I and many others would regard as explicitly and unreservedly Jewish films (e.g., *Crossing Delancey* and *Kissing Jessica Stein* [2001]), are often not seen as such by mainstream reviewers. Such reviewers miss not only sly in-jokes but also an onscreen circumcision or a Shabbat dinner. Sometimes, though certainly not always, the "unselfconscious, normalised, 'casual' or 'matter of fact' Jewishness" that Abrams heralds becomes obscured into uncomplicated and privileged whiteness. This is true of directors as well as cinematic characters: Zach Braff was lambasted for his Kickstarter campaign to help make his assertively Jewish film *Wish I Was Here* (2014) because he was read as a privileged white Hollywood insider who had no right to such grassroots financing. The formidable challenge to making explicitly Jewish films is a production constant veiled by the argument that Jewishness has become normalized in contemporary American cinema.

Perhaps most important, the normalization thesis belies the fact that the American Jewish cinematic tradition is still perceived as impoverished. In March 2019, a Twitter conversation about Jewish film was initiated with a request for "favorite non-WWII Jewish films." The responses were instructive. *Fiddler on the Roof, Yentl*, and *The Chosen* were well represented, as was *The Hebrew Hammer*. Happily, several of the films included in this book—for example, *School Ties, The Pawnbroker, Crossing Delancey, Crimes and Misdemeanors, A Serious Man* (2009), *Avalon* (1990), *Kissing Jessica Stein*—were listed. But it strikes me as significant that one respondent wrote in one tweet, "I can think of Jewish actors, but movies? Oy, I'm a huge film fan, but . . . ," and in another freely admitted, "Not on top of my game as a film-loving Jew. Not a lot of really good films about Jews, ya know? Yeah, you know."

The normalization thesis, which has the potential to see the representation of Jews onscreen as the only cultural work that matters, might inadvertently lead to this sense that there are "not a lot of really good films about Jews." We create lists and surveys that provide evidence that Jews are everywhere on a screen near you, but they nevertheless remain insubstantial because we move from one example to another without paying enough attention to the cultural work that particular forms of representation do onscreen and off. Vincent Brook suggests that "the *qualitative* level of this cultural accretion, especially as it relates to Jewish identity, is less assured—and less reassuring." Although somewhat less skeptical than Brook, Daniel Itzkovitz acknowledges a cinematic trend of "aggrandizing but flattening out of Jewishness."[20] And, too often, the critical establishment, which rightly bristles at the idea that Jewish films are only made to provide role models, performs a simple reversal and privileges films that present an ironic slice of Jewish life. Normalization becomes equivalent to satire, while films that wrestle with spiritual questions or cultural history are too often dismissed as "nostalgic," "sentimental," or "shmaltzy." Commentary on *Keeping Up with the Steins* (2006) exemplifies this trend, with several critics relishing the satirical first part of the film but then bemoaning the supposedly premature retraction of its "fangs."

In making an argument for a "cinema of engagement," Sarah Kozloff usefully challenges irony's "reputation as the culturally advanced mode, the mode of the intellectuals, while earnestness is for the Victorians and the booboisie."[21] She encourages us to think anew about the importance of narrative, identification, and emotional connection in relation to the cultural and political work of movies. Notably, in the director's commentary on *Wish I Was Here*, Zach Braff apologizes for the sentimentality of a scene that involves explaining death and burial to a child. We might usefully ask why sentimentality—feeling or excessive feeling—requires a directorial apology while excessive irony or violence does not. *Movie-Made Jews* unashamedly promotes a cinema of Jewish engagement, with a refusal to dismiss films that include but also move beyond Jewish funny business. Some of the films that have been panned or ignored, especially by the mainstream press, I regard as taking Jewish experience seriously; often, they engage in self-critique, signaling that they tap into an established tradition of Jews arguing with and among themselves. Of course, reception histories become emblematic of that tradition as well. The cinema of Jewish engagement featured in *Movie-Made Jews* promotes identification with diverse Jewish positions. As such, it performs a different type of normalizing for Jews.

Another, related critical impediment to seeing a usable tradition of American Jewish cinema is the tendency to define Jewish films too narrowly, often counting only those films that explicitly and primarily represent Judaism. Barry Levinson, director of *Avalon* and *Liberty Heights* (1999), nails the Jewish double bind so often encountered in the making and reception of Jewish films. "With a movie with Jews . . . , you are almost stuck between a rock and a hard place. . . . They're going to be too Jewish, not Jewish enough, it's almost a no-win situation. . . . I remember someone said, 'We didn't know they were Jewish in *Avalon*,' and I said, 'Well, do they have to wear yarmulkes in all the scenes? How many religious artifacts have to be in the film?'"[22] Warren Rosenberg's commentary on Levinson's *Liberty Heights*, a movie that begins and ends with Rosh Hashanah services filmed in historic Baltimore synagogues and that represents young men negotiating their Jewishness in a climate of not so genteel antisemitism, illustrates this trend: according to Rosenberg, *Liberty Heights* contains "as little actual Jewish content as any of the previous Levinson films" and is "clearly uninformed by the practice or study of Judaism."[23] Such critical opinions, which seem inclined to embrace and reproduce a lachrymose view of American Jewish cinematic history, beg the question of what constitutes a Jewish film—and, by extension, what sort of Jews are seen and recognized as Jews.

Movie-Made Jews is, quite intentionally, a work of cinematic and religious pluralism. By highlighting a diverse cinematic tradition that makes Jews in a variety of ways, I strive to not only accurately represent the story of American Jewish cinema but also view movies as a resource for healing a community riven by religious and political fault lines. In these pages, those who might be identified as "just Jews" reside alongside those who are traditionally—and sometimes untraditionally—observant; tensions as well as reconciliation between warring Jewish tribes are part of the tradition limned here. Ultimately, I consider a film such as *Keeping Up with the Steins*, a narrative grounded in resisting the commercialization and cheapening of the Jewish coming-of-age ritual, the bar mitzvah, or a film such as *Arranged* (2007), an Orthodox women's marriage plot with a twist, as no more but also no less assertively Jewish than Woody Allen's *Whatever Works*. That 2009 Allen film, which proffers secular Jewish imaginings as being a light unto a divided nation and a form of resistance to the likes of Donald Trump and his minions, seems startlingly relevant today.

As I write this in 2020, the Jewish question of Woody Allen (smartly represented in John Turturro's *Fading Gigolo* [2013]) seems considerably less urgent to address than the "Me Too" question. Allen's sexual ethics (or lack thereof) has been revealed not only by his predilection for cinematic narratives of older men lusting after younger women but also by his marriage to Soon-Yi Previn, adopted daughter of his ex-wife Mia Farrow, and by the widely publicized charges of sexual assault by Dylan Farrow, Allen's adopted daughter. In her open letter to the *New York Times*, Dylan Farrow writes:

> Woody Allen is a living testament to the way our society fails the survivors of sexual assault and abuse. So imagine your seven-year-old daughter being led into an attic by Woody Allen. Imagine she spends a lifetime stricken with nausea at the mention of his name. Imagine a world that celebrates her tormenter. Are you imagining that? Now, what's your favorite Woody Allen movie?[24]

I quote this letter directly because I don't want to gloss over the seriousness of the decision to include Woody Allen in this study. I argue here that not only films themselves but also the reception of them are significant, and scholarship is part of a film's and a director's reception. By including Allen in the usable cinematic tradition I am charting here, I am doing my part to canonize and even laud his work; as a Jewish feminist, I owe my readers a clear explanation for such inclusion.

Of course, I am hardly the first to wrestle with the Woody question. In the Twitter thread on Jewish movies cited earlier, one respondent wrote, "I would have said every Woody Allen movie, but I don't think I'm allowed to say that anymore." One response was a broken-heart emoticon and a two-word reply: "I relate." And in the pages of the *Forward*, Ezra Glinter writes:

> For those of us who have written about Allen or praised him or invested ourselves in his work, it's hard not to feel tainted. And this isn't just a problem

for a writer—it's a problem for everyone who ever has, or ever will, watch and love a Woody Allen movie. It's a problem for Jews, who have made Allen an icon of American Jewish culture. It's a problem, as Farrow makes clear, for the entertainment industry that supports and honors Allen. Right now Woody Allen is a problem for us all. And I don't know what the solution to that problem is.[25]

I think that the only intellectually honest solution to this problem is the one that Glinter performs but does not necessarily embrace or feel comfortable with—acknowledge it rather than disallow conversation about or serious engagement with the works of a major cinematic figure who has influenced countless other cinematic figures, including many crucial to this study. I could jettison *Crimes and Misdemeanors* and weaken but not eviscerate a mini-tradition of films that indirectly and responsibly wrestles with the legacy of the Holocaust in an American context. I could jettison *Whatever Works* and weaken but not eviscerate a mini-tradition of films that not only are assertively Jewish but also have the chutzpah to turn a Jewish gaze on mainstream Gentile culture. Yet, even if I jettison those works, what do I do with *Fading Gigolo*, a film that sensitively depicts a Hasidic woman's insistence on determining her own religious and sexual agency, directed by John Turturro, but in which Allen appears and served as a script consultant? If I'm not allowed to talk about Woody Allen, then how do I talk about *Kissing Jessica Stein*, whose protagonist was conceived as a brainy neurotic or Woody in a woman's body?[26] Am I allowed to talk about Allen-influenced filmmakers, one of whom is Zach Braff, noted for his menschy sets? Emily Nussbaum puts it well as she "wrestle[s] with [her] own history with the work of terrible men," Woody Allen included: "A critic can't be clean; you can't scrub history off your skin."[27] Ultimately, I believe that a usable tradition can include meaningful aesthetic and cultural resources that are the products of deeply flawed, even deplorable, human beings. As a viewer and a critic, as a Jew and a feminist, I refuse to throw the baby out with the bathwater, but I also refuse to whitewash history, cinematic or otherwise.

My decision to put documentaries into dialogue with fiction films here also merits some explanation. Although documentaries are often assumed to represent "reality," and fiction films are viewed as, well, fiction, we need to recognize the potential "truth" of fiction film as well as the aesthetics and constructedness of documentaries.

Michael Renov, one of the foremost scholars of documentary art, argues that documentary "employs many of the methods and devices of its fictional counterpart," including such "fictive ingredients" as "character ... emerging through recourse to ideal and imagined categories of hero or genius, the use of poetic language, narration, or musical accompaniment to heighten emotional impact or the creation of suspense via the agency of embedded narratives (e.g., tales told by interview subjects) or various dramatic arcs (here, the 'crisis structure' comes to mind). Many more examples could be offered: the use of high or low camera angles..., close-ups which trade emotional resonance for spatial integrity... the use of editing to make time contract, expand, or become rhythmic."[28] A documentary director's choices can help to enhance or diminish Jewishness. For example, in Rob Epstein's Oscar-winning documentary *The Times of Harvey Milk* (1984), the choice of the queer Jewish writer and actor Harvey Fierstein as narrator contributes to the Jewish representation of Milk, an out martyred politician.

Films explicitly based on historical events or figures most obviously point to the porous boundaries between the cultural work of fiction film and that of documentary (I realize that talking about porous boundaries between historical and fictional texts is a dangerous game in this era of fake news; however, I also think that intelligent people can and must learn to distinguish between responsible, historically informed narratives and pernicious conspiracy theories, lest the current moment demolish the capacity of imaginative work onscreen to produce knowledge and empathy). Attending to how and whether Jewishness is represented in historically based work can provide a vivid demonstration of how Jews are made—or unmade—in and by the movies. A biopic such as Gus Van Sant's 2008 *Milk* (for which *The Times of Harvey Milk* was a crucial source text) needs to be discussed in terms of what it does—and, more to the point, doesn't do—in terms of representing Milk's Jewishness. Decisions about when and how to deviate from the historical record and when to be faithful to it can be Jewishly significant. However, as my discussion of *Milk* illustrates, what's onscreen is only part of the story; the reception of *Milk* by spectators aware of Milk's Jewishness affirmed queer Jewish identity and political history.

Just as we need to recognize documentaries as works of art, so do we need to acknowledge that fiction films have tissues of connection to the real world. The making of many of the fiction films discussed here included some form of targeted research. The writers of *Kissing Jessica Stein* interviewed Jewish lesbians as they were developing the script.[29] The director of *Zebrahead* (1992) spent time with diverse high school students early in the filmmaking process.[30] Mazursky brought members of the cast to meet survivor communities as preparation for filming *Enemies, A Love Story*.[31] A fascinating trend in the production of fiction films that feature Orthodox characters is the hiring of expert consultants to avoid culturally misinformed representations.[32] This was true of *Fading Gigolo*, *Arranged*, and *Romeo and Juliet in Yiddish* (2010). Such research does not (and should not!) foreclose debates about stereotypes avoided or performed or the politics of particular representations; nonetheless, it indicates that these filmmakers are aware that story and image matter in the world and that they have given thought to their movie-made Jews. Ultimately, directors, writers, and editors of both documentary and fiction films make aesthetic choices that impact onscreen Jews and the reception they receive. In addition to the aesthetic overlap between documentary and fiction film, we should also consider that spectators experience these different movie forms alongside one another, especially at Jewish film festivals.

Film festivals represent and make communities; Jewish film festivals represent and make communities of Jews—and their allies. Attending a Jewish film festival is one among many ways of "doing" Jewish. The prototype for Jewish film festivals was the San Francisco Jewish Film Festival, which got its start in 1981.[33] Philadelphia followed suit, and now many cities, including New York, San Diego, Miami, Atlanta, Austin, Houston, Washington, Boston, and Portland, Maine, to name just a few, are home to such festivals. The "invigorating" cross-generational conversations that Ilan Stavans associates with Jewish film are part of festival planning. According to directors of Jewish film festivals, a movie's ability to "spark discussion" is an important criterion for selection.[34] For some, an annual Jewish film festival is a ritual—as such, it might exist alongside High Holiday services, a Passover seder, or the lighting of the hanukkiah, or it might be one of the only Jewish rituals observed during the year. Put another way, a Jewish film festival plays a role in the making of cultural Jews as well as those who define themselves along a spectrum of religiosity. At the 2004 Conference of Jewish Film Festivals, a panel was devoted to goals of Jewish film festivals, and the idea that festival attendance should be viewed as a "gateway to affiliation" (i.e., a step on the path to becoming a member of a synagogue) was debunked.[35] Rather, this panel affirmed the idea that "cultural Judaism [is] a legitimate, self-sufficient expression of Jewish identity, which should be supported as such," and Jewish film is seen as a means of making cultural Jews.

The role of Jewish film festivals in not only exhibiting and marketing newly released films but also canonizing Jewish films should not be underestimated. Many Jewish film festivals present annual awards for best film or audience favorites; increasingly, festivals also include retrospective offerings as part of their programming. Such retrospective offerings indicate that a film is considered a classic and help to establish its status. In other words, Jewish film festivals help to make Jewish film traditions as well as movie-made Jews. Many, if not most, of the fiction films and documentaries featured in these pages premiered and/or won awards at a major Jewish film festival; several—including *The Pawnbroker*, *Crossing Delancey*, and *Crimes and Misdemeanors*—have been included as retrospective offerings at major Jewish film festivals.

While Jewish film festivals are key institutions in the making and sustaining of audiences for an American Jewish cinematic tradition, the differently crucial role of film festivals that are not specifically or even primarily Jewish also needs to be recognized. Sundance, a preeminent and historic institution for independent film, has provided both production grants and exhibition space for many of the films discussed in these pages. Notably, in 2001, two of the films that made a splash at Sundance were *The Believer* and *Trembling Before G-d*, causing Larry Mark to quip in the *Forward* that the Sundance logo "sport[ed] a small Jewish star."[36] The Tribeca Film Festival, the brainchild of Robert De Niro (and others) to reinvigorate the life of lower Manhattan after 9/11, was the premiere site for *Keeping Up with the Steins*. *Heart of Stone* (2009) premiered and won the Audience Award at Slamdance, which advertises itself as a festival "by filmmakers, for filmmakers," and began as an alternative exhibition site for quality Sundance-rejected films. The fact that so many explicitly American Jewish films have been supported and even lauded by non-Jewish festivals indicates that American Jewish cinema is an important part of our national cinema and needs to be critically recognized as such. The production and reception history of many of the films discussed in *Movie-Made Jews* also indicates that American Jewish film promotes significant intercultural conversations and that Jewish allies are also made at and through the movies. Ultimately, a Jewish movie is neither just a movie nor for Jews only.

Films that make good on the festival circuit—Jewish and otherwise—are often picked up for wider theatrical runs and/or digital distribution. Certainly, streaming has many angsting about the future of the film industry; indeed, some wonder whether film even has a future. Such worries have long been a feature of the critical conversation around American Jewish cinema. An important volume edited by Sarah Blacher Cohen in 1983 was pessimistic about the continuity of American Jewish cinema. Alan Spiegel perceived Jewish presence in the contemporary American film of his day as "a vanishing act" devoid of Jewish particularity.[37] Sanford Pinsker put Mel Brooks at the center of American Jewish film and read that parodic tradition as "a cinema of exhaustion."[38] And Blacher Cohen viewed the golden age of American Jewish culture as embodied by the Yiddish theater and opined, "At the present time ... it would be unrealistic to expect the mainstream Jewish-American stage and screen to hatch very many of these genuine Jewbirds which were so plentiful in the parent nest, the Yiddish theater.... Indeed, its more emancipated, less informed heirs are more comfortable with nondescript starlings and loud-mouthed parrots who imitate accents but utter nonsense."[39] In sharp contrast, Lester Friedman's *Hollywood's Image of the Jew* (1982) ends with the declaration that "the celluloid history of the American Jew always has one more chapter." Patricia Erens is more cautiously optimistic in *The Jew in American Cinema* (1984): she ends her book by emphasizing the "new visibility of the screen Jew ... and a future which holds forth the *possibility* of a continued and creative interest in the screen Jew." In 2004, Friedman and David Desser seem to throw their lot in with the doubters. They conclude their second edition of *American Jewish Filmmakers* with the pessimistic possibility that "we have witnessed the final flowering of an American Jewish cinema."[40] While I disagree with some of Nathan Abrams's assumptions about normalization in *The New Jew in Film*, that book provides ample, compelling evidence that the 1990s and the new millennium brought neither a vanishing act nor the exhaustion of parody. And my view here of *Crossing Delancey* and *Romeo and Juliet in Yiddish* gives the lie to Blacher Cohen's pessimism that Yiddish-inflected Jewbirds are a thing of the past or can only hearken back to the past; rather, these works suggest that American Jewish cinema is a living tradition capable of continuity and change. New business models—such as the grassroots marketing employed for *Keeping Up with the Steins* and the Kickstarter campaign that enabled *Wish I Was Here* (2014) to come into cinematic being—are part of that change. Digital distribution also provides some real opportunities for American Jewish film in particular. The fact that so many of the Jewish films discussed here are available on diverse streaming platforms means that the cultural work of American Jewish film can be home-based—as are the holidays of Passover and Hanukkah—and can happen 24/7.

Since my goal is to chart a usable tradition of continuity and change rather than a narrative of progress, I have organized the chapters of this book thematically rather than chronologically, while remaining attuned to chronology within chapters. And although *Movie-Made Jews* considers documentaries and fiction film equally important parts of the American Jewish cinematic tradition, I've made no attempt to represent them equally or even include both in all chapters. Antisemitism, the subject of chapter 2, has long been considered both a potential maker and keeper of Jews, the glue that might hold a community together, and a potential unmaker of Jews, that which encourages Jews to leave the fold for a better or, at least, a more expansive life. The recent and alarming resurgence of what some consider "the longest hatred" has reenergized this debate. In "Looking at Antisemites and Jews," I briefly discuss the vexed social problem film *Gentleman's Agreement* before focusing on its heir, *School Ties*, a film that situates antisemitism as a history of Jewish passing and resistance. The chapter also includes the controversial film *The Believer*, based on a true story of a Jewish neo-Nazi, as well as Marc Levin's documentary *The Protocols of Zion*, which controversially points the camera at post-9/11 conspiracy theorists, neo-Nazi groups, evangelical Christians, and Jewish Hollywood insiders. Levin's film seems especially prescient viewed from the post-Charlottesville, post-Pittsburgh era. Taken together, these films explore the impact that diverse forms of antisemitism have on how Jews see themselves and how Gentiles view not only Jews but also their own subjectivity. The making of Jews and their allies through antisemitism is the onscreen story; it is also an important part of the production and reception history of these films. Directors, actors, and viewers attest to the impact of these films on their own continuing education about this particular and persistent form of hate.

Although *Gentleman's Agreement* appeared just a few years after the Shoah, attempted genocide is the absent presence of that film. Of course, since then, Holocaust films have proliferated, and the crucial but also potentially problematic outsize role that such representations have on making American Jews (not to mention non-Jewish perspectives on dead and live Jews) is often debated. In chapter 3, "Looking at the Shoah from a Distance," I turn my attention to a set of fiction films that deals with the Holocaust through indirection. Such an aesthetic orientation is particularly apt to represent a historical cataclysm that impacted U.S. consciousness in general and U.S. Jewish consciousness in particular but happened elsewhere. Sidney Lumet's *The Pawnbroker* is one of the first films to focus on the figure of the survivor and thus the aftereffects of the Shoah rather than the historical event itself; it also explicitly addresses flatfooted, facile forms of identification. The production history of Paul Mazursky's *Enemies, A Love Story* is a case study of attempts to de-Judaize the Holocaust and resistance to that impulse. Both the film itself and its making exemplify a cinematic Holocaust education that distinguishes between European survivor communities and U.S.-born Jews. *Crimes and Misdemeanors*, one of Woody Allen's most explicitly Jewish films, uses a case of femicide to explore post-Holocaust theology and ethics. The chapter concludes with a discussion of the Coen Brothers's *Barton Fink* and *A Serious Man* and the cinematic imagery that performs the indirect trauma of the Shoah haunting American Jewish consciousness.

As I have already indicated, the story of Hollywood is often seen as a prototypical narrative and medium of American Jewish assimilation, the unmaking of Jews. However, chapter 4, "Focusing on Assimilation and Its Discontents," argues that American Jewish cinema has also become a site for chronicling the losses associated with assimilation and a possible staging ground for the remaking of Jews. Taken together, Pollack's *The Way We Were*, Mazursky's *Next Stop, Greenwich Village*, Micklin Silver's *Crossing Delancey*, and Levinson's *Avalon* and *Liberty Heights* tell a story of assimilation and its discontents; significantly, these film narratives engage not only interfaith, intercultural romance but also media history—the Hollywood blacklist as well as the development of television. Even as these films cast a Jewish critical eye on the values and types associated with the dominant culture, their production histories reflect the double binds that attend movie-made Jews.

In chapter 5, "Assertively Jewish Onscreen," cultural and religious Jews are unapologetically represented, often in close proximity. Allen's *Whatever Works* is a conversion of the WASPS tale, with neurotic, cosmopolitan Jewishness so culturally normalized that others assimilate to it, while Turturro's *Fading Gigolo* views Judaism not as an outmoded joke but as a sustainable way of life freely chosen. The question of who should assimilate to whom dominates Annenberg's *Romeo and Juliet in Yiddish*, while the contemporary spiritual wrestling of Jews is the focus of *Keeping Up with the Steins* and *Wish I Was Here*. New business and marketing strategies empowered the directors of these films, not all of whom are Jewish, to realize and share cinematic visions that some assumed were "too Jewish" and not ironic enough.

The Jews onscreen in chapter 6, "Queering the Jewish Gaze," are assertively Jewish and queer, and they refuse—though not without significant struggles— to give up essential parts of themselves. The chapter begins with two fiction films—*I Now Pronounce You Chuck and Larry* (2007) and *Kissing Jessica Stein*—that do important antihomophobic work but nonetheless fail to fully realize a vision of sustained queer Jewishness. A comparison of Epstein's documentary *The Times of Harvey Milk* and Van Sant's biopic *Milk* shows how the cultural Jewishness of this iconic queer politician has been cinematically conveyed and whitewashed. While Alisa Lebow and Cynthia Madansky's title *Treyf* (1998) conveys the sense that queer Jews find themselves at odds and in keeping with diverse forms of Jewish tradition, *Trembling Before G-d* and *Hineini* put into sharp focus the specifically religious struggles that observant queer Jews encounter as they demand to be seen. The latter two documentaries provide ample evidence that films make and remake Jews. Life imitates documentary art once again as observant queer Jews have become known as "tremblers," and the production and screenings of *Hineini* have prompted important conversations about Jewish pluralism in educational institutions, settings in which Jews are consciously and intentionally made. The fact that *Trembling* has served as a resource for queer religious wrestlings in non-Jewish communities reminds us yet again that a Jewish film is not just a movie and not for Jews only.

Chapter 7, "Cinematic Alliances," focuses on the making of Jews in relation to other groups. The chapter begins with the vexed history of Black-white Jewish cinematic relations, including a screening of *Schindler's List* to Oakland high school students that became a flash point for issues of identification and lack thereof with the Holocaust and its victims, and by extension, Jews. I then turn my attention to Beth Toni Kruvant's *Heart of Stone* (2009), a documentary about another high school, New Jersey's Weequahic, and the work of a heroic, visionary Black principal, aided by Jewish alums, to turn a failing school into one that equips its students to choose life beyond an often death-dealing street. The making of Yoav Potash's documentary *Crime after Crime* (2011) played a role in the eventual freeing of Debbie Peagler, a woman imprisoned for the killing of her abuser. While this documentary chronicles the evolving professional and personal relationship between a Black Christian inmate and her traditionally observant white Jewish lawyer, the fiction film *Zebrahead* (1992) movingly resists the myopic dictum of a so-called educator who advises Jews and others to "stick to your tribe, that's how you know who you are." After 9/11, cinematic alliance narratives focus on the obstacles and opportunities for

Jewish-Muslim relations. While Jews and Muslims share the challenges of being religious minorities in the United States, they are often perceived and perceive themselves as divided because of Middle East politics. Both Diane Crespo and Stefan C. Schaefer's *Arranged* (2007) and Joel Fendelman and Patrick Daly's *David* (2011) refuse to see movie-made Jews in isolation. The production and reception of the films discussed in this chapter often performed the complexities represented onscreen; this mini-canon of alliance films illuminates how and why Jewish movies matter and how often they are simultaneously multicultural movies.

Chapter 8, "Epilogue: Cinematic Continuity and Change Through a Feminist Lens," focuses on two arguably Jewish feminist documentaries of 2018: Paula Eiselt's *93Queen* and Julie Cohen and Betsy West's *RBG*. The documentary *93Queen*, like the fiction films discussed in chapter 5, is assertively and unapologetically Jewish, while Ginsburg's Jewishness is referenced glancingly even as it is indisputable that *RBG* was received as a Jewish film by members of the tribe. Like *Milk*, *RBG* functions as a limit case for American Jewish films. Viewed in tandem, *93Queen* and *RBG* demonstrate the narrative of cinematic continuity and change that *Movie-Made Jews* has charted. While an explicitly Jewish gaze resides behind the camera and on the screen more often than it has in the past, sometimes the Jewishness of a movie still lies mainly in the eye of the Jewishly literate beholder.

The fiction and documentary films discussed here make Jews through antisemitism, Holocaust indirection, assimilation and its discontents, as well as through the unapologetic assertion of Jewishness, queerness, and alliances. Taken together, these films constitute a Jewish gaze that is pluralistic and often lovingly self-critical. Writing about Black women's critical spectatorship and an oppositional gaze, bell hooks posits that "one learns to look a certain way in order to resist."[41] White Jews have historically made movies and, in part because of this racialized cinematic history, are positioned simultaneously as cultural insiders and outsiders. Given such history and cultural positioning, the collective gaze represented here might be thought of as not only or primarily oppositional but also expansively Jewish. To be sure, characters, directors, and spectators look critically at and resist identifying with dominant WASP culture. However, that insistence on Jewish difference is also an intensive look at intra-Jewish difference. Because what is present—and absent—onscreen influences how we look and how we learn to look, it matters that a diversity of Jews along the cultural and religious spectrum are seen and recognized by one another and by non-Jewish eyes.[42]

As we go to our local theater, attend a Jewish film festival, insert a DVD into our computer, or watch streaming videos on our tablets, Jewishness becomes part of the multicultural mosaic rather than collapsing into a generic whiteness or being viewed as a life apart. Although *Movie-Made Jews* argues that a usable American Jewish film tradition extends far beyond *Fiddler on the Roof, Yentl, The Chosen*, and *Hebrew Hammer*, it is not a comprehensive survey, and I have purposely opted for depth over breadth. Although I fully expect that some readers might find some favorite flicks missing from these pages, I hope all will discover some unusual suspects and that my commentary will provide new ways of looking at American Jewish films that aren't included here or have yet to be made. By selectively revisiting canonical pre-1990 films and amply representing films of the new millennium that merit critical attention, *Movie-Made Jews* illuminates an American Jewish film tradition that continues and changes before our eyes.

Marc Levin, talking about *Protocols of Zion* in 2005, hoped that his documentary could function as a containment of hate and that film could be part of our "creative arsenal."[43] I am finishing the writing of this book in 2020 and in an era marked by white supremacists chanting "Jews will not replace us" in Charlottesville; congregants being gunned down for praying while Jewish in Pittsburgh and in Poway, California; visibly Jewish walkers being attacked on the streets of Brooklyn; and swastikas appearing all over the country. Both the research for *Movie-Made Jews* and the teaching of American Jewish films in classrooms and in the community give me faith that film can be an antidote to hate and a creative arsenal that makes Jews and our allies through a myriad of images. Our jazz singers, our serious men, our crimes and misdemeanors not only show us the way we were when we crossed Delancey but also help us to focus on our next stop, whether we're leaving a yarmulke behind on our way to Greenwich Village or whether we're trembling before G-d.

2

Looking at Antisemites and Jews

••••••••••••••••••••

In Henry Bean's *The Believer* (2001), an Orthodox Jew turned neo-Nazi (based on a true story—I kid you not) advises his antisemitic comrades that "without . . . hatred, the so-called chosen people would vanish from the earth." Movies about antisemitism and the reception of them worry this question about the impact of Jew-hating and representing it onscreen. Does antisemitism keep the Jews more than Shabbat? If so, what sorts of Jews are made by founding identity on hatred and victimization, and can such Jews survive when antisemitism wanes? Put another way, does the experience, cinematic and otherwise, of Jew-hatred increase or decrease Jewish solidarity and commitments to a people and its practices? Relatedly, what impact does the representation of antisemitism have on non-Jews? Does real talk about antisemitism mitigate or incite Jew-hatred? Do movies about antisemitism make Jewish allies or help to reproduce antisemites?

Any discussion of movies *about* antisemitism and their impact needs to take into account the foundational role that antisemitism has played in American Jewish film history. As Steven Carr has compelling argued, the so-called Jewish question, with its obsession about whether and how Jews might be integrated into national bodies, morphed into the Hollywood question: "The Hollywood Question simply updates the Jewish Question and its attendant set of assumptions. Instead of overtly asking whether Jews can participate in the regular affairs of daily life, the Hollywood Question asks whether Jews, given their quasi-racialized difference, should participate in the regular affairs of mediated life. The Question . . . constructs Jewishness for Jews."[1]

Notorious antisemite Henry Ford codified the Hollywood question through the influential editorials of prejudice that appeared in his *Dearborn Independent* newspaper during the 1920s; those editorials were later collected in *The International Jew*. In such pieces as "The Jewish Aspect of the 'Movie' Problem" and "Jewish Supremacy in the Motion Picture World," Jewish media conspiracy tropes were promulgated: for example, "The motion picture influence of the United States—and Canada—is exclusively under the control, moral and financial, of the Jewish manipulators of the public mind," and "The American Public is as helpless against the films as it is against any other exaggerated expression of Jewish power."[2] And with a stroke of brilliant bigotry, the *Independent* strove to preempt charges of antisemitism: "The movies are of Jewish production. If you fight filth, the filth carries you straight into the Jewish camp because the majority of the producers are there. And then you are 'attacking the Jews.'" As historian Dennis Klein points out, the very charges that Hollywood was a pernicious agent of cultural change made it difficult for the dream machine to address the Christian question of antisemitism "without evoking [Ford's] characterization of the movies as 'Jewish supremacy' or a Jewish conspiracy."[3] In an effort to evade the cinematic censorship that those obsessed with the Hollywood question threatened to impose, studio heads embraced the Motion Picture Production Code, administered by Joseph Breen, who shared Ford's antisemitic views: Breen referred to Jews variously as "vile people," "scum of the earth," and those who "seem to think of nothing but making money and sexual indulgence."[4] In short, the controlling interests of antisemites in the early years of Tinseltown should not be underestimated.

However, the Hollywood question extended its tentacles well beyond the 1920s and 1930s. In 1944, as attempted genocide was occurring in Europe, Gerald K. Smith, founder of the National Christian Crusade and the America First Party, published the "Rape of America by Hollywood" in *The Cross and the Flag* (one of the dirty secrets of U.S. history is that levels of domestic antisemitism soared as our armed forces were fighting fascism abroad).[5] After World War II, the anti-Communist witch hunt of the House Committee on Un-American Activities (HUAC) and the subsequent blacklist were motivated, at least in part, by antisemitic sentiments; Jews, Communists, and queers were viewed as overlapping and intertwined undesirables.[6] Six members of the Hollywood Ten, those who were imprisoned for refusing to answer HUAC's questions, were Jewish; both Jews and Gentiles involved with *Crossfire* and *Gentleman's Agreement*, two anti-antisemitism films of 1947—Edward Dmytryk, Adrian Scott, Elia Kazan, and John Garfield, to name names—were among those ensnared by HUAC.

The Hollywood question and its attendant obsession with Jewish control of the film industry is still with us, though there have been dramatic shifts in the form and tone it takes as well as dramatic shifts in the form and tone that resistance to it takes. It's worth noting that Jewish movie talk is full of debates about whether a particular film or film comment is part of the problem, part of the resistance, or both. To be sure, when Marlon Brando, using a whole set of loathsome racial and ethnic epithets that I won't repeat here, claimed in 1996 that Jews who "run" and "own" Hollywood have shamefully stereotyped all marginalized groups except their own, there wasn't a lot of debate about the meaning of his remarks. And Mel Gibson's antisemitism is so infamous that a comedian's quip "Mel Gibson blames—you know who he blames" was greeted with roars of knowing and resistant laughter at the 2016 Golden Globes.[7] But when Seth MacFarlane's voice has Ted, the raunchy stuffed animated movie bear, introduce himself at the 2013 Oscars by saying "I was born Theodore Shapiro and would like to donate to Israel and continue to work in Hollywood forever," and then ask copresenter Mark Wahlberg if he's Jewish, the reception of the bit was varied. Some viewed it as a joke that exposed the open but politically incorrect Jewish secrets of Hollywood, some viewed it as a joke mocking the antisemitic conspiracy theories about Jewish Hollywood, while others—including the Anti-Defamation League (ADL) and the Simon Wiesenthal Center—saw nothing funny about the reproduction of antisemitic sentiments.[8]

While the Hollywood question shadows American Jewish cinema in general, it has particular resonance for antisemitism films in particular, since such films can be viewed as an assertive response to the question or a manifestation of it. The Hollywood question asks Jews to police themselves and other Jews, to worry that movie talk about antisemitism will elicit antisemitism, to wonder whether Jews are somehow to blame for antisemitism or can prevent it if only they make themselves over into one image rather than another (though what this image should be is hard to say). In this chapter, I focus on four anti-antisemitism films: the 1947 Oscar winner, *Gentleman's Agreement*; *School Ties* (1992), a film indebted to and an updating of *Gentleman's Agreement*; *The Believer* (2001), an unsettling intertwining of Jewish self-hatred and self-love with neo-Nazi movements; and Marc Levin's *Protocols of Zion* (2005), a documentary exploration of the post-9/11 rise in antisemitism that, from the vantage point of the Trump era, seems prescient. Taken together, these films (inclusive of their production and reception histories) show that cinematic narratives about antisemitism can and do make Jews and their allies. However, those that represent diverse forms of Jew-hatred interspersed with strategic glimpses of Jewish life contribute to a usable rather than a lachrymose cinematic tradition.

Gentleman's Agreement (1947)

As a scholar and a Jewish viewer, I have a love-hate relationship with the social problem film *Gentleman's Agreement* (1947) because it seems ambivalent about whether the social problem is antisemitism or Jewish difference. Certainly, *Gentleman's Agreement* is among the most well-intentioned films in Hollywood history. Yet, as the saying goes, the road to hell (where, according to Christian fundamentalists, Jews end up if they don't change their ways) is paved with good intentions.

Gentleman's Agreement was a prototype for the social problem film, a genre often disdained by film critics. In part, such disdain is based on the perception that the genre espouses liberal rather than progressive values, that is, focuses on individuals rather than systems. The social problem film is also derided for being narrative-driven and for being earnest rather than ironic. Film scholar Sarah Kozloff challenges this bias in film studies by reaffirming the real-world value of films that "directly *engage* in a fight against political and social injustice ... seek to emotionally *engage* the viewer in their fictions, the better to raise spectators' consciousness and inspire action."[9]

Such a defense of the social problem film seems not only appropriate but perhaps even required for the 1947 film that sought to perform—and, to some extent, succeeded in doing so—the work of its protagonist, Phil Green, a Gentile journalist passing as a Jew in order to "blow the lid off" the scourge of genteel antisemitism. *Gentleman's Agreement* is based on the best-selling book by Laura Hobson, an American Jew who learned all about antisemitism as a coed at Cornell and, later, relearned those lessons listening to an antisemitic epithet uttered not on the street but rather on the floor of the House of Representatives.[10] The impetus for turning Hobson's American Jewish novel into what became an Oscar-winning film featuring such Hollywood heavyweights as Gregory Peck and Dorothy McGuire came from Gentiles: director Elia Kazan as well as producer Darryl Zanuck, whose presence at Fox caused it to be dubbed "the goy studio."[11] Some in the Jewish community were acutely aware and afraid of the risks associated with such work and opposed the cinematic airing of national dirty laundry related to antisemitism. As Jewish film historian Patricia Erens reports, the pressure on Zanuck to abandon making *Gentleman's Agreement* led him to add a scene in which a Jewish industrialist tries to kill the story that Green is working on; he, rather than the series on antisemitism, is shut down by both Green and his publisher.[12] The production history of *Gentleman's Agreement* (as well as that of *Crossfire*) indicates that the decision to tackle antisemitism onscreen should not be taken for granted.

Of course, 1947 was just two years after the end of World War II and the Holocaust. The latter is not mentioned explicitly in *Gentleman's Agreement*; however, the Shoah is the absent historical presence of the film, which strives to be responsible in not conflating genteel discrimination with the machinery of genocide. As Jewish film historian Lawrence Baron points out, the film's press kit makes appropriate distinctions in its description of the plot: "'Phil finds prejudice cropping up fast—flicks here and there of insult that tap constantly on the nerves. No yellow armbands, no marked park benches, no Gestapo, no torture chambers—just a flick here and there.'"[13] When Phil's mother suffers a heart attack from which she will recover, she asserts that she "didn't know pain could be so sharp." In essence, this is the argument of the movie—that while Jews recover from being denied housing or, relatedly, a room at the inn; from the easy assumption that Jewish doctors are guilty of "overcharging or stringing out visits"; from changing names in order to secure employment; from the assumption that they did PR for the war effort to avoid serving in the theater of war; from being called "dirty Jew" and "stinking kike," their pain is sharp, and the majority needs to not only recognize that pain but also take action to stop inflicting it.

Although *Gentleman's Agreement* was couched as a cinematic action to raise the consciousness of and unmake genteel antisemites, Jewish community leaders worried that the Hollywood question was so culturally ingrained that anti-antisemitism films might have the opposite effect. In response to such concerns, studies were commissioned to determine the impact of such narratives. The results of those studies supported a social activist agenda and assuaged Jewish fears: for most respondents, watching films such as *Gentleman's Agreement* and *Crossfire* reduced rather than augmented antisemitic attitudes.[14] Yet the furor over the making of *Gentleman's Agreement* and its potential reception reminds us that the phrase "It's just a movie" belies much of film history in general and Jewish film history in particular.

Given what I have written here, the commonsense Jew in my head (who, in keeping with my geographic origins, has a strong Brooklyn accent) says, "Nu, what then is there not to like. You have a film that lessens antisemitism, that doesn't conflate U.S. antisemitism with the Holocaust, and that addresses itself to the majority on behalf of a minority. You're meshugge for criticizing it." My own experiences bringing this film into classrooms in Georgetown, Texas (where it sometimes feels like it's 1947 when it comes to Jewishness), not to mention the antisemitic tropes that increasingly get play in contemporary political culture, provide further evidence that the work this film strives to do is still needed, that is, in some quarters, the news that Jews are like everyone else is, well, news.

However, as a film scholar who cares about Jewish difference, I'm simultaneously convinced that the way *Gentleman's Agreement* delivers such news, without qualification, is playing a dangerous game that makes Jews primarily in the image of antisemitism. When Phil decides that to get the scoop on antisemitism, he'll play at being a Jew, he assumes that "all I have to do is say it." In other words, Jewish identity is reduced to the statement "I am a Jew." Although in some contexts that was and is a potentially powerful statement, a lot of culture and history, not to mention ritual, does a vanishing act when "I, Jew," is all there is to Jewish identity. Consider, for example, the moment when Phil's precocious son, Tommy, asks Phil, "What's a 'Jew'?" (a word he hears for the first time in relation to antisemitism). Phil's answer: "There are lots of different churches," and Jews "call their kind of churches synagogues or temples." When Tommy assumes that, unlike Jews and Catholics, Americans aren't hated, Phil strives to distinguish between nationality and religion. This explanation to Tommy—and to viewers—is designed to cement the notion of American Jews as full, patriotic citizens (showing Dave Goldman, Phil's best friend and his model for a Jew, in military uniform reinforces this point). Making Jewishness and synagogues a church flavor is in keeping with the universalizing, melting pot model of the post–World War II era. Yet the film doesn't even sustain this reduction of Jewishness to religious orientation. There are no synagogues anywhere to be found here, no Torah, no Shabbat, not a rabbi, yarmulke, or tallit in sight.

Rather, in the cinematic world of *Gentleman's Agreement*, the experience of antisemitism distinguishes Jews from non-Jews.[15] Dave may share Phil's dark eyes and dark hair, but he can't find housing in New York. Although Professor Lieberman (played by Sam Jaffe), a physics professor visually suggestive of Albert Einstein, claims that his face betrays his Jewish heritage, science rather than Judaism is established as his religion. Yet, what really calls him back to the tribe is that it would be perceived as an advantage not to be a member. Not as honorable or privileged as Lieberman, Elaine Wales, Phil's secretary, reveals that she was born Estelle Wilasky and that she couldn't get a job until she changed her name. Her internalized antisemitism (she fears being lumped with the "kikey ones" and is astonished to discover that Phil was only playing at being a Jew) enables the protagonist to truly become an honorary male Jew according to the logic of the film: his Jewish expertise is antisemitism, about which he lectures to Jewish and non-Jewish women alike (respectively, Wales and his girlfriend Kathy). Dave, too, teaches Kathy about antisemitism, although he employs the Socratic method and argues that talking back to antisemitic bigots will cure her liberal dis-ease (not coincidentally, her activist response to this lecture resuscitates her relationship with Phil).

The strength of *Gentleman's Agreement* is simultaneously its weakness: it locates the Jewish question clearly in the Christian majority, but in doing so, it leaves no imaginative or onscreen room for living a Jewish life that includes anything beyond antisemitism. The social group becomes defined solely by the social problem, which is a well-intentioned but ultimately troubling way for movies to make Jews.

School Ties (1992)

School Ties has been dubbed the *Gentleman's Agreement* of the 1990s.[16] It, too, is a passing narrative, but rather than featuring a Righteous Gentile passing as a Jew to expose antisemitism, here we have a Jew striving to pass as a Gentile in order to transcend economic and educational disadvantages imposed by anti-semitism. Although Jewish difference beyond the experience of antisemitism is not dominant in the film, it does provide strategic nods to Jewish culture and Judaic practice wholly absent from its precursor.

Set in the 1950s, *School Ties* presents itself as a period piece. Although the film focuses on the antisemitism of an elite New England prep school, it begins in working-class Scranton with a brawl that the protagonist David Greene, played by Brendan Fraser, gets into with antisemitic biker thugs right before he heads to the other world (established with extreme long shots) of St. Matthew's High School. David is given this educational opportunity, which he and his father hope can be extended into a spot at Harvard, because of his prowess on the football field. He has been recruited as a quarterback to restore the athletic honor of St. Matthew's, which unlike some of its peers, is willing to enroll a Jew for a winning season, though not openly.

As his name suggests, David Greene is a composite of Phil Green from *Gentleman's Agreement*, the non-Jewish journalist who passes as a Jew in order to blow the lid off antisemitism, and Dave Goldman, Phil's best friend and the Jew upon which he models himself. As Jewish film historian Omer Bartov points out, *Gentleman's Agreement* could have chosen to focus on Dave rather than Phil, but he acknowledges that the social impact of the film was likely greater with Phil as a figure of identification for Gentile audiences.[17] The shift from a Gentile to a Jewish protagonist in *School Ties* facilitates the inclusion of some Jewish content. Just as important, it enables a Jewish gaze to focus on the majority and find it wanting.

The Christian-centeredness of St. Matthew's—where students are expected to wear school ties to chapel—is so normative that it need not speak its name. A potent and unselfconscious antisemitism accompanies the assumption that all are Christian. When David is grooving to "Smokey Joe's Cafe," the music playing on a Victrola, casual conversation about the acquisition of the machine, which included being "jewed down" by someone who was "not even Jewish," clues him in to the casual antisemitism of his peers. At this point, David's classmates do not yet know that he is Jewish. Rather, as the new quarterback, he is hailed as the "great white hope," a symbolic reminder that religious politics are simultaneously racial politics. Later, when David's schoolmates talk about their collegiate aspirations, one of them disavows Harvard because of "all those Jews and Communists—and that's just the faculty." Their entrenched belief that "it's kind of hard to miss a Heeb" is richly but bitterly ironic, especially as David borrows a school tie from his roommate, a metaphor for his ability to pass. After David has been outed as a Jew, his roommate castigates him for not being honest. The contradictions of his genteel bigotry are on full display as he asserts both that "Jews are different; everything about them is different" and declares that David claiming his Jewish identity at the outset wouldn't have made a difference. David's pointed reminder of the unselfconscious "jewed down" language puts his room-mate's hypocrisy—and David's Jewish double bind—into sharp relief.

This double bind, with its push and pull of making and unmaking David as a Jew, is fostered by the Jewish and non-Jewish adults in his life. When David's Scranton coach is preparing him for St. Matthew's, he counsels him to "play your cards close to your vest," implicitly instructing him to hide his Jewishness. When he asks David about any potential "diet problems—anything you can't eat," code for how Jewish/observant are you, he is visibly relieved by David's humorous response: a disavowal of turnips. While Jewish difference in the form of kashrut (dietary laws) is recognized here, it has the potential to make David too Jewish to pass. As he is leaving Scranton by bus—a sign that his economic mobility has limits unimaginable to most of the St. Matthew's brood—his father urges him to fit in but then tells him in Yiddish to "go in good health." This poignant moment represents the collision between assimilationist imperatives and desires to preserve cultural difference. Similarly, his father refuses to fully wrestle with the reality that the Jewish ties that bind and David's school ties are at odds when a football game representing a historic rivalry falls on Rosh Hashanah. Rather, his father simply commands David "to show respect and get to Temple." When David strives to compromise—he plays and wins the game and then prays in the chapel after hours—the headmaster castigates him with a question: "Was it worth it—breaking a tradition to win a football game?" From coach to father to headmaster, the men in David's life slowly but surely turn competing school and ethnoreligious ties into a noose.

However, in this 1990s *Gentleman's Agreement*, David, Jew by birth rather than Gentile donning Jewface for a limited time, escapes this noose by turning his focus outward. In keeping with the wonderful Jewish tradition of answering a question with another question, David's eloquent and effective response to the headmaster is "Your tradition or mine?" In this simple reversal, David reminds the headmaster—and the viewer—that the passing narrative is an effect of the tradition of antisemitic exclusions rather than Jewish moral failings or cowardice. Throughout the film, the privileged elite are portrayed as dishonorable and cowardly, despite or because of all their advantages. When David is outed as a Jew by Charlie Dillon, played by Matt Damon, the prep school gang is revealed to be better-dressed but no more sophisticated or progressive than the Scranton biker club. Dillon, with his declaration that David is a "lying, back-stabbing kike" and a "Heeb," is a mirror image of the thugs with whom David fights prior to his departure from Scranton. And once he is outed at St. Matthew's, he is greeted with a sign featuring a red swastika and the words "Jew Go Home." The form that this hate speech takes illuminates that the turf battles of the Scranton street and the relatively recent nationalist and genocidal history of the Third Reich are on a continuum with the battles of the private boys' club.

Turf war is revealed as fundamental to exclusions at St. Matthew's and beyond. David is Charlie's athletic and romantic competitor: while passing, the former replaces the latter as quarterback and as the beau of the blonde beauty Sally Wheeler. Eliminating potential or actual competition in order to rig the game of life and continue the tradition of illegitimate privilege motivates these cinematic chosen few just as it did those who historically fought for quotas lest "the Jews" make their home in the Ivy League. Although he never carries a torch, Charlie is in the mold of those who marched through Charlottesville chanting, "Jews will not replace us."

The climax of the film focuses on a cheating scandal, an apt metaphor for the war between those trying at all costs to hang on to unearned privilege and those trying to work their way into the halls of power. Although Charlie is the creator and user of a history exam cheat sheet, he tries to save his skin by projecting his guilt onto David: after David accurately reports that he saw Charlie cheat, Charlie accuses David of being the real offender. Honor code tradition at St. Matthew's requires students to police themselves, and David agrees to abide by this tradition. Although David's roommate begs the boys to separate the Jewish question from the issue of guilt, identity politics plays a seminal role in deliberations as the St. Matthew's boys try to determine whether to "dump Dillon for a dirty Jew." To add insult to ethnocentric injury, these future captains of industry will not vote openly; by secret ballot, they deliver their verdict that David is guilty.

When David is told to turn himself in to the headmaster, he agrees to at last truly join the club even as he once again asserts his Jewish perspective on the status quo: "I'll honor *your* traditions, I'll go to the headmaster and I'll *lie*" (my emphasis). While neither tradition nor democratic process serves fair play, the belated honesty of the house prefect, who saw Dillon cheat, refutes David's false confession, and he, along with the prefect, are not punished for their legitimate honor code violation of not immediately reporting Dillon for academic dishonesty. The headmaster strives to save a system that has been shown to be rotten at its core by professing his desire to forget the whole ugly episode and by recruiting David as the consummate upholder of its code: "David, you represent the best of what we hope for at St. Matthew's; don't think about leaving." But David will have none of this revisionist gentleman's agreement; rather, he insists that his presence will be a constant reminder of this institutional history, and he likewise insists on naming the agreement that has really been struck: "You used me for football, I'll use you to get into Harvard." As the expelled Dillon exits the campus, he comforts himself and strives to discomfort David by affirming that he will go on to have a good life while David will "still be a goddamned Jew." However, David has remade himself into a Jew who speaks truth to power even as he negotiates the double bind caused not by Jewish difference but by antisemitism.

The production history of *School Ties* serves as a reminder that American Jewish film history is a narrative of continuity and change rather than one of straightforward progress. Although such Hollywood heavy hitters as Sherry Lansing and Dick Wolf were invested in the project, they had to contend with "multiple rejections from every studio," and it took nine years to make the movie.[18] Despite such difficulties and studio disinterest, young actors of the time actively sought roles in the film, and those who were ultimately part of the cast considered it a professional coup. *School Ties* served as the breakout opportunity for Brendan Fraser, Matt Damon, and Chris O'Donnell (it also included Ben Affleck, who had much screen time but few lines).[19]

Many of those behind the scenes of the film acknowledge that David Greene's fictional struggles resonated with their own historical Jewish educational experiences. The script derived from Dick Wolf's experiences at Phillips Academy in Andover, Massachusetts. Director Robert Mandel reports that his college experience at Bucknell included "a 10 percent Jewish quota" and "closed fraternities." Having grown up on the Jewish streets of New York, he explains, "At the time I was very confused, but I just accepted it as being part of life." Lansing's time at her alma mater, Northwestern, paralleled Mandel's: she experienced a closed Greek system and discovered that Jews and Blacks had to meet higher admission standards. Brandon Tartikoff, who was chairman of Paramount during the making of *School Ties*, remembers, "It was such an eerie coincidence that when I got to Paramount, this project that I had nothing to do with in the first place looked like it was a homage to my own experiences at prep school." Recalling the chilly climate for Jews at Lawrenceville School in Lawrenceville, New Jersey, in the early to mid-1960s, Tartikoff says, "There were 15 Jewish students in a school of about 650 kids. . . . I went there seven months after my bar mitzvah. The anti-Semitism wasn't as overt as it was in the film. But you heard people making remarks; there were fist fights; people called you 'dirty Jew.' I was a pretty popular kid, on a couple of varsity athletic teams, but there was this steady undercurrent of anti-Semitism. It made me aware that I grew up quite insulated. It made me aware that I was in a distinct minority."[20]

While *School Ties* is a period film and might lead some to view antisemitism as a vestige of the past, those behind the scenes of the film indicate that genteel forms of antisemitism did not end with the 1950s and that their own schooling in such bigotry extended well beyond high school and college. Stanley Jaffe, former president of Paramount, indicates that tales of housing discrimination that attended his move from LA to New York in the late 1970s and early 1980s were the catalyst for his commitment to *School Ties*: "I was looking for an apartment in New York, and four or five people began telling me about not getting the apartments they wanted for one reason: they were Jewish. The apartments were on the Upper East Side. . . . I thought, why not do a film dealing with this subject in the same way *Gentleman's Agreement* did?" Lansing reports that just a year prior to the premiere of *School Ties*, she was told by a "very nice" woman at a tennis match in the Hamptons that "she didn't want her son to go to some school because there [were] too many Jews." When Lansing objected, "How could you say this in front of me? I'm Jewish," the woman could only respond, "Oh, come on."[21] Apparently, the assumption that "it's kind of hard to miss a Heeb" endures, and *School Ties* onscreen and off reflects how antisemitism and resistance to it make both Jews and movies.

According to some of the young *School Ties* actors, making movies about antisemitism can also raise the consciousness of Gentile allies. Brendan Fraser attended a boarding school that "while . . . non-denominational . . . reflected a strong society of Anglicans. We used to recite the Lord's Prayer every day." *School Ties* caused him to reflect on his Jewish schoolmates and how they may have experienced his school's culture. Matt Damon recalls being exposed to well-disguised but potent antisemitism that unwittingly worked its way into a scene of *School Ties*. In the film, Dillon outs David in the shower room, at one point calling him "a fucking kike." That epithet was ad-libbed by Damon, and he was shocked that he was capable of coming up with such unscripted hatred.[22]

Although the narrative of *School Ties* takes place in the 1950s, its knots extend well beyond the setting and set of the movie. In 2012, New York State's Pine Bush Central School District refused to protect students from antisemitic bullying, including beatings, swastikas, and epithets, a failure that ended up in court and resulted in a 2015 settlement that included not only monetary damages but also court-supervised training and curricular programs.[23] In March 2019, the *New York Times* reported that a recent court filing shows that "despite the district's efforts, anti-Semitism remains a stubborn problem at Pine Bush, as similar complaints about anti-Jewish bias are on the rise across New York State and elsewhere in the country."[24] At a high school in Minnesota, social media posts related to a Valentine's Day dance that included Nazi salutes and Hitler jokes show Jewish students no love; in Tennessee, a Jewish student who objects to the Nazi salutes of classmates is the one sent to the principal's office; in Massachusetts, a Jewish Student Union sign at a high school is vandalized with swastikas; and, in a California high school made infamous by a drinking game featuring a swastika formed by beer mugs, antisemitic flyers are posted.[25] Given such a cultural climate, *School Ties'* representation of David Greene talking back to an educational system that seeks to make him into a "goddamn Jew" speaks to the contemporary moment as well as to the very different times in which the film was set and made.

The Believer (2001)

That parting shot from Dillon in *School Ties*—"you'll still be a goddamned Jew"—seems a particularly apt description for Danny Balint, protagonist of

Henry Bean's *The Believer* (2001), an extended case study of a Jewish neo-Nazi whose fascination with fascism becomes, according to the director, his "form of practicing Judaism."[26] If a critical problem with *Gentleman's Agreement* is too little Jewishness and Judaism, then the equally critical problem with *The Believer* might well be that there is too much Judaism alongside this narrative of internalized antisemitism. The intertwining of extreme love and hate for Judaism and Jews (which is Bean's point) pushes the envelope on questions of how Jews and antisemites are made.[27]

As if the premise of a Torah-educated Jew doubling as a neo-Nazi weren't troubling enough, this narrative conceived as Bean's "love poem to my religion,"[28] and regarded as a "primer for anti-Semitism" by the Simon Wiesenthal Foundation,[29] is based on a true story. Danny Burros, a Grand Dragon of the Ku Klux Klan and a member of the Nazi Party, was unveiled as a Jew by a *New York Times* reporter in 1965 and subsequently committed suicide as he promised he would if the reporter printed the story of his origins.[30] Bean's Danny Balint (played by Ryan Gosling) also ends up self-destructing, although he does not shoot himself as Burros did. Rather, Balint positions himself to be blown up by the bomb that he has planted in a synagogue, but only after he gets his neo-Nazi Hebrew-learning girlfriend and his fellow Jews to safety. The headlines behind the film encouraged Bean to shoot the film in a rough-cut documentary style that included generous use of handheld camera footage and scenes in black and white that belie the ambivalence and ambiguity at the heart of this film.[31]

Reviews of the film often complain that the motivation for Danny's hateful political orientation is not explained. However, Danny's turn to neo-Nazism is clearly a symptom of the argument he is having with Jewish history and culture, not to mention God. Flashbacks to Danny's yeshiva days show him objecting to the narrative of the binding of Isaac, which he regards as emblematic of God's sadism and Jewish masochism. Whether he is beating up a yeshiva student who represents his former self or is taunting Holocaust survivors who tell their stories as part of a court-sanctioned sensitivity training program, neo-Nazism is Danny's attempt to recast Jewish masculinity. Although he claims that those who lost children in the Shoah should be learning from their latter-day tormentors to fight back rather than teaching so-called sensitivity, Danny finds himself haunted by their stories. When, toward the end of the film, he imagines himself in their world, he casts himself as resisting and getting shot. Although he tries to distance himself from the Jewish people and their victimization, he seems to identify with them existentially.[32]

Similarly, he cannot resist the siren call of the Torah. At a moment when he and his thugs are desecrating a synagogue, he is appalled by the ignorance of his cohorts and their wanton rather than mindful destruction. His act of saving and savoring the Torah scroll outs him as a Jew to Carla, his neo-Nazi girlfriend, and incites her to become his Hebrew student.

At one point, Danny tells Carla that she should cover herself in front of the Torah, and she asks, "Who gets contaminated: Gentile or Jew?" This question becomes a critical one about the film itself and its impact. In interviews, Bean fantasizes that the film could contaminate confirmed antisemites: "My dream . . . is to show it to the Aryan Brotherhood, or the Ku Klux Klan, or neo-Nazis in England. They would start out by saying, 'Yeah, right, he beats up a Jew, great. He's saying all these things, great.' And then they'd say, 'Wait a second, he's Jewish? He knows all these things about Judaism? And this Judaism sounds sort of interesting?' And in the end, they'd walk out, and their grip would be loosened. They wouldn't know what to think."[33] The detailed Judaic content that Danny often provides during the most virulent depictions of antisemitic violence (on kashrut when the yeshiva student is being beaten in a kosher dairy restaurant; on Torah calligraphy during the Torah-desecration scene) is the stuff that Bean imagines might loosen the grip of hate. Bean is undecided on whether this film lies within the Jewish genre of the *d'var* Torah or the Purim-spiel.[34] No matter the genre, he regards the film as a "paean to Judaism."[35] In keeping with that intention, he took special care to ensure that no authentic Torah was defiled in the making of the film. Those scenes, shot in the Ansche Chesed Synagogue in New York, included a facsimile of a Torah scroll that did not contain the word of God.[36] Bean also made sure that no cursing occurred during that scene and that the camera was directed away from the open Ark.[37] From his perspective, Judaism is given a fair and respectful hearing in the making of the film as well as in the film itself. And at least some critics questioned whether the film is too Judaic for some viewers: as film critic Daniel Steinhart puts it, "Some of the Judaic discourse may be too particular for viewers who aren't versed in the Torah."[38]

However, other critics regard the inclusion of so much Judaism as a possible peril. J. Hoberman writes that "the film does run the risk of suggesting that Jews are to blame for anti-Semitism," and Sanford Pinsker notes the "worry— rightly, I'm afraid—about those who will take the film as an invitation to, or confirmation of, their own anti-Semitic leanings." Kirk Honeycutt writes, "It also is unsettling to listen to any movie that wallows in obscene anti-Semitic slander with little attempt to balance these tired accusations with any rational challenge. Perhaps Bean assumes that his audience holds a proper point of view. That's a dangerous assumption in today's world."[39]

This critical debate about how the movie might matter—whether it had the potential to unsettle, confirm, or create antisemitic feeling—was reflected in the distribution drama that rivals the production difficulties that plagued both *Gentleman's Agreement* and *School Ties*. Initially, *The Believer* had a charmed cinematic life. It premiered at the Sundance Film Festival, garnering the Grand Jury Prize for Drama. Quips Bean, "If the showing of the film at Sundance was the birth, then winning the grand prize was the bris."[40] However, shortly after the film was previewed for the Simon Wiesenthal Center, the distribution deal with Paramount that was fairly far along fell through. Rabbi Allen Cooper of the Wiesenthal Center deemed *The Believer* a pedagogical failure and found the scene of the seeming Torah desecration objectionable. In contact initiated by Paramount, Cooper shared his misgivings, and Paramount decided to pass on this controversial film, a decision that initiated its own controversy, with innuendos rife in the media about Jewish institutional censorship (the ADL's decision to include the film in an LA Leadership training program, declaring that the film portrayed a "disturbing subject" without "legitimizing or glamorizing the hate-filled protagonist, anti-Semitism or the lifestyle of skinheads," complicated this narrative).[41] Showtime stepped into this distribution vacuum and picked up *The Believer*, with plans to show it during the 2001 High Holiday season. However, airing a film that depicted anti-Jewish terrorism, including the bombing of a synagogue, was judged to be ill-advised in the immediate aftermath of 9/11, and its cable premiere was postponed until the Passover season[42]

It might seem odd that a film about Jewish antisemitism would be marketed as either High Holiday or Passover fare. However, this marketing strategy was in keeping with Bean's view that Balint's extremist wrestling is quintessentially Jewish: "His argument with Judaism grows out of his religiousness, out of a serious engagement with the Torah. . . . He wants to argue with the text, and that's such a Jewish thing. It doesn't just come out of his desire to be a football player and to get a blonde. It's something much closer to home."[43] For Bean, Danny Balint is a very different type than David Greene of *School Ties*. Notably, Ryan Gosling, himself a Mormon, was helped to get into character by an Orthodox youth.[44] Bean reports that when he tested out Balint's theological tirades on a group of Orthodox young men, they affirmed that such sentiments were part of their own Jewish development.[45] According to Gosling, "Many Jewish people have told me that this is a film about being Jewish."[46] Bean has indicated that the audience at the Jerusalem Film Festival was "perfect": "They completely got it, every little joke."[47] Jewish film critic Michael Fox found the Jewish neo-Nazi's take on assimilation—hating Jews makes them stronger, the best way to get rid of them is to love them—the most promising albeit underdeveloped part of the film.[48]

During the production of *The Believer*, Bean found himself wrestling with these very questions. On the one hand, he was making what he regarded as a very Jewy movie; on the other hand, he posited that "being Jewish wasn't a big deal anymore. Was that good or bad? . . . what did it mean to be a Jew if it wasn't a problem? Without suffering (even the vicarious kind), what became of one's 'Jewish identity'? If the Jews were free and, if the oppression and the vast culture that grew up around it disappeared . . . then it seemed we had two choices: we could let it go at last and lose ourselves in the great sea of the nations, or we could perform the *mitzvoth*."[49] For Bean, the antisemitic discourse that rose from the ashes of 9/11 caused him to reappraise his view that Jewishness had become normalized and to consider that "maybe we weren't free after all."[50] Mormon Ryan Gosling learned while making the film that those who are always out as Jews, who presumably choose to perform many of the mitzvot on a daily basis, know all too well the price they may pay for being mitzvot-made Jews. As Gosling tells it:

> In the two months' preparation I added 20 pounds of muscle, had a shaved head and had a hate tattoo on my arm. Walking around New York, the reactions of people, the fear you instill in them is scary. I remember going into a camera store, it was like a Hassidic camera store, and *I wasn't even thinking*. I just went in to get some film, and all the people in there were visibly sweating, I was trying to be nice and I couldn't understand why they were so nervous. Then I looked at my arm and I realised why. *I'm ignorant*, I kind of didn't believe that this existed now, I thought it happened a long time ago. It's not true, people are still living in fear, and it's still an issue.[51]

Although David Greene and Danny Balint are profoundly different movie-made Jews, the non-Jewish actors who played them onscreen became unwitting witnesses to the ongoing offscreen impact of Jew-hatred. For better or worse, a Jewish education, including a cinematic one, needs to include lessons about antisemitism, but that needn't be the sole Jewish content available. Ironically, *The Believer*, a vexed and complex film about Jewish antisemitism, dramatically and controversially provides that object lesson.

Protocols of Zion (2005)

Both Ryan Gosling's realization that antisemitism is still an issue and Henry Bean's rethinking of his assumption that Jewishness has been normalized are foundational to Marc Levin's documentary *Protocols of Zion* (2005), described by one critic as "a peripatetic meditation on anti-Semitism."[52] This film, about the resurgence of Jew-hatred after 9/11, began in a New York taxicab. The driver, Egyptian-born and obviously well-educated, offered what he considered a well-known "fact": that no Jews died in the World Trade Center bombing. When Levin challenged this assertion, the driver invoked the *Protocols*, a conspiracy theory authored by the Russian czar's secret police but falsely attributed to Jews supposedly dedicated to world domination. Levin was astonished and troubled that anyone could take this "comic book" seriously.[53] Consequently, he embarked on a journey to "employ a gonzo kind of dialogue with those who believe in the book, and come out and end the film on the third anniversary of 9/11."[54] Accompanied by his father, Al Levin, Marc Levin films bracing encounters with a street vendor who has sold out of copies of the popular *Protocols* as well as with youths on the street who find evidence for Jewish control everywhere they look: in Pepsi, which stands for "Pay every penny to support Israel," and in the phonetics of then New York mayor Giuliani's name, "Jew-Liani."

It's tempting to dismiss such trash talk as the margins of the margins. However, such a dismissal becomes less convincing as the word on the street is complemented by Malaysian prime minister Mahathir Mohamad claiming at a 2003 Islamic conference that "today Jews rule the world by proxy and get others to fight and die for them," scenes from a popular Egyptian TV miniseries that perpetuates the blood libel by representing Jews slitting the throat of a child for Passover matzos, and interviews with leaders of such U.S.-based hate groups as Jew Watch and the National Alliance. *Protocols of Zion* also includes footage of Kofi Annan, former United Nations secretary-general, addressing the United Nations Seminar on Anti-Semitism in 2004 with the sobering perspective that there is an "alarming resurgence of this phenomenon [antisemitism] in new forms and manifestations." Levin's openly emotional viewing of the beheading of journalist Daniel Pearl, who was forced to declare himself a Jew prior to his onscreen assassination, reminds us that he—and we—should not be dispassionate viewers of hate; that we are made, in part, by what we watch.

In keeping with the documentary strategies of Michael Moore, Levin adroitly allows his interview subjects to reveal and often indict themselves in ways that are shocking and sometimes humorous. The editor of an Arab American newspaper that published the *Protocols of Zion* in installments supposedly did so to "educate" his readers; recognizing that the *Protocols* are "fake and not true" (and planning to print that information at the end of the last installment), he notes that Jew-hatred is not a solely Muslim problem. He goes on to explain that all those who hate Jews, in the Muslim world, in Europe, in the United States, "are jealous because Jews control everything." Then there's Shaun Walker, whom Levin and his crew bravely interview at the headquarters of the National Alliance in an area of West Virginia without cell coverage (they understand this as both a filming opportunity and a potentially violent trap). This sequence, which many critics consider among the strongest in the film, features a white supremacist who, although an heir to Brownshirt George Lincoln Rockwell, has learned to present himself as an ordinary guy neatly attired in a white shirt and red tie. Although the *Protocols*, a "core" and "timeless" book, is sold out, Walker proudly shows off the National Alliance merchandise currently available, including a sticker that identifies the white race as the "Earth's most endangered species" as well as Aryan Wear boots with swastikas and SS bolts impressed on their soles. Troublingly, Walker's business model seems to be working, although he betrays the limits of his historical knowledge when he confidently asserts that he "doesn't see Hitler as suicidal."

FIG. 2.1 Antisemitic merchandise for sale in *Protocols of Zion* (2005)

To those of us committed to alliance politics, an interfaith activist who considers outrage about the blood libel miniseries to be an "overreaction" is particularly dispiriting: Mehdi Eliefifi's view that "the whole world will turn upside down ... just because something was mentioned about Jewish," while "nobody cares" about equating Muslims and terrorism, is a classic script of competing victimization. Levin's segment on *The Passion of the Christ* also provides a less than encouraging view on interfaith work. On the one hand, James Carroll is shown as acutely aware that charges of deicide are an "old lie" that must not be reinforced and that Christians need to "learn a new way to read the Passion narrative." On the other hand, Pastor John MacArthur, who expresses "regret that [he's] not Jewish" since "all [his] heroes are Jewish," also professes his belief that it's "true" that "salvation is in Christ and Christ alone." In this way, Levin adroitly highlights that charges of deicide, an "image of evil Jewish conspiracy," serve as a precursor of the *Protocols*, while also showing that the Christian narrative of loving Jews so much that you need to save them from their waywardness involves a perverse intertwining of philosemitism and antisemitism. Notably, as Levin tries to get Hollywood insiders such as Larry David, Norman Lear, and Rob Reiner to discuss Mel Gibson's *Passion of the Christ* as well as the larger, often antisemitic-tinged question of Jews in Hollywood, he finds himself doing a "telephone hora" in which he is shut out of the circle.

Given Levin's cinematic chutzpah, he does not shy away from the elephant in the room of antisemitism, "the endless cycle of violence between the Israelis and Palestinians," as he terms it in a voice-over. Noting that the Hamas Charter cites the *Protocols*, he interviews young Sunset Park Palestinians who are in mourning and in rage after the Israeli assassination of Hamas leader and founder Sheik Ahmed Yassin; he also talks to participants in the Israel Day Parade. Extremist views are evident on both sides: signs that charge "Nazi Israel" as "Guilty of Genocide" are counterpointed with those who believe that "Kahane was right" in his advocacy of expelling Palestinians. However, more thoughtful, genuinely anguished voices on both sides are also featured: Palestinian American youths who talk about the fear they feel when the phone rings, with inevitable news of dead relatives, grieving mothers, and house demolitions, as well as Jewish Americans appalled that a mere "fifty, sixty years after the Holocaust, the world has forgotten what Israel means to the Jewish people" and hyperaware that messages of "peace and love" belie images of Jewish heads— Nicholas Berg's as well as Daniel Pearl's—"rolling on the internet for all to watch."

Levin intends his film not as an instrument of conversion but as one of inciting conversation.[55] Ironically, the most meaningful and hopeful onscreen conversation takes place among those incarcerated at Trenton State Prison, a place where the *Protocols* and its ideology are readily available. Here critical distance is provided on scripts of Black-white Jewish enmity, with one prisoner indicating that when you "grow up Black in America, you've heard Jews have done this and the Jews have done that all your life, whether they have or not," and wisely noting that Jewish involvement in the slave trade is not an all-or-nothing history. Other gems from this exchange include the mantra that "conversation is not combat" and a comment on the inefficacy of hate: "hating you doesn't let me play basketball, or read another language or get out of prison." In this sequence, the Quran is invoked as a vehicle of embracing difference "so [people] would know one another, not despise one another."

Some of Levin's evidentiary work to refute the *Protocols'* narrative of Jewish domination provides much-needed humor to counter what, in the first cut of the film, threatened to become a numbing "overdose of hate."[56] Returning to the scene of southern Florida and senior citizens so confused by butterfly ballots that they mistakenly cast votes for the antisemitism-spouting Pat Buchanan belies the view that Jews relentlessly exercise political muscle. To counterpoint the blood libel associated with Passover, Levin not only remembers his own family seders but also uses footage from the Jewishly diverse Downtown Seder, an annual New York event. There, he interviews drag queen Rebbetzin Hadassah Gross (aka Amichai Lau-Lavie), who explains that Passover is an "invitation to become free" and that, at this time of year, she scrubs her own toilets because "you have to deal with your shit."

The inclusion of Al Levin, the director's father, identified tongue in cheek in the credits as "The Elder," also provides some relief from the hate as well as background for the director's personal stake in this film. While prior to 9/11 Marc Levin only understood antisemitism as a historical phenomenon, Levin "the Elder" remembers the street as a place where he was verbally assaulted with such epithets as "Jew-boy and Christ-killer." Of course, as the film makes clear, such local antisemitism was promoted nationally by such public figures as radio priest Father Coughlin and Henry Ford. Yet Al Levin also gives voice to a lineage of activism and resistance to hate. A moving sequence unequivocally refutes the 9/11 myth that no Jews were killed through interviews with a 9/11 widow as well as with a medical examiner who also serves as a cantor. Following that sequence, Al Levin and the director are shown at the grave of Herman Levin, Al's father and Marc's grandfather. Herman's headstone is emblazoned with an injunction that seems to have been passed on from generation to generation: "God means go do good."

Yet whether Levin's *Protocols of Zion* is good for the Jews is a matter of debate. In the film itself, Levin includes a kabbalist who warns him away from such provocative material as well as those Jewish Hollywood insiders whose refusal to discuss antisemitism or *The Passion of the Christ* seems like a throwback to the production history of *Gentleman's Agreement* while also anticipating the reception history of Levin's documentary. In interviews, Levin reports that parts of the organized Jewish community were not eager for the film to be seen and discussed, and that this pushback from what was considered one of the film's most predictable niche audiences "stunned" its distributor, Thinkfilm.[57]

Levin himself seems to have conceived of an anti–niche marketing strategy from the outset. His determination not to "ghettoize it as a Jewish film" led to some provocative and unorthodox events.[58] As with so many films discussed in this book, Sundance and the San Francisco Jewish Festival were early and significant exhibition sites, which led to screenings across the country, including such places as the Jewish Community Center in Omaha, Nebraska. However, a less conventional screening took place at HBO's New York headquarters ahead of the film's release in theaters and on HBO: this event included invitations to members of the Nation of Islam and the New Black Panther Party, including then chairman of the party, Malik Zulu Shabazz, a 9/11 conspiracy theorist who insisted that the U.S. government had perpetrated the attack and who cast doubt on the number of Jewish victims of 9/11. Abraham Foxman, then executive director of the ADL, objected to such invitations: "The subject of the film is too serious for show business. There's enough anti-Semitism in the movie without bringing in a live example."[59] Some accounts of the Q& A session after the screening and a panel discussion that included an Orthodox rabbi and a Muslim interfaith educator seem to justify concerns about staging conversations about explosive issues. Anthony Kaufman of *Indie Wire* reported that the rabbi on the panel and Nation of Islam members seemed incapable of really hearing one another, "as if totally, utterly blocked to the other's presence. If *Protocols of Zion* is supposed to spur discussion, I don't think it matters much if no one is listening to each other." Saul Austerlitz, writing for the *Forward*, categorized "the questions [as] running more toward rambling rants."[60]

However, Levin's interpretation of these encounters was guided by lower expectations and his guiding principle of conversation rather than conversion. He pointed to the fact that while some predicted and expected this encounter to become violent, it was civil. In responding to a debate about terms used to refer to Muslims who embrace terrorism—Rabbi Cooper incorrectly used the term "Islamicist," for which he, according to some, "offered a half-hearted apology"—Levin expressed his view that "an important discussion would not have taken place if we had not been open to all kinds of people coming to the screening. If we can't have this dialogue here in New York City, how do we ever expect the Sunnis and the Shiites and the Kurds to work things out in Iraq?"[61] Levin's faith in conversation over conversion as his cinematic goal was also affirmed by a screening to an NYU group of Palestinian students who "initially deemed the film one-sided," but then started a dialogue among themselves about political strategy, asking, "Do we really want to peddle this medieval shit? Because it makes us look like idiots. And if our agenda is to fight Israel and get a Palestinian state, this is retarding our cause."[62] From the vantage point of 2020, when the line between anti-Zionism and antisemitism has become increasingly blurry and pernicious, a film that instigates reflection on this phenomenon merits attention.

Perhaps most edifying to Levin was a Chicago screening of *Protocols of Zion* to a group of 500 inner-city public school students. According to their teacher, "These students are not hard-core bigots or Jew-haters. But it is amazing how many have heard these rumors about the Jews and 9/11 and how many have absorbed elements of the classic anti-Semitic stereotypes. This film absolutely blew their minds and provoked one of the most profound discussions I've ever witnessed."[63] Such a response seems to affirm Kevin Crust's argument that while this film is unlikely to change the minds of haters, Levin, "in creating a document of refutation, . . . offers an alternative voice for anyone who might be fooled."[64] Thus, in 2005, long before the widespread epidemic of fake news that now plagues the nation, Levin was fighting that good fight with film. While *Protocols of Zion* may not unmake committed antisemites, it might prevent the reproduction of that type.

Although Levin insists that he "didn't want to ghettoize [*Protocols of Zion*] as a Jewish film"—it is "more about hate and the world we live in"—the making of the documentary did contribute to remaking him as a Jew.[65] While he indicates that his "rediscovery of Judaism" was underway prior to his work on *Protocols*, his interview with Shiya Ribowsky, the New York City medical examiner and cantor who gets a fair amount of screen time toward the end of the film, propelled him to reprioritize a Jewish life beyond the antisemitism at issue in *Protocols*. Ribowsky is affiliated with the Gramercy Park Brotherhood Synagogue where Levin's children had their b'nai mitzvah. Given that Levin had been thinking during the filming that he "was getting deeper and deeper into

[his] Jewish heritage and [he] wasn't a member of a synagogue," he decided to reaffirm his commitment to formal and institutional Jewish life by returning "to a place we were once connected to."[66]

One of the most common critiques of *Protocols of Zion* was that it lacked focus. Ty Burr of the *Boston Globe* suggests that "the film bites off more than it can comfortably chew," and Ed Gonzalez and Nick Schager ask, "Is the film ultimately about post-9/11 anti-Semitism? Or historical hatred? The Israel-Palestinian conflict? Or the titular book itself?"[67] However, I would argue that what reviewers deemed the film's lack of focus is actually a reflection of the chameleon-like nature of antisemitism, which has become even more evident and worrying in the Trump era. Post-Charlottesville, post-Pittsburgh, post-Poway, and amid an epidemic of antisemitic attacks in New York, Levin's 2005 film seems newly and alarmingly relevant. Many of the critiques that were questionable or misguided in 2005—for example, the notion that "Levin spends too much time with Shaun Walker, the head of the 'white power' group National Alliance, whom he keeps prodding for neo-Nazi soundbites" or the statement, "As hateful as these people are, one wonders how significant they really are"—seem naive, at best, as we deal with Richard Spencer and his ilk.[68] Levin's assertion that "this is a battle of ideas, not just a battle of reason," and that "we need to use culture—art, humor, film—as part of our creative arsenal"[69] usefully reminds us that *Protocols of Zion* as well as *Gentleman's Agreement*, *School Ties*, and *The Believer* were never just movies. Rather, they function as a microhistory of how Jews have been objects of hate as well as how they have internalized and resisted such hate. Recognizing that Jews and allies are produced alongside these films is an important part of the story, one that goes beyond what we see onscreen.

3

Looking at the Shoah
from a Distance

•••••••••••••••••••••

In high school, Steven Spielberg was traumatized by the antisemitic physical
and verbal assaults that he experienced at the hands of his peers. Shame about
being targeted as a Jew motivated him to hide this trauma from his parents as
well as from many seemingly close friends; it also distanced him from his Jewish heritage early in his career. Joseph McBride, Spielberg's biographer, suggests
that, as a young filmmaker, Spielberg followed in the footsteps of the early Jewish Hollywood studio heads: he embodied assimilation and represented Jewish experience in code, if at all.[1] A little more than a decade before *Schindler's
List* (1993) changed the Holocaust cinematic scene, Steven Spielberg gave us
E.T. (1982), the tale of an alien being who finds himself on earth, enjoys the
pleasures of young companions and the sweetness of Reese's Pieces, but nonetheless wants to return to his homeland and be among his own kind. At one
point, E.T. is reduced to an ashen, emaciated figure in a hospital bed, hooked
up to an IV and monitors; even in this state of mortal peril, he yearns for the
end of his exile. Viewed retrospectively, E.T. might be coded as an immigrant
or even a survivor of the Shoah. While E.T. goes home at the end of his movie,
Schindler's Jews honor their Gentile rescuer in Jerusalem during the final scene
of *Schindler's List*.

The making of *Schindler's List*, based on the novel by Thomas Keneally,
remade Spielberg as a Jew. The Shoah haunted Spielberg from the time of his
youth. Images of the atrocities were always with him, the Holocaust was a subject of dinner conversation in the years immediately following the war, and he

spent time in the company of survivors.[2] Nonetheless, he was well into his career before he undertook *Schindler's List* and came out as a Hollywood Jew. In interviews, he shares the intense emotion associated with the making of this film and credits it with provoking Jewish pride rather than Jewish shame.[3] *Schindler's List* led Spielberg to found the Shoah Visual History Foundation, dedicated to preserving the testimony of tens of thousands of survivors; Spielberg considers this the most important work he has done.[4] He has used film to make the history of World War II in general and the Holocaust and its aftermath in particular widely accessible, and it's worth noting that the experience of an American Jewish GI is included in Spielberg's *Saving Private Ryan*.

In *Schindler's List*, Spielberg attempts to provide us with a straight-on representation of the Shoah, and he wants his viewers to feel as he did while making the film: "I re-created these events, and then I experienced them as any witness or victim would have. It wasn't like a movie."[5] Shot almost entirely in black and white and including handheld camera sequences, the film consciously creates the feel of a documentary. It tries to take us into the bureaucratic machinations of a genocidal regime, including those who gave orders, those who followed orders, and a Nazi sympathizer who turned into a Righteous Gentile when he could no longer make sense of rationalized murder. Perhaps most powerfully—and controversially—it takes us deep into the crematoria, as naked Jewish women, along with their moviegoing viewers, learn that they are to be among the saving remnant when water rather than gas mercifully emerges from the highlighted shower head.[6]

Although Universal bought the rights to Keneally's novel in 1983, Spielberg had considerable doubts about making the mainstream movie he felt needed to be made about such historically traumatic material. Once he decided to do so, he was discouraged by Hollywood insiders; one studio head reportedly suggested a donation to the U.S. Holocaust Museum might make better sense than fronting such an expensive film that was not likely to realize its production costs.[7] Only Spielberg's heavy-hitter status in Hollywood enabled him to do this project, which, of course, became an astonishing success and set the stage for Holocaust movies to become a viable and profitable subgenre. Spielberg should be credited with donating all of his own proceeds from the film to such organizations as the Holocaust Museum and his Survivors of the Shoah Visual History Foundation.[8]

Like the groundbreaking, wildly successful, and critically controversial *Holocaust* miniseries (1978), *Schindler's List* provoked a set of soul-searching questions about whether and how to represent the Shoah. Does the injunction to never forget demand that we try to re-create history visually? What is fair, responsible use of the Holocaust and existing archival images, and what is sensationalism? What stories illuminate a complex, multinational, multicultural historical event, and what stories run the risk of distorting history by universalizing attempted genocide and providing catharsis where none should be available? What is the line between depicting historical horror and manipulating or traumatizing viewers? When does show business become Shoah business, a transformation that desecrates the memory of those who perished and turns those who survived into commodities? And what does Holocaust consciousness mean for Americans in general and American Jews in particular, since this tragedy happened elsewhere?

This last question is of particular interest given that movies have, paradoxically, both de-Jewed the Holocaust—as they have Americanized and universalized it—and made it *the* Jewish story; indeed, for some, Holocaust film and Jewish film are synonymous. Some of the earliest American mainstream movies related to the Shoah—for example, George Stevens's *The Diary of Anne Frank* (1959) and Stanley Kramer's *Judgment at Nuremberg* (1961)—were directed by former members of the U.S. Army Signal Corps; Stevens shot and edited footage of the liberation of the concentration camps that subsequently was used in war trials, including at Nuremberg.[9] However, these first movies on the Holocaust followed prewar conventions and were reluctant to get ensnared in the Hollywood/Jewish question. As Jewish cultural critic Alan Mintz points out, viewing *Judgment at Nuremberg* when it first came out felt like a monumental recognition of the tragedy felt acutely by Jews in the postwar era. However, it is shocking, retrospectively, to realize that "Jew" dares not speak its name in the film.[10] Similarly, the film adaptation of Anne Frank's diary was short on Jewishness and long on optimism, best represented by the line that Anne still believes in the goodness of people.[11] Thirty years later, even Spielberg's *Schindler's List* focused on a Gentile, righteous though he became, with the Jewish Isaac Shtern as his celluloid sidekick.

A cinematic history of a Holocaust without Jews—not to mention tendencies to sugarcoat stories of the Shoah with optimistic narratives of redemption—has, ironically, upped the ante for representing the horror of the Holocaust in the most realistic and graphic terms possible. In the contemporary moment, Holocaust imagery and narratives are seemingly omnipresent, and many fear that we are becoming anesthetized to the horrors of the Final Solution at exactly the moment when the number of living witnesses to the Shoah is dwindling. Even as the need to memorialize increases, there is also legitimate concern about Holocaust-made U.S. Jews for whom, as Mintz puts it, "the slaughtered European Jew became a kind of doppelganger."[12]

Cultural theorist Gary Weissman has argued that intense needs to remember the Holocaust provoke what he calls "fantasies of witnessing," a desire on the part of film spectators to feel as if they are actual witnesses to atrocities.[13] The making of *Schindler's List* exemplifies the desire to have the Holocaust film experience be one that seemingly transcends time and space. In lieu of such fantasies, some notable fiction films—Sidney Lumet's *The Pawnbroker* (1964),

Paul Mazursky's *Enemies, A Love Story* (1989), Woody Allen's *Crimes and Misdemeanors* (1989), and the Coen Brothers's *Barton Fink* (1991) and *A Serious Man* (2009)—thematically and aesthetically position American Jews in the shadow of the Holocaust. These films do the work of Holocaust memory, but they do so indirectly and at a distance, expanding and complicating relationships to a history not our own. Holocaust survivors in America, ethical and theological questions that arose from the ashes of the Shoah, the often impoverished state of American Jewish post-Holocaust life and its inability to fully grasp the atrocity abroad, even questions about moviemaking in the Holocaust and post-Holocaust eras—this is the stuff of these Holocaust indirection films. And while the Holocaust remains present though at a remove in these films, Jewishness and even Judaism are often front and center.

The Pawnbroker (1964)

Sidney Lumet's *The Pawnbroker*, adapted from the 1961 novel by Edward Lewis Wallant, premiered four years after the trial of Adolf Eichmann. Both the locale of the trial—Israel—and the testimony of survivors established the specifically Jewish losses of World War II and the Holocaust. In sharp contrast to earlier cinematic treatments of the Holocaust such as *The Diary of Anne Frank* and *Judgment at Nuremberg*, Lumet's film has a Jewish type—some would even say Jewish stereotype—at its center. However, while a conventionalized Jewish figure is profoundly present here, this film is equally notable for what's absent. As the film's editor Ralph Rosenblum makes clear, "In keeping with the screenplay and the original novel, not one of the gross Nazi atrocities was portrayed.... There were no ovens or executions or horrid human experiments. The story revealed the destruction of an identity, and in this respect the delicacy of fiction was more overwhelming than the stink of explicit horrors."[14] Lumet's film is distinctive for its groundbreaking use of flashbacks to represent the psychic afterlife of the Holocaust; its temporal and geographic distance from the Holocaust is accompanied by a critique of specifically American forms of remembering, forgetting, and not knowing.

The opening scene is European pastoral: a family picnic eventually revealed to include three generations, with elders who are identifiably observant Jews. A sequence of shots adds members of the family to the landscape, a cinematic reversal of the genocidal murders that have decimated this family, with one exception: Sol Nazerman, whose mind twenty-five years later is exposed as the source of these images and memories. From the vantage of a Long Island suburban home and a pawnbroker's shop in Harlem, Sol wrestles with the angels and demons of history that sometimes seem uncannily reincarnated in the present.

Sol's urban American world is a diverse one. It includes multicultural clients who are uniformly desperate; a Black gay mobster and his mostly white underlings who use the pawnshop for their money-laundering business; his new assistant, Jesus Ortiz, who promises his mother that he will give up his life of petty crime but nonetheless becomes involved in the robbery of the pawnshop that will cost him his life; Tessie, Sol's lover, who cares for her dying survivor father (played by Baruch Lumet, the director's father); and an all-American social worker who makes Sol one of her projects, despite his wishes to the contrary.

Almost an automaton in his daily life as a pawnbroker who "take[s] a dream, give[s] a dollar," Sol is at war with the calendar, which is about to shift into October and the twenty-fifth anniversary of the European graveyard that left him bereft and traumatized. Shots of Sol's urban present recall the atrocities of the past. As the camera pans through the streets of Harlem, a shop window piled with shoes recalls the iconic images of footwear belonging to Jews who perished in the crematoria. The bars that enclose Sol in the pawnshop similarly reek of camp imagery.

The blurring of past and present is most powerfully accomplished through flash or shock cuts, quick memory shots that intrude on action in the present and eventually give way to more sustained flashbacks. Although critics often assume that Lumet adapted and mainstreamed the cinematic strategies of such European art film directors as Alain Renais and Jean-Luc Godard, Lumet himself credits this flashback innovation to his background in early television, "when we were doing cuts as fast as a finger could move."[15] Shots of a local Harlemite striving to climb a fence to evade hoodlum attackers and the soundtrack of a barking dog give way to Sol's memory of witnessing the hunting of a friend vainly trying to climb the barbed wire that enclosed the camp. When a desperate pregnant woman comes to pawn her diamond engagement ring that turns out to be glass, the image of her hands gives way to multiple hands poised above barbed wire. The hands of the many who have been captured by the Nazis are stripped of their rings as a prelude to genocidal violence. When Ortiz's girlfriend, a prostitute, tries to seduce Sol with the intended siren call of "Look, don't cost you nothing to look," Sol hears a Nazi soldier once again asking him if he wants to see; in his mind's eye, Sol's head is thrust through a glass window so that the soldier can show him his beloved wife, Ruth, being scrubbed down in a shower as a prelude to sexual assault. Contrary to the prostitute's assurances, looking and seeing cost Sol a great deal. On the subway, Sol relives the journey on the deportation train packed with human flesh and once more feels his grip loosening on his son David, the screams of Ruth echoing in his ears then and now.

In the final minutes of the film, after his assistant Jesus has lived up to his name and has died trying to save Sol from a botched robbery scheme, Sol cradles the head of this young savior. In the aftermath of Jesus's death, viewers once again witness Sol's memory at work. However, this time, the images relived and reviewed are parts of Sol's present: the impoverished supplicants pawning their goods; his lover, Tessie; Marilyn, the social worker. Silent screams of anguish accompany Sol impaling himself on the spike that holds the bureaucratic paperwork of the pawnshop. The pawnbroker who has been characterized as a "bastard" by Lumet now openly bears stigmata on his body as well as his psyche.[16]

Understandably, the imposition of a Christian frame on this survivor's life as well as paralleling Shoah scenes with those of urban ghetto blight troubled some viewers. Despite Lumet's assertions of intentions to the contrary, these aspects of the film encouraged some to view *The Pawnbroker* as cementing cinematic trends that Christianize and Americanize the attempted genocide of European Jewry.[17] However, such a view gives short shrift to the film's project to explicitly address—and critique—diverse forms of American ignorance and appropriation of the Holocaust.

American—even Jewish American—forgetting of the trauma of the Shoah is at issue early in the film. Sol's dream of a pastoral family picnic that turns into historical gothic with the arrival of the Nazis is followed by a scene in which his sister-in-law talks about her murdered sister in one breath and of a European tour in the next. Her husband considers a trip to Europe as cultural and professional capital, and she betrays herself as nostalgic for the "shrines, the old cities . . . there's an atmosphere we don't have here . . . age lends its own charms . . . you can almost smell the difference." For Sol, Europe is rife with the "stink" of death; for his sister-in-law, her family, and by extension much of the United States, Europe's siren calls of culture and civilization erase recent genocidal history.

The Pawnbroker also represents the younger generation as having little to no knowledge of this history to erase. One of the young men of color who ultimately rob the pawnshop wants to know where Sol got "those numbers tattooed"; Jesus also betrays his ignorance of the Holocaust when he follows up on the earlier query by asking how he might join the "secret society" that he assumes must be associated with those numbers. His assumption that such numbers are a sign of chosen privilege rather than murderous oppression is in keeping with the unconscious and culturally sanctioned antisemitism that empowers him to ask, "How come you people come to business so naturally?" Sol is also the object of blatant Jew-hatred, even in post-Holocaust America: a junkie who is a regular customer of the pawnshop responds to Sol's proposed payment for a radio with the explosive "blood-sucking sheenie, money grubbing kike." Notably, Sol's older customers are quite aware of the nightmares of history in general and the likely impact they have had on him in particular. One man, hyperconscious that this Harlem pawnbroker was a European professor in another time and place, strives to engage him in intellectual conversation, and a loquacious woman identifies him as a "hard man" in need of God's pity; such awareness causes her to forget her pawn ticket and the two dollars she was desperate enough to accept for a pair of cherished candlesticks. While elders in Harlem understand that Sol has been made, not born, a pawnbroker, the younger generation's historical illiteracy threatens to reproduce antisemitic stereotypes that did not perish with the death of 6 million. The representation of such American forms of forgetting or not knowing in 1964 resonates in the contemporary moment when 64 percent of millennials surveyed cannot identify Auschwitz.[18]

The potential universalizing and Americanizing of the Holocaust as a metaphor for suffering is critiqued through the figure of Marilyn Birchfield, a social worker who has more understanding of Sol's history than most but not as much as she thinks she does. Nazerman meets with Marilyn four times. In the first meeting, at the pawnshop, she identifies herself as a "new neighbor" asking for help from local businesses for a youth center, an "investment in the future." Although Nazerman avows that he has no concern with the future— we know that his future and children were extinguished in Europe—he nonetheless hands Birchfield a check, whether to get rid of her or out of some residual commitments to youth and *tzedakah* (righteousness) we can't be sure. When she suggests that he might want to coach basketball at the center, his response— "You must be joking"—is rude but nonetheless on target in its identification of her as an out-of-touch reformer, a pastoral all-American (as her name suggests) rather than one well-equipped to negotiate multicultural difference in the urban ghetto. During their second meeting, also at the pawnshop, Birchfield witnesses the antisemitic rant of the junkie. She not only apologizes to Sol for the junkie's behavior but also for her own tactlessness at their last meeting, and she proposes having lunch in the park later in the week. When they meet for that lunch, their distance from one another is visually enforced by the tree that divides them.[19] She explicitly recognizes him as a concentration camp survivor; when he does not offer his story, she offers her own, that of a lonely young woman whose solitude was broken for a brief time by the love of a husband who died prematurely. While she assumes that they can bond over the universalism of loneliness and loss, Nazerman brutally—but to my mind honestly and accurately—insists that "there is a world different from yours, much different, and the people in it are of another species." Despite her admission that she is out of her depth, she returns to her own experience, which Nazerman dismisses as "nothing," a moment that seems to justify Lumet's characterizing him as a bastard.

Nazerman's final meeting with Birchfield occurs after a traumatic encounter with the money-laundering pimp, Rodriguez. During that meeting, Sol tries but fails to extricate himself from a relationship that he has come to understand as complicit with forms of sexual abuse and violence visited upon his wife in the camps. Like the Nazi guard, Rodriguez insists on compelling Nazerman to "look"—at both Rodriguez and himself. Disoriented by the accumulating

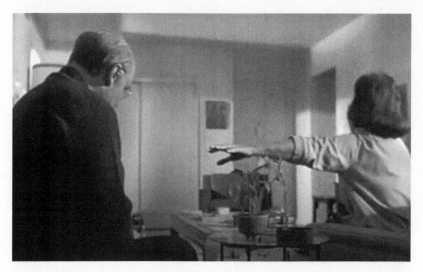

FIG. 3.1 The gulf between survivor and social worker in *The Pawnbroker* (1964)

convergences of past and present, Nazerman stumbles through the night streets of New York to Birchfield's apartment and collapses. Birchfield once again mis-identifies his malady as the same as hers—loneliness. Nazerman rectifies this faux identification by outlining for her the "memories [that] flood my mind": "Everything that I loved was taken away from me and I did not die, nothing I could do, nothing." Overcome by "listening to [him] and not being able to do anything for [him]," Marilyn holds out her hand to Nazerman but then lets it drop.[20] If they are joined at the end of this scene, it is only by their mutual recognition of the distance that separates them, as well as their mutual inability to intervene in the history of atrocity.

Twenty years after the war ended, post-Nuremberg and post-Eichmann, Americans, in the throes of their own domestic upheavals, can no longer be fig-ured or figure themselves as only and always optimistic liberators. Despite the Christian motifs and imagery that continue from Wallant's literary text to Lumet's cinematic vision, in *The Pawnbroker*, all-American saviors can neither erase nor appropriate the Jewish specificity of the Holocaust survivor's experi-ence and trauma. Notably, Lumet's reflections on his own career indicate early resistance to scripts of Jews being saved by their all-American compatriots. He explains his shift from actor to filmmaker: "I knew at that time that if I stayed in acting, the best I could hope for was getting the part of the little Jewish kid from Brooklyn who got shot down by the mean Japs or Nazis, and then Clark Gable would pick me up and then with tears in his eyes would rush forward and single-handedly wipe out their machine gun nest. That was an area of drama that didn't particularly interest me."[21]

Compelled to look not only at Sol but also at Marilyn and Jesus, viewers of *The Pawnbroker* are encouraged to acknowledge that, especially from this side of the Atlantic, the Shoah can only be glimpsed partially and indirectly. For Lumet, the ethics of Holocaust representation demand that the illusion of realistic representation be refused: "The original script for *The Pawnbroker* said to use real footage of the concentration camps—newsreel footage—and I wouldn't do that because it seemed so totally exploitative. Those people didn't die so that we could use them in the movie."[22]

Enemies, A Love Story (1989)

Like Sidney Lumet, Paul Mazursky was determined not to provide a fantasy of witnessing the Shoah in his 1989 adaptation of Isaac Bashevis Singer's novel *Enemies, A Love Story*. He committed himself to "no shots of the Holocaust. No shots of children being dumped into a hole. No shots of escape." As he put it to Sam Wasson, "The trick for me in adapting the book was to visualize the Holocaust without showing it, but in a way that didn't make it corny or melodramatic"[23] Using the aesthetic and narrative strategy of indirection, Mazursky portrays survivors as haunted, complex human beings wrestling with personal and theological crises that distance them from native-born American Jews.

Herman Broder, played by Ron Silver, is initially torn between two lovers in New York: Yadwiga, the Christian Polish peasant who sustained him in his past as he hid in a hayloft and now keeps his Brooklyn home, and Masha, a sister survivor who lives in the Bronx with her aging and demanding mother. The opening scene, in which Nazi forces mercilessly massacre screaming Jewish women, is quickly revealed to be the stuff of Herman's nightmares, history from which he cannot fully awake. Reminiscent of *The Pawnbroker*'s use of flashback and dream sequences, this scene establishes that the psychic crawl space of traumatic memory is as real as the gritty New York subway system.

The plot of Herman's Holocaust afterlife thickens when his wife, Tamara, who was reportedly killed along with their two children, turns out to be very much alive—at least physically. Like Herman and Masha, Tamara is haunted; the operation that she needs to remove the bullet that wounded but did not kill her indicates that the violence of the past still lies within and must be excised.

In the aftermath of one of his short-lived religious moments, Herman opines that the "Talmud is a great book but doesn't explain what a man should do with two wives." Jewish textual tradition is just as ill-equipped to provide guidance when the third is added to the mix. The limits of Talmud are certainly mined here for a bit of comic relief from the desperately schizophrenic lives wrought by attempted genocide. However, such heretical humor also points to the spiritual vacuum left by the Shoah: while Masha assumes that suffering is an attribute of God and thus the extermination of U.S. Jews cannot be ruled out, Herman simultaneously denies and defies God. The minimalist seder that includes only Herman, Tamara, and the now converted—and pregnant—Yadwiga suggests that history threatens to empty Jewish ritual of its capacity to redeem and to liberate.

The domestic Jewish landscape, especially the U.S. rabbi for whom Herman is a ghostwriter, contributes to this post-Holocaust spiritual wasteland. Critics have rightly noted the death-in-life nature of a ghost and the ways in which Herman's work life mirrors his incapacity to establish a solid sense of self and intimate relationships.[24] However, it's also worth noting the insubstantiality—ghostliness—of a Central Park West rabbi who writes neither his own sermons nor the scholarly articles that appear under his name. Alan King, whose own training ground was the Catskills, is brilliant casting for this parody of a spiritual leader. Calling Herman a "greenhorn," the rabbi predicts that he'll "marry a shiksa" and then decides that he needs to speak on "mixed marriages, the plague of the Jews." That intermarriage could have the status of a "plague" in the imme-diate aftermath of the Shoah is a potent reminder of the chasm between the expe-rience of native-born American Jews and that of European Jews.[25]

That chasm is narratively ubiquitous throughout *Enemies, A Love Story*. When one well-heeled man realizes that Herman has two wives—he does not yet know that there are three—he remarks, "Refugees certainly know how to live in this country." Giving the lie to that glib American sentiment, Herman is shortly thereafter literally and figuratively caught in a storm, and he hears the bloodthirsty barking of dogs, a reminder of the Nazis from his opening nightmare.

Similarly, when Herman and Masha take a bus to the Catskills, bucolic American Jewish life replete with rhumba and ping-pong is contrasted with Masha's heavy drinking and her sense that she is "still among the dead." Nota-bly, a group of women engage in Jewhooing, a means of defining one's Jewish-ness through citing celebrities of the tribe, as David Kaufman has compellingly argued.[26] John Garfield is one of the featured Jewish movie idols in this seem-ingly lighthearted resort game. Of course, the cinematically literate viewer watching *Enemies* in 1989 (and beyond) likely knows that Garfield, formerly Garfinkle, died tragically young, in part a victim of fascism at home in the form of HUAC. When Masha first arrives in the Catskills, she asks, "Where are the Nazis?" The citing of John Garfield seems like an indirect answer to her ques-tion. Both the shadow of the Holocaust and the antisemitic Communist witch hunt in Hollywood haunt the American Jewish pastoral of the Catskills. How-ever, even as *Enemies, A Love Story* links domestic fascism with its much darker European double, it distinguishes talk of Tinseltown from traumatic memories of the Shoah.

The next generation, both the one lost in Europe and the one waiting to be born in the United States, also dominates the film's narrative. The murder of David and Sarah, Herman and Tamara's son and daughter, haunts their survivor parents, as Herman's private mourning on erev Yom Kippur poignantly captures. Masha experiences a faux pregnancy; her mother indicates that she wanted a grandchild, "if only someone to name for the murdered Jews." Early in the film, Yadwiga expresses her heartfelt desire to convert and bear Herman's child. At the end of the film, Yadwiga gives birth to a baby girl shortly after Masha commits suicide, and the child bearing the name of Herman's "crazy but interesting mistress" will be raised by Yadwiga and Tamara. Although Herman reneged on a double-suicide pact with Masha, at the end he is represented only by the cash he sends and an empty sheet of paper. Counterpointing the void at the heart of *Enemies, A Love Story* is a close-up of baby Masha. Film historian Omer Bartov considers this ending to be an "attempt to recreate the past" that is "both false and impossible."[27] However, the infant seems to me to be less a replacement for Masha, David, and Sarah and more a living memory of them. The historical chasm of the Shoah is not bridged by but rather exists alongside Jewish continuity fostered by a contemporary Ruth and Naomi. Jews can still be made, but they cannot redeem the losses of the Holocaust.

Living memories of the Shoah not only are contained in but also were central to the making of *Enemies, A Love Story*. Ron Silver, a Jewishly committed actor, needed no Holocaust education, but Mazursky made sure that Lena Olin (Masha) and Angelica Huston (Tamara) received tutorials in Jewish history and culture, including a trek to a Lower East Side deli in New York where refugees noshed and survivors with numbers on their forearms waited tables.[28] Rita Karin, born Rita Karpinowicz, played the role of Mrs. Schreir, a Brooklyn neighbor; the Polish-born Karin, whose parents perished in the Shoah, was involved with the Yiddish theater first in postwar Poland and then in the United States.[29]

Such care with the cast and its education was in keeping with Mazursky's commitment to resist the whitewashing of historical specificity. Touchstone Pictures, a division of Disney, paid for the film rights to Bashevis Singer's novel and also paid Mazursky and Roger Simon to write the script. Despite this initial investment, Michael Eisner balked at the estimated $10 million price tag for this period piece and suggested that Mazursky "update" the material to lower costs. "I almost fainted when I heard that," said Mazursky. "I'm reminding you this is a movie about Holocaust survivors."[30] The film was ultimately released by Twentieth Century Fox.

Billy Wilder, that émigré master of a very different indirect Holocaust film tradition known as noir, admired *Enemies, A Love Story* but predicted that it wouldn't sell because it lacked star power.[31] Despite lackluster results at the preview, producer Joe Roth recognized the film as a "masterpiece" and rightly assumed that the studio would at least break even.[32] However, the marketing for this masterpiece was also lackluster, and the film earned Oscar nominations, including for Best Adapted Screenplay, but no wins. While film reviewer Michael Fox notes (and rues) the omission of *Enemies, A Love Story* from the canon-constructing documentary *Imaginary Witness: Hollywood and the Holocaust*, *LA Times* film critic Kenneth Turan includes *Enemies* among his "Ten Great Jewish American Films."[33] And Ilan Stavans, who writes about discovering a diverse Jewish diaspora at the movies, identifies *Enemies* as one of the cinematic experiences that has provided "invigorating" discussions with his son.[34] Ultimately, the making of Jews through moving images of surviving in America happens from generation to generation both onscreen and off.

Crimes and Misdemeanors (1989)

Few directors are as associated with Jewishness, both positively and negatively, as Woody Allen. For some, Allen is a case study of Jewish self-hatred, a Judas figure who disrespects Judaism and promulgates antisemitic stereotypes of Jewish perversion in both his life and his work.[35] Others credit him with making Jews sexy through a body of work that not only serves as a catalyst for secular Jewish identification among Jews but also, in Vivian Gornick's provocative words, makes "Jews of Gentiles."[36] *Crimes and Misdemeanors* (1989), a film that many regard as among Allen's finest, is also, arguably, his most Jewish and Judaic-friendly. This movie, a murder plot with a subplot about documentary filmmaking, is a compelling meditation on the theological and ethical crises engendered by the Holocaust.

Born in 1935, Allan Stewart Konigsberg, who later transformed himself into Woody Allen, came of age during World War II and its aftermath. Extended members of his family were Holocaust survivors and were aided by his parents. In a 1990 article in *Tikkun* that he wrote to contextualize an earlier *New York Times* op-ed in which he critiqued Israel, he begins with a portrait of a prosperous survivor who nonetheless had "the predictable haunted look," a haunting from history that Woody clearly shares from a distance. Although in that essay Allen expresses skepticism about overemphasizing Jewish difference, he professes the belief that Holocaust survivors merit a secure Jewish homeland of their own and his acute awareness that Righteous Gentiles during the Shoah inspired awe but were not numerous enough to spare 6 million. For Allen, the Holocaust confirms the misanthropic assumption that "people are no damn good" rather than the optimism of Anne Frank.[37]

The Holocaust, like other serious subjects such as sex and death, is often treated with humor, albeit bitter humor, by Allen in his movies, and Holocaust consciousness has sometimes been represented as a symptom of Jewish neurosis or even paranoia. Alvy Singer's obsessive-compulsive behavior in *Annie Hall* includes turning Marcel Ophüls's epic documentary on French collaboration *The Sorrow and the Pity* into his own private cult classic. The title character of *Deconstructing Harry* suggests that the Holocaust record of 6 million is made to be broken. And Sandy in *Stardust Memories* notes that only by the grace of being born in Brooklyn rather than Poland did he avoid being turned into a lampshade. Given such a tradition of one-liners, Allen's serious engagement with Judaism and questions regarding an ethical life lived in the shadow of the Shoah in *Crimes and Misdemeanors* is noteworthy.

Judah Rosenthal (played by Martin Landau) is a successful, seemingly happily married ophthalmologist, a cosmopolitan man of science who has left behind his Orthodox religious upbringing. His stewardess mistress, Dolores (Angelica Huston), is so desperate to hang onto him that she threatens to reveal not only his romantic but also his financial improprieties. Rabbi Ben (Sam Waterston), his friend and patient, advises him to confess his infidelities to his wife and trust in her forgiveness. His no-goodnik brother Jack, played by the leather-jacketed and leather-faced Jerry Orbach, advises the extinction of the seemingly insuperable impediment Dolores and ultimately arranges her murder. While Judah is initially horrified and undone by his own complicity with murder, he chooses to resume his prehomicide life. Before he does so, however, he revisits his childhood home and flashes back not to the Holocaust nightmares of *The Pawnbroker* and *Enemies, A Love Story* but to a seder during which God's presence in the post-Holocaust world was debated. Aunt May, a rabid materialist, insisted that the Nazis' getting away with the murder of 6 million Jews refutes any possibility of believing in a world informed by divine justice, while Sol, Judah and Jack's father, affirmed his faith in a God-centered, ethical world. Baited with the possibility that he's wrong, Sol insisted that his life still would be better and richer with such a worldview.

The boundaries between flashback memory and the present moment fall away as the contemporary Judah steps back in time and space and asks his assembled relatives about murder, to their great confusion and consternation. According to the Talmud, for those who have taken a single life, it is as if they have destroyed a world (just as those who save a single life save a world). The connections powerfully forged between the murder of Dolores and the world-destroying Shoah through this seder scene are in keeping with Jewish tradition. Just as Jews recounting the Exodus story are supposed to experience for themselves liberation and redemption, so does Judah, as the not-so-innocent bystander to Dolores's murder, become reimmersed in the theological and ethical debates of his childhood in particular and the post-Holocaust world in general.

The narrative thread devoted to Cliff, a small-time documentary filmmaker played by Woody Allen, is similarly framed in relation to the Shoah. Cliff, enlisted to shoot a film about another director, his uber-successful brother-in-law Lester (Alan Alda), turns this assignment into an exposé. Rather than filming the great man at work, Cliff intercuts shots of Lester at his womanizing, narcissistic worst with those of a donkey as well as Mussolini. While Judah is complicit with murder, Lester, from Cliff's perspective, violates the sanctity of artistic life with his superficial sound bites and his overly commercialized consciousness. In sharp contrast to the charlatan Lester, Cliff's preferred documentary subject, philosophy professor Louis Levy, seems to be the real intellectual deal. The sole member of his family to survive the Holocaust, Levy nonetheless philosophically affirms the meaning of life in a world without a loving God figure.

A very different type than Sol in *The Pawnbroker* or Herman in *Enemies, A Love Story*, Levy seems to have constructed an extraordinarily affirmative philosophy in the face of genocidal history; this inspirational outlook convinces Halle, Cliff's extramarital love interest and the editor with whom he is working on Lester's documentary, to help Cliff secure funding for this project. However, Levy's suicide and his profoundly antiphilosophical suicide note—"I've gone out the window"—torpedoes Cliff's documentary, while suggesting to Halle the necessary incompleteness of any philosophical system. In "Reflections of a Second-Rate Mind," the previously mentioned essay that appeared in *Tikkun*, Allen reveals this view as his own. Significantly, that haunted survivor of Auschwitz living the good life in a bistro on the Upper East Side of Manhattan was the catalyst for his stated belief that "no philosopher ever to come along, no matter how profound, could even begin to understand the world."

The Louis Levy story line in *Crimes and Misdemeanors*—modeled in part on the life and death of Primo Levi, the Italian writer-chemist whose *Survival in Auschwitz* is a classic of Holocaust literature—recalls and upends the Hollywood tendency to turn the Shoah into redemptive or feel-good grist for the cinematic mill. However, Judah's murderous, self-serving nihilism does not become the final solution to the philosophical and theological crises crystallized by the Holocaust. At the end of the film, Judah and Cliff meet at the wedding of the daughter of the now-blind Rabbi Ben. Upon hearing that Cliff is a filmmaker, Judah, who is more than a bit tipsy, offers Cliff a movie idea based on his recent life: a successful man commits a terrible crime, finds himself tormented by it for a time in keeping with the moral lessons of his religious upbringing, but then, when he finds that no punishment is forthcoming, resumes his former life with the knowledge that the God of his father is truly dead. True to form, Cliff complicates the ethics of this "chilling story" by positing a Levyesque plot twist: in the absence of God, human beings must construct their own moral universe, and thus the criminal confesses and takes his punishment like a moral man. Judah dismisses this alternative ending as a fantasy and Cliff as a man who has seen too many Hollywood movies. However, Allen's own *Crimes and Misdemeanors* gives Levy the last word in the form of a voice-over:

We are all faced throughout our lives with agonizing decisions. Moral choices. Some are on a grand scale. Most of these choices are on lesser points. But we define ourselves by the choices we have made. We are, in fact, the sum total of our choices. Events unfold so unpredictably, so unfairly. Human happiness does not seem to have been included in the design of creation. It is only we, with our capacity to love, that give meaning to the indifferent universe. And yet, most human beings seem to have the ability to keep trying, and even to find joy, from simple things, like their family, their work, and from the hope that future generations might understand more.

Cliff and Judah's discussion of ethics in relation to film conventions suggests that, for Allen, movies can function as a secular form of Torah study, with post-Holocaust questions and debate trumping any fundamentalist answers.[38]

Martin Landau, whose Austrian-born father helped to bring relatives and Torah scrolls to safety from Nazi-occupied Europe, views *Crimes and Misdemeanors* as the "first time [he] ever saw Woody Allen embrace his Jewishness. In *Annie Hall*, there is a scene where his character is at dinner with a Protestant family, and suddenly he feels self-conscious and imagines himself wearing payis, like he's embarrassed to be Jewish." However, from Landau's perspective, in *Crimes and Misdemeanors*, "a rabbi serves as the moral voice of the film."[39] In sharp contrast to Landau, some regard the portrayal of Ben as further evidence of Woody's disdain for Judaism and those committed to Jewish identification. In that view, Ben's blindness is a metaphor for his refusal to see the reality of a world without God, and the final shots of him happily dancing at his daughter's wedding to the tune of "I'll Be Seeing You" are seen as evidence of Allen's mean-spirited irony.[40]

While viewing Ben as *the* moral voice of the movie strikes me as an overstatement—Cliff and Louis Levy offer moral though not God-centered perspectives at the close of the film—Ben's voice is certainly part of the dialogue. In good Talmudic fashion, Woody seems intent here on preserving the minority view. Moreover, while Ben's vision loss might be viewed as connoting the blind faith of a fool, it's worth remembering the tradition in Western culture, represented by Oedipus and Tiresias, that sees blindness as a special form of insight. Ben as a serious ethical man rather than a comic figure stands in marked contrast to other rabbis and devout Jews in Allen's films both before and after *Crimes and Misdemeanors*. And compared with the other films discussed in this chapter, Ben's integrity and Jewish life are portrayed very differently—and much more positively. Sam Waterston's Ben puts to shame the rabbi played by Alan King in Mazursky's *Enemies, A Love Story* and, as will be shown shortly, the rabbis represented in the Coens's *A Serious Man*. In *Crimes and Misdemeanors*, God is indicted much more harshly for a world marked by murder and genocide than those movie-made Jews who continue to have faith in divine justice or a human-bound ethical system.

Barton Fink (1991) and A Serious Man (2009)

Like Woody Allen, Joel and Ethan Coen, known as the corporate entity the Coen Brothers, tend to be either loved or hated by filmgoers in general, and Jewish filmgoers in particular. Raised in a Jewishly observant Minnesotan home by two professors, these blood and aesthetic brothers called upon the Jewish community from which they sprang to help fund their first film, *Blood Simple*. Adamant on remaining independent from Hollywood studio production, though not distribution,[41] the Coen Brothers, who have been aptly and amusingly described as "joined at the quip," are the darlings of the indie film circuit.[42] Those who consider the cult celebrity status of the Coens as much ado about nothing hold that their films promote style over substance and remain locked into an allusive, self-contained world of film, a postmodern void, a contemporary black cinematic hole with stylized shots of unrelenting violence.[43] However, as I argue here, two of their Jewciest movies—*Barton Fink* (1991) and *A Serious Man* (2009)—use their trademark stylized shots and narratives of man-made and natural violence to indirectly represent American Jewish takes on cataclysms abroad.

Barton Fink, a film about a New York Jewish leftist playwright who goes to Hollywood, suffers writer's block, and becomes entangled with an insurance salesman revealed to be a psychopathic killer, provided a "vacation" for the Coens from the complications associated with scripting *Miller's Crossing*.[44] Although the film was far from a box office hit, it received numerous awards, including the prestigious Palme d'Or at Cannes for best film. Fink, played by John Turturro, is loosely based on the playwright Clifford Odets, one of the many serious writers who found themselves at odds with the artistic values— or lack thereof—of Tinseltown.[45]

The Coens intentionally set *Barton Fink* on "the eve of the apocalypse, since, for America, 1941 was the beginning of the Second World War."[46] This cinematic period piece portrays the isolationist tendencies of an intellectual that mirror the state of the nation and, especially, Hollywood. Although Fink is supposedly interested in the common man, the working stiffs who deserve a theater of their own, he cannot shut up long enough to listen to the stories of Charlie Meadows (John Goodman), his next-door neighbor in the sweltering Hotel Earle. With its oozing, peeling wallpaper and a creepy bellman played by Steve Buscemi who first emerges from underground through a trapdoor, the hotel announces that we are in noir country, significantly the genre developed and refined by such Jewish émigrés fleeing Nazi Europe as Billy Wilder and Fritz Lang.[47]

As the plot of *Barton Fink* thickens and Audrey, the ghostwriting mistress of a Faulkneresque character, ends up in Barton's bed first as lover and then as corpse, the narrative fulfills the noirish promise of the locale. The likeliest suspect for the murder is none other than Charlie Meadows, the insurance salesman who makes good on his promise that "fire, theft, and casualty don't just happen to other people." As Fink finds out from Detectives Mastrionotti and Deutsch, Meadows is the pastoral alias for Madman Karl Mundt, a serial killer who beheads his victims and thus literally cuts off the life of the mind. The Italian and German last names of the detectives link the LAPD with the Axis powers and their American counterparts; this link is strengthened when one of the detectives disdainfully notes that Fink is a Jewish name and that the Earle is not restricted, that is, not a Gentiles-only establishment. Both detectives are slain by Mundt late in the film, and a "Heil Hitler" from the killer is part of the send-off given to Deutsch.

The year 1941, a killer with a German last name, and antisemitic detectives suggest that the shadows of the Shoah are making their way across the Atlantic to American shores. By the end of the film, courtesy of Mundt, the hallway of the Hotel Earle is aflame, a literal holocaust at home. When we remember that shoes have lined that hallway on a nightly basis, that some shots of the hallway dimly lit by symmetrically arranged fixtures give it the look of a railway tunnel, and that the revelation of Audrey's bloody body is preceded by camerawork of movement down a drain/sewer/tunnel, we retrospectively realize that Holocaust imagery has been present throughout the film, though not at the same intensity as when Barton walks a path through the raging inferno. Fink is a survivor figure, made more so by the likelihood that his family has perished at the hands of Mundt, who reports that he visited those "good people"—at Fink's suggestion—when he was in New York. The viewer of the film, like Barton Fink and U.S. Jews, can only read and interpret the signs of the Shoah retrospectively and from a distance.

Fink's meetings with Hollywood mogul Lipnick (brilliantly played by Michael Lerner) punctuate scenes in the Hotel Earle, including encounters with Meadows/Mundt. Given such narrative placement, these meetings reveal *Barton Fink* as a film that is, in part, about the workings of Jewish Hollywood and its response to Nazi threats. Much ink has been spilled about the motivations of Jewish studio heads who avoided using their influence to cinematically represent the impending doom facing their former brethren, the Jews of Europe. This complicated story needs to take into account U.S. isolationist tendencies, with its accompanying antisemitism, that dominated the period. Suspicions that the alien immigrants of Jewish-controlled Hollywood would lead America into another world war were promoted by such notorious antisemites as Father Coughlin, Henry Ford, and Congressman John Rankin (it's worth remembering that as late as 1944, Rankin received applause rather than protest from the House of Representatives when he used the word "kike"). In 1940, Joe Kennedy, ambassador to Great Britain, met with Hollywood Jews and warned them that any anti-Nazi activity would cause increased antisemitism at home. It is also relevant that motion picture production codes, overseen by Joseph Breen, the Hollywood censor who was himself no stranger to antisemitic sentiments, prohibited any denigration of national groups in film; in practice, this rule effectively rendered criticism of fascist violence off-limits. We must also remember that most of the powerful Hollywood studio heads were devoted assimilationists at heart who tended to internalize antisemitism. Moreover, business interests—including and especially film distribution in Germany—were guiding principles in the making and editing of U.S. films. Thus the Warners pulling out of Germany after one of their salesmen, Joe Kaufman, was beaten to death by a Nazi mob in 1936 and their greenlighting *Confessions of a Nazi Spy* have long been regarded as the exception to the rule of Hollywood appeasement. More recently, film scholars Thomas Doherty and Ben Urwand have waged a war of words over whether it makes sense to regard the Hollywood Jews as collaborators with the Nazis.[48]

Barton Fink's first encounter with Lipnick signals that this vexed Jewish Hollywood history is part of this noirish plot. In interviews, the Coens indicate that Lipnick was conceived as a composite figure of Harry Cohn, Louis B. Mayer, and Jack Warner, and that their screenplay was informed by Otto Friedrich's *City of Nets: A Portrait of Hollywood in the 40s*. In the film, the fast-talking Lipnick refers to himself as hailing from New York but also from "Minsk, if you want to go all the way back, which we won't if you don't mind, and I ain't asking." Horrifying and overwhelming the mousy Fink during that first meeting, Lipnick refers to himself as the "biggest and meanest and loudest kike in this town." Later in the film, he appears in military uniform and informs Fink that he is now to be addressed as colonel. He has arranged for an army commission and has gotten wardrobe to provide him with the costume that goes with this role. Gleefully, the Coens report that this "surreal" scene actually comes from the annals of the movie industry. As Otto Friedrich tells it in *City of Nets*:

> Jack Warner . . . responded to the call to service by saying that he wanted to start out as a general. He added that he would be happy to telephone the White House to get President Roosevelt's approval. Persuaded to settle for the rank of lieutenant colonel, and assigned to a public relations post in Los Angeles, Warner proceeded to the studio tailoring shop to get himself outfitted for his new role. Though his military duties never called him far from his office in Burbank, he let it be known that he liked to be addressed as "Colonel" while he produced films like *Winning Your Wings* and *Rear Gunner*. On the day that a full colonel came to the studio to discuss future film projects, though, when Jack Warner graciously welcomed his visitor by shaking his hand, and the

visiting colonel said, "you should have saluted me"—that was the day Jack Warner resigned his commission.[49]

Although *Barton Fink* depicts writers and studio executives at odds with one another, when it comes to wartime narcissism and historical denial or, more charitably, repression, Fink and Lipnick are close doubles. While Lipnick dons a non-military-issue uniform to play a faux part in the war effort against the "Japs" (not the Nazis), Fink celebrates the completion of his wrestling picture script at a USO dance. Notably, Audrey's gruesome death, a box Meadows leaves with Fink when he goes to New York with the retrospectively macabre assignment of dealing with things that have gone awry at the "head office," and a picture of a bathing beauty at the beach that hangs above his desk in the Hotel Earle have all served to release Fink's creative juices and to end his bout of writer's block. When he emerges from his maniacal typing spree, he dances wildly with a woman dressed in red. A sailor tries to cut in; when Fink insists that this is *his* dance, the sailor informs him that he is shipping out tomorrow, implicitly appealing to respect for the war effort and the sacrifices some men are making. Fink self-indulgently asserts that he is celebrating "the creation of something good" and that his mind is his uniform. Despite Fink's lofty ideals, war is a metaphor and an aesthetic performance no less for him than for Lipnick.

Affronted by Fink's presumption, another soldier decks him, and a chaotic fight ensues, from which Fink adroitly extricates himself. A shot of the mouth of a trombone leads back to the hallway of the hotel, which will shortly become the fiery front lines of the domestic home front. However, the film doesn't end there. Rather, the scene shifts from Shoah-like images back to the studio, where Lipnick expresses nothing but disdain for Fink's script, indicating that wrestling with one's soul does not belong at the center of a B movie wrestling picture and that the world does not revolve around what goes on in that "kike head of his." The film ends with Fink on the beach, encountering there in the flesh the bathing beauty of the picture. Fire, casualty, and theft *have* happened to other people, but they are in close proximity to Fink—most notably, Audrey as well as his parents and uncle. Yet Fink, like real and imagined Hollywood Jews—that is, Lipnick, Cohn, Mayer, and Warner—remains in the world of conventionalized pictures, even as the Coen Brothers commit themselves to independent cinema and to not making the same picture twice. As a film about the movie industry during the early years of the Holocaust era, *Barton Fink* suggests that, for the Jewish Hollywood studio heads, surviving in America entailed dealing indirectly, if at all, with historical horror.

As a reminder that indirect Holocaust meditations are connected to more straightforward Holocaust-themed films, it's worth noting that, after seeing *Barton Fink*, the Italian director Francesco Rosi decided to cast John Turturro as Primo Levi in his film *The Truce*, based on Levi's autobiographical novel *The*

Reawakening, which details his journey from Auschwitz back to Italy. As Rosi puts it, "What struck me about Turturro when I saw the movie *Barton Fink* were his eyes, which manage to communicate a certain innocence, and to pass from irony to the most intimate, internal drama. . . . I didn't want to lose the gaze of Primo Levi, who is an observer, but is an observer totally interested in human life, totally curious about human experience, of all that happens around and within himself, which is typical of a great writer."[50] Casting decisions together with narratives and imagery remind us of the links as well as the stark differences between the Holocaust indirectly imagined in America and cinematic attempts to represent historical atrocity and its direct aftermath.

The structure of *A Serious Man* (2009) reminds us, albeit with considerable tongue in cinematic cheek, of Jewish communities that are worlds apart. The prologue of *A Serious Man* consists of a faux Yiddish folktale set in a pre-Holocaust shtetl; there the debate between husband and wife, which is not settled, is whether Reb Groskover is man or dybbuk. The main narrative, set in 1967 in a Midwestern Jewish community, focuses on the trials and tribulations of Larry Gopnik, a physics professor up for tenure as his wife announces she wants a divorce, his son professes more interest in *F Troop* than in his upcoming bar mitzvah, his brother gets in trouble with the law for violating both antigambling and antisodomy laws, and his daughter spends her time washing her hair and planning for a nose job. Larry's "professional and personal tsuris" culminates with an ominous call from his doctor about the chest X-rays taken at the beginning of the film and the sighting of a literal tornado bearing down on the community. As many reviewers and critics have noted, this tale of almost unrelenting woe, delivered with postmodern, comic twists, figures the Coens's serious man as a contemporary Job. The final tornadic imagery in dialogue with the prologue, as well as antisemitic neighbors who both hunt and infringe on property lines, suggests that postmodern parody here becomes an indirect form of post-Holocaust consciousness.

The prologue and its relation to the rest of the film is an interpretive enigma. The Coens explain it variously and contradictorily as like the cartoon that used to precede the feature presentation of classic Hollywood movies; as unambiguously signaling with its identifiably Jewish locale and characters that this is a Jewish story; as offering a contrast between the recognizable, predictable presence of Jews in a shtetl and the counterintuitive existence of Jews on the plains; and as providing some "resonance" with the story of Minnesota Jews that unfolds.[51] The oncoming tornado may or may not destroy the Jewish community clearly based on St. Louis Park, the Minnesota suburb where the Coens came of age (Joel Coen's bar mitzvah kiddush cup makes a cameo appearance in the film).[52] However, if we read the film as coming full circle—which the medical subplot encourages—then the final whirlwind reminds us of the forces that demolished the forms of Eastern European life depicted in the prologue. It's also worth remembering that the year in which the film is set—1967—was, for U.S. and Israeli Jews, a year in which a second Holocaust was feared: preparations for the 1967 Six-Day War included evacuations of children, the digging of graves, and the distribution of gas masks, some contributed to Israel by Germany in a historically ironic reversal.

Other scenes reinforce the sense that this contemporary Jobian saga—as well as postwar Jewish suburban life—is informed by the shadows of the Shoah. At one point, Larry dreams that he is helping his brother Arthur escape by boat to Canada. Initially, this seems to refer to Vietnam refuseniks who dodged the draft by heading farther north; however, as Arthur sets on his way, he is shot. The shooters are the "goys" next door, and the dream ends with neighbor Brandt, reminiscent of *Barton Fink*'s madman Mundt, pointing at Larry and telling his son that "there's another Jew."

Such historically induced nightmares are in keeping with the sense of otherness that these Midwestern Jews experience even in their upwardly mobile, suburban enclaves. When Larry's wife's beau is killed in a car accident (paralleled by a less serious accident involving Larry, thus pointing to the seemingly mysterious or random workings of God or fate), the shiva minyan is interrupted by detectives looking for Arthur. When Larry explains that the family is sitting shiva, the detectives' response is an incredulous and comic "What?" After Larry translates that "we're bereaved," the detectives take their leave, papering over their ignorance of Judaic ritual with their departing wisecrack, "Do your thing."

Of course, in Coen Country, Jewish illiteracy is not only a problem for Gentile characters or those viewers who make serious use of the special DVD feature titled "Hebrew and Yiddish for Goys." Rather, Jewish ignorance is so rampant even and especially in the Jewish community that the "What?" gag played by the Gentile detectives is first played to the hilt by Jews who are mystified by the notion of a get, a Jewish ritual divorce. When the term is first used by Larry's wife, Larry responds with a quizzical "What?" That interrogative is repeated by both an assistant rabbi and a Jewish lawyer, who uproariously insists that a get is not a legal concern (only Judaically literate insiders who understand that a get is a pillar of Jewish law, aka halakhah, will get this particular joke from the mouth of Adam Arkin, who plays the divorce lawyer).

The Jewish institutional world is a spiritual wasteland, as both Larry's search for cosmic meaning and his son Danny's bar mitzvah preparation make clear. A Hebrew school teacher who faces the blackboard rather than the class as he deadens students with the conjugated verbs of a revived language, the tropes of Torah half-heartedly learned from a recording by cantor Yossele Rosenblatt, and a coming-of-age ceremony filmed at a tilt to convey the perspective of a stoned bar mitzvah boy suggest that the making of post-Holocaust Jews in the faux lightness of Jewish suburban being is tricky business. Many Jewish viewers of the Coens's generation profoundly identified with this lachrymose narrative of Jewish education; notably, recent articles on the crisis of Jewish education cite this aspect of *A Serious Man* as if it were a case study![53]

Paralleling Danny's less than transcendent bar mitzvah experience are Larry's visits to a triad of rabbis that structure both his search for meaning and much of the film itself. In what might be viewed as a Goldilocks rabbinical tale, the first rabbi is too young and focused on the wonder contained in the parking lot; the second rabbi, with his tale of a message sent to a dentist through a "goy's teeth," is too elliptical; and the third rabbi, Marshak, a wizened, sage-like figure, is too busy thinking to even meet with Larry and can only offer Danny lyrics from Jefferson Airplane and the advice to be "a good boy."[54] Like the Central Park West rabbi in Mazursky's *Enemies, A Love Story*, these post-Holocaust American rabbis seem not to be serious enough men to provide wisdom to those facing Jobian challenges, not to mention the next generation in their charge.

The closing credits include the line "No Jews were harmed in the making of this film," a faux legal claim that some refute given the grim comic gaze visited upon this Midwestern Jewish subculture that even the Coen brothers who sprung from it deem strange. The fact that this film has been embraced by many as an accurate period piece adds salt to the wounds of those who worry that such depictions are bad for the Jews. The Coens are both hyperaware and profoundly dismissive of such worries. Taking their cue from David Mamet, their response to what they regard as stereotypical Jewish anxiety is "Too bad, you big crybaby."[55]

Yet many others consider the Coen Brothers in general and *A Serious Man* in particular a sign that the silence around Jewishness that marked Holocaust-era Hollywood and beyond has come to an end. For, as I have shown, while Holocaust imagery may be indirect and even coded here, Jewishness is not. From Rashi to a neo-Yiddish folktale to rabbis with foibles to a bar mitzvah service, there's no hiding the Jewishness of this movie or its production. The Coen set has been described as a "menschy" one.[56] Just as Joel Coen's kiddish cup was used, so did Aaron Wolff, the actor who plays Danny, chant the Torah portion that marked his own becoming a Jewish man, thus blurring the line between making Jews onscreen and off.[57] The bar mitzvah ceremony sequence featured an authentic cantor, and the congregational extras were recruited from the local Jewish community. In fact, without direction, when the Torah scroll was raised at the end of the bar mitzvah scene, the audience stood—as they would during a real rather than a cinematic service.[58] That seemingly small production detail tells a much larger story about the staying power of Jewish performances among Americans who should never forget either the Shoah or the fact that their collective national experience of it was overwhelmingly indirect and at a distance. However, the pressure to assimilate, cinematically and otherwise, was—and arguably still is—the paradigmatic narrative of American Jews. The films to which I turn next put this drama and its discontents onscreen.

4

Focusing on Assimilation
and Its Discontents

• •

A progressive—and dominant—narrative of American Jewish film history offered by such diverse critics as Joel Rosenberg, Henry Bial, and Nathan Abrams views cinematic Jews as moving from assimilation to normalization.[1] According to this narrative, Hollywood studio heads, chasing and creating the American dream, promoted the erasure, downplaying, or coding of American Jewish experience onscreen. Neal Gabler, in his classic book *An Empire of Their Own: How the Jews Invented Hollywood*, cemented this narrative.[2] As J. Hoberman and Jeffrey Shandler astutely note, both Gabler's book and the documentary based on it, *Hollywoodism*, "portray Hollywood's studio executives as victims, both of American anti-Semitism . . . and of their own embrace of the false god of assimilation into the American mainstream."[3] Once the studio system ended and the age of New Hollywood began, in dialogue with a renewed cultural emphasis on roots and ethnic pride, Jews came out as Jews onscreen. For Rosenberg, this shift "toward unselfconscious representation of Jewish experience," which began in the 1970s, shows that "Jewishness is not a problem but rather a natural component of a wider social landscape."[4] Building on Rosenberg's insights, Abrams reads the "veritable flood" of representations of New Jews after 1990 as "post-melting pot and post-assimilatory" and as a "visual manifestation of the comfort of US Jewry by the late twentieth century, that Jews had arrived, and were *at home* in the United States."[5]

To be sure, Jewish characters, Jewish jokes, and Jewish tragedy (particularly in the form of Holocaust narratives) proliferated in the 1970s and beyond. But not all Jewish representations are equal, equally significant, or equally desirable. If Jews are everywhere to be seen, are they nowhere in their particularity? In other words, proliferation may not necessarily be progress. We also need to acknowledge that Jewish representations are not received uniformly: what some perceive as the welcome inclusion of Jews as no big deal is to others a sign of a toxic normalization of assimilation and antisemitism, resulting in the reproduction of pernicious stereotypes and hyper-self-consciousness about being either "too Jewish" or "not Jewish enough." A narrative of American Jewish film history as inevitably one of progress also underestimates the challenges that directors and screenwriters often experience as they strive to realize their Jewish vision onscreen.

A set of films that simultaneously represent assimilation and resistance to it—*The Way We Were* (1973), *Next Stop, Greenwich Village* (1976), *Crossing Delancey* (1988), *Avalon* (1990), and *Liberty Heights* (1999)—suggests that American Jewish film history is a narrative of continuity and change rather than one of progress when production and reception are considered alongside what appears onscreen. These films, set in the past or in seemingly old neighborhoods, have often been derided as nostalgic. However, rather than pining for what was, they chronicle the losses and pain associated with assimilation as they neither hide nor are solely defined by Jewishness. The Jewish gaze of these films is achieved not only by looking at Jews but also by focusing on dominant Gentile culture and characters that are found wanting. Ironically, while some of the films considered here were deemed "too Jewish" during preproduction and were made against all odds, critical debates abound about whether these films are Jewish enough or even Jewish at all! From my perspective, the questions about the losses and limits of assimilation that are asked by and about these films are the very stuff of a usable tradition. Assimilation has historically been viewed as the unmaking of Jews; revisiting and critiquing those complex processes through diverse and moving images have the potential to remake Jews.

The Way We Were (1973)

I find it hard to be dispassionate about Barbra Streisand, and I have plenty of critical and cultural company. Babs is a lightning rod for adoration, immortalized in *Saturday Night Live*'s "Coffee Talk with Linda Richman." Those sketches gave voice to Jewish women's identification/overidentification with the actor, singer, and director who seemed to do things her way—name, nose, and all.[6] I still remember watching *A Star Is Born* (1976) as a teen and not knowing whether I was more taken with Kris Kristofferson or Barbra's/Esther's frizzy hair that matched my own and gave me hope that my unruly mop wouldn't always be the bane of my existence. I also remember watching *Yentl* (1983) and seeing a woman don a tallit—prayer shawl—for the first time. And, paradoxically, Streisand herself helped me to view the makeover in *The Mirror Has Two Faces* (1996) as unnecessary and counterproductive, even if it did weaken the knees of Jeff Bridges. Popular Jewish feminist writing indicates that my response was part of the zeitgeist—Letty Cottin Pogrebin glories in the powerful performances of Babs's Jewish Big Mouth, and Anne Roiphe revels in Babs making Jewish beauty a cultural reality.[7] More recently, Babs has been credited with making Jewish "sexy" and "fashionable."[8]

But adoration certainly isn't the only response to Barbra—the flip side is so prevalent that film critic Vivian Sobchack frames her own arguably excessive ambivalence about Babs with "the troubling question: why do so many people in our culture (Jews and non-Jews alike) *hate* Barbra Streisand."[9] If "Coffee Talk" represents Babs's adoration scene, then the "Mecha-Streisand" *South Park* episode is the prototypical scene of abhorrence for a woman who, for some, exceeds the bounds of feminine power, taste, and class. Here, Streisand is cast as a Godzilla-like monstrosity threatening the town and mobilizing superheroes to defeat her rapaciousness.[10]

How we view Babs likely impacts our response to one of her cinematic alter egos, Jewish Communist Katie Morosky in *The Way We Were*, directed by Sydney Pollack. Here Katie/Babs shares the screen with all-American WASP Hubbell Gardiner/Robert Redford. Sometimes maligned even by its fans as schmaltzy, sentimental, and nostalgic (code words for too Jewish?), the film should be recognized as historic for its Jewish feminist battles in the so-called New Hollywood and as an early exemplar of a postassimilationist cinema.

Billed as an opposites-attract love story, *The Way We Were* opens with a glamorous, straight-haired Katie entering a club and glimpsing from afar Hubbell Gardiner dozing on a bar stool in full naval uniform. This establishing shot foregrounds not only the "we" of the title (and the titular song that earned an Oscar) but also that Hubbell is a symbol of a dozing nation, even in the midst of the Second World War. A flashback to their college days, when Hubbell was an adored member of the crew team and an up-and-coming writer, while Katie was an antiwar, anti-Franco activist associated with the Young Communist League, ensues. Her lack of social capital is conveyed by her passionate political speech being hijacked by a sign that reads "Any peace but Katie's piece"; her lack of desirability and her outsider status are furthered by her painful role as waitress to Gardiner's privileged clique. Although Katie and Hubbell are worlds apart, they share the space of a competitive creative writing classroom, in which Hubbell comes out on top for his clearly autobiographical short story, "An All-American Smile." The opening of that work summarizes his character and the role that he will play throughout the film: "In a way he was like the country that he lived in. Everything came too easily to him. But at least he knew it. Every month or so he worried that he was a fraud."

The WASP man's burden of awareness of *his* lack and the Jewish woman's attempt to reform him into an authentic being of substance are the constituent ingredients of this romantic and American tragedy. And to my mind, that's what makes this movie revolutionary—the All-American Smiler is the object of the gaze of the nice Jewish girl. Paul Cowan rightly notes in *Golden Land on the Silver Screen*, a film about how and why Jewish movies matter, that Katie is "always in Redford's world," and thus that *The Way We Were* is a "profoundly anti-assimilationist statement" in a "most Protestant setting."[11] While that setting diminishes the Jewish value of the film for Cowan, the Jewishness of this film resides as much in the Jewish gaze on the majority as it does in the looks of Katie Morosky/Barbra Streisand. Put another way, while Katie's Jew-fro is prominent at the beginning and the end of this film, it is equally important that her view of the world as a politically, though not always romantically, progressive Jewish woman is the perspective of the film.

To be sure, this shift in who looks at whom (and how) didn't happen without a fight, and the production history of *The Way We Were* is illuminating for what was and wasn't possible in the post–studio system, director-dominated New Hollywood. The screenplay was largely written by Arthur Laurents, a Brooklyn-born, gay Jewish graylisted writer (i.e., one who wasn't officially blacklisted but nonetheless had his career impacted by the anti-Communist witch hunt that dominated Hollywood in the 1940s and 1950s). His Cornell education as well as his coterie's experience with HUAC informed the story.[12] When production started, Pollack was determined—as was Laurents—to make this film "the first-ever blacklist movie, the first one to show how it was."[13] However, although it *was* the first film to deal with the blacklist (it preceded *The Front* by three years), the romance plot dominated the political narrative, in part because that's what tested well in San Francisco, in part because producer Ray Stark and Columbia Pictures were gun shy about the film becoming too radical. As a result of the latter, Katie's being named as a Communist sympathizer, then being pressured to name names and refusing, and divorcing Hubbell to avoid compromising his career never made it into the final script. At one point, Laurents was fired as screenwriter, and a group of writers dubbed "Pollack's Eleven," which included Dalton Trumbo, one of the original Hollywood Ten who refused to cooperate with HUAC and were jailed for their noncompliance, took over. However, the script became incoherent, Laurents was brought back, and Trumbo's pages—in which Hubbell turned informer—were scrubbed.[14]

Intertwined with the offscreen drama of representing the Hollywood witch hunt was Pollack's desire to appease Redford, who had to be convinced to take the role, which he considered more symbol than flesh-and-blood character. While Hubbell proclaims onscreen that being with Katie was "too hard," Redford didn't want to risk being cinematically dominated by Streisand offscreen:

"What I was really worried about was the whole concept of basing a movie on Barbra as a serious actress. . . . She had never been tested" (apparently, *Funny Girl* didn't count!). At the outset of the project, Redford told Pollack, "Her reputation is as a very controlling person. She will direct herself. It'll never work."[15] As politics and Redford's role were negotiated, the set became "an unacknowledged battlefield" in which Laurents—and Streisand—did battle on behalf of Katie and her vision.[16] Notably, Laurents accused Pollack of assimilating to Redford's and Hubbell's view of the world: "You're going to build up Redford's part because you're in love with him. I don't mean homosexually but he's the blond goy you wish you were. The picture is Barbra's no matter what you do because the story is hers. Be careful you don't destroy it trying to give it to him."[17]

Script changes designed to bolster Hubbell/Redford sometimes did diminish Katie's/Streisand's appeal. A fight between Katie and Hubbell at Beekman Place, for example, was originally written to be between just the two of them rather than a public performance of political and personal dogmatism.[18] However, for those of us who think that a lapse in decorum is ultimately a small price to pay for sustaining the impulse to talk back and to repair the world, Katie's flaws enhanced rather than impeded identification. Precisely what made her difficult was a large part of her appeal, and even Hubbell's struggle with her and with the vision she represented acknowledges this. When a pregnant Katie decides to go to Washington in support of the Hollywood Ten, a decision that signals the end of her assimilation to Redford's world and the end of them as a couple, Hubbell and J.J., a friend from college and now his partner (played by Bradford Dillman), watch home movies of a fiery, frizzy-haired Katie. During this scene, J.J., in the midst of ending his marriage to college sweetheart Carole Ann, affirms Katie's beauty and her real value compared with that of his trophy wife.

In *The Way We Were,* Katie's hair tells the tale of assimilation and resistance. In college, she sports a frizzy mane that then gets ironed in Harlem, stays straight through a sojourn in Hollywood, and then returns to its natural state in the film's final sequence. At the end of the movie, Katie is protesting nuclear arms in New York, and Hubbell, now with an all-American blond girlfriend, is working in television and can't summon the courage to make himself known to their daughter, who is being well-fathered by Katie's husband, David X. Cohen. When Hubbell and Katie talk during the club scene that opens the movie, he asks her whether ironing her hair hurts. Katie laughs at his masculine cluelessness about female beauty rituals. Yet, the question metaphorically illuminates the gains and losses of giving up Jewish female unruliness for the spoils of a Waspy particularist American dream that previously presented itself as the only possible success story. Astonishingly, *The Way We Were* ultimately insists that ironing one's Jewish hair *does* hurt, that although giving up that

American dream and the "goyishe guy" that goes with it *is* experienced as a real loss, losing one's self and values would be an even greater one.

Back in New York in full Jewfro and activist mode, Katie reverses an earlier scene in which she, desperate to hang onto Hubbell, insists that she will change. However, while Hubbell refuses to advocate for such change for her—"Don't change, you're your own girl, you have your own style"—he ends up opting for the assimilation mode himself. Desperate to keep his job as the screenwriter for the film based on his novel, he gives into pressure exerted by J.J. and Bessinger, the director. Echoing Katie's most frenzied moment, he sells out his own literary progeny (a precursor to his abandonment of his daughter): "I know what your concept is, I'll make the changes . . . no resistance." At this juncture, the critique of assimilation that has been centered on Katie extends to Hubbell, and a Jewish feminist gaze has been refocused on him. Ultimately, Katie, the ugly duckling, is exposed as having been a swan all along, while Hubbell is revealed as a pretty WASP boy who betrays his own potential. Pauline Kael writes, "When Redford's glamour is overdone and his white teeth glitter, the movie seems to share Katie's infatuation, and you have to laugh at yourself for what you're enjoying."[19] Such laughter admits, even compels, an ironic distance on Hubbell that might be the real political power of this movie.

Whether the Jewishness of this movie makes it past Katie's curls has been the subject of much debate. Felicia Herman believes that the "Jewishness in Streisand's films seems confined at the most to a kind of secular liberalism . . . that leaves no room for the particularism of Jewish experience, religious, cultural, or otherwise; at the least, Jewishness is reduced to stereotype." According to Herman, "The divorce occurs more for reasons of gender than of religion or ethnicity."[20] Similarly, Jeanne Hall, who reads the film as a vexed political romance, suggests that the film and critics are confused about the source of opposition between Katie and Hubbell, "attributing their 'irreconcilable differences' variously to conflicting 'personality types,' contrasting ethnic, religious or regional backgrounds, and even to physical inequality or incompatibility."[21] Both Herman and Hall underestimate the intertwining of gender, personality, geography, politics, and perceived physical desirability with Jewish questions. Moreover, as Laurents makes clear in his discussion of Katie's genesis, at least some of these interconnections were intended: "Katie could only be a Jew because of her insistence on speaking out, her outrage at injustice, her passion, her values. . . . Besides, it was . . . high time that the movies, the only industry founded by Jews, had a Jewish heroine."[22] His own progressive brand of secular Jewishness was infused into Katie: as he puts it, "It wasn't Judaism of any kind that made me a Jew or the kind of Jew I was."[23]

Yet even some of the religious particularism that Laurents disavows and that Herman insists is nowhere to be found in Streisand's oeuvre makes it into *The Way We Were*. Early in their relationship, Katie wishes Hubbell a happy Rosh

FIG. 4.1 A Rosh Hashanah gift in *The Way We Were* (1973)

Hashanah and gives him a typewriter. Of course, gift-giving is not associated with the High Holidays, and Paul Cowan, one of the only commentators to even notice this odd scene, reads it as tension between Katie's Jewish and American identities. However, it's worth remembering that the Days of Awe are all about renewal and the turning associated with teshuvah (repentance), and that, throughout the film, Katie advocates for Hubbell's artistic integrity. This gift of a typewriter on the Jewish New Year enjoins him to not take the easy way out, to not assimilate politically, creatively, or romantically. His ultimate decision to sell out his own novel, to give short shrift to principles (the very definition of peoplehood, according to Katie), to write for TV, and to end up with a "lovely" girl is just as culturally coded as Katie's big mouth and big Jewish hair.

Despite criticism centered on what was missing in *The Way We Were*—Jewishness, a more significant engagement with the blacklist, a more assertive feminism—the film was a commercial success and became nothing less than a cultural touchstone, nowhere better represented than in the "Ex and the City" episode in season 2 of *Sex and the City*.[24] In that episode, Carrie (played by Sarah Jessica Parker, another cultural Jew) is trying to come to terms with Mr. Big's engagement to supermodel Natasha. During an alcohol-infused brunch, Miranda responds to Carrie's question of "why her" with "one word: Hubbell." After Miranda, Charlotte, and Carrie rehash the plot of the much-beloved film and do their own rendition of the title song for Samantha (who doesn't watch "chick flicks"), Carrie has the epiphany that the narrative of the film is the prototype for her relationship with Big. She is the complicated, curly-haired Katie, and Natasha is the simple girl. More than a bit tipsy, Carrie goes to the Plaza, the scene of Big's engagement party and the setting for the last scene of the film, and asks Big the big question: "Why wasn't it me?" Without realizing that he has figuratively walked onto a culturally overdetermined movie set, he responds with the Hubbell-like "It just got so hard . . . and she's . . ." The gaps in his speech betray both what he cannot and will not fully articulate about his own romantic values. Carrie proceeds to enact the last scene of the film, lightly touching his hair and uttering words of sad resignation and indictment: "Your girl is lovely, Hubbell." When Big, now recast as Hubbell, says he does not understand (he, like Samantha, has not seen the film), the critique of Hubbell that was implicit in the film now becomes explicit: "And you never did." As Carrie walks away, the camera shifts to a policeman trying to calm his braying horse, a scene accompanied by Carrie's voice-over: "Maybe the problem was he couldn't break me. Maybe some women aren't meant to be tamed. Maybe they need to run free until they find someone . . . just as wild to run with." The onus and deficiency here lie with Mr. Big, while Carrie—and, by extension, Katie—is figured as positively wild. Hubbell and Mr. Big are the object of the Jewish women's gaze and are found wanting. Not a bad ride for 1973 and beyond.

Next Stop, Greenwich Village (1976)

While Katie's hair tells a story of assimilation and its discontents in *The Way We Were*, Larry Lapinsky's headgear choices in the opening scenes of *Next Stop, Greenwich Village* (1976) intimate the adroit Jewish balancing act at the heart of that semi-autobiographical film by director Paul Mazursky. As Larry, the film's protagonist, is packing to make the exodus from Brooklyn to Manhattan, in part to pursue an acting career and in part to flee his Jewish mother (much more on her to come), he extracts a yarmulke from his drawer, puts it halfway on his head, then quickly removes it and returns it to the drawer. Later, on the subway, he pulls a beret from his coat pocket and dons it. Although this move from yarmulke to beret would suggest that Larry is leaving his Jewish self behind, *Next Stop, Greenwich Village* is one of Mazursky's Jewiest films, both explicitly and in coded ways. As in *The Way We Were*, damaging assimilation scripts are written for Jews and Gentiles alike; however, such scripts are not American Jewish cinematic destiny.

Arthur Laurents, a Brooklyn boy himself, has commented, "The journey to Manhattan is easier from Texas than from Brooklyn," and Larry's departure from Brownsville would seem to confirm that sentiment.[25] For Larry, Jewish mother and drama queen Faye Lapinsky—listed only as Mom in the credits and memorably played by Shelley Winters—is both a catalyst for and an impediment to his departure. She not only becomes hysterical as he is about to make his brief northwest journey but also keeps showing up at his Village apartment to critique his living quarters, feed him (of course), and query him and his girlfriend about their sex life and nonexistent wedding plans. This seemingly stock rendition of the Jewish mother figure put off some critics. Stanley

Kauffmann's take on Shelley Winters and her character here is strikingly similar to his view of Streisand/Katie: this material is "stale" and "unbearable."[26] For Gene Siskel, Winters's Jewish mother schtick is "the one big flaw in the film. . . . Winters' role asks her to do nothing you haven't seen before." According to him, whenever Winters arrives in the Village, "the mood of the picture . . . swings from one of exploration of young people's feelings to borscht belt comedy."[27]

Yet others, including this Brooklyn-born Jewish feminist, see something more than stereotype in Mrs. Lapinsky and Shelley Winters. Pauline Kael hits the critical nail on the head when she writes that Mrs. Lapinsky's "unused brains have turned her into a howling freak, but you can recognize in her the sources of her son's talent and wit. And, even seeing her through her son's agonized-with-shame eyes, you don't get too much of her—or, rather, you can't get enough of Shelley Winters' performance. . . . Fat, morose, irrepressible, she's a force that would strike terror to anyone's heart, yet in some abominable way she's likable. She's Mrs. Portnoy seen without hatred."[28] Kael's critical commentary accords with the perspective of Sarah Roth, Larry's girlfriend (played by Ellen Greene): during her first volcanic meeting with Mom, Sarah says that she now knows where Larry gets his sense of humor and later tells Larry that his mother is "unbelievable but also smart and kind of interesting."

During a fantasy scene in which Mom makes an appearance in her son's acting class, Larry and Mazursky demonstrate a good bit of critical consciousness on and revision of the cinematic staple of the Jewish mother. Talking back to a misogynist, antisemitic tradition and with a nod to Babs's Fanny Brice and Shakespeare's *Merchant of Venice*, Winters opines: "You think I'm your standard Jewish mother . . . a funny lady who just shouts and shrieks and wails. Am I not flesh? Am I not blood, a human being with feelings, feelings like you. . . . You think I took you to all those double features so I could get out of the house. No, no. I want to be in show business, too." Here Mazursky is analyzing rather than merely reproducing a type and exposes the long-winded and long-suffering Jewish mother as a being who acts out her thwarted desire. Mrs. Lapinsky is based on Mazursky's own mother, whose death liberated him to put her and his complex feelings about her onscreen. Recognizing the role that history played in constructing his Jewish mother in particular and the type in general, Mazursky avers, "In another time in another place, she might have been one of those fabulous characters like Dorothy Parker or [Robert] Benchley. She was like a Gypsy lady who operated on instinct, but most of the time she had good instincts."[29]

Mrs. Lapinsky's aesthetic instincts need to be recognized as coexisting and even overlapping with her over-the-top hysterical performances. Fittingly, she is an opera lover, and her histrionics are continuous with her genre of choice. Notably, mother and son are simpatico when it comes to aesthetics. Although

critics such as David Desser and Lester Friedman list the food and clean under-
wear Mrs. Lapinsky brings to Larry's Village apartment, she also brings opera
records, and meaningful mother-son bonding occurs during shared aesthetic
experiences.[30] When the Black gay Bernstein Chandler (played by Antonio Fargas) whisks Mrs. Lapinsky onto the makeshift dance floor that Larry's apartment becomes during a rent party, Mom shows herself capable of a whole new
set of moves. Her love of movies and flair for melodrama are a model for Larry's own impromptu performances; these include a successful screen test as a
Brandoesque juvenile delinquent and, less appealingly, as the enraged lover who
loses control when Sarah confesses that she has slept with a writer, Robert, and
chokes her before coming back to himself and getting her a glass of water. Larry's considerable talent as well as his destructive rages makes him a chip off the
old maternal block, and Mrs. Lapinsky is established as an aesthetic and dramatic double rather than a mere stereotypical impediment to her Jewish son's
dreams and development. Larry melodramatically asks "the great god in heaven"
to have mercy upon "a Jewish boy." Yet Mazursky's film also manages to have
rachmones (Yiddish for compassion) for—or at least understanding of—the
"twisted brain" of the Jewish mother figure, who is arguably maligned more by
critics than by a filmmaker who dares to explore—albeit with humor—her
existential anguish alongside that of her progeny.

While the film begins with Larry's exodus to the Village, it ends with his
journey westward to Hollywood. Rather than rant, Mom urges him to "remember where he comes from," gives him strudel that she has made, and recites the
story of his—and Mazursky's—grandmother who crossed the Polish border
hidden under sacks of potatoes and who avoided the bayonets that Cossacks
used to unearth the human goods fleeing oppression. In his own way, Larry
heeds his mother: while initially asserting—at top volume—that he has no use
for her strudel, he eats it in the final scene of the film. Accompanying that old-
world homemade sweet are the delectable sights and sounds of a fiddler practicing his art on Brooklyn streets. Eastern Brooklyn with traces of Eastern
Europe is where Larry and Mazursky come from, and those origins are narratively and cinematically rendered and preserved.

The assimilationist road not taken is perhaps best dramatized as Larry awaits
his turn at the casting call for a part that he ultimately gets. There he talks with
a more experienced actor, Clyde Baxter (formerly Charles Belitnokoff). When
Clyde asks him if he's going to change his name, Larry explicitly calls upon the
open secret of Hollywood: "Why, is it too Jewish?" When Clyde demurs and
euphemistically cites "difficult names" as a reason to transform one's identity,
Larry humorously invokes Edward G. Robinson as a successful actor who has
a difficult name. Moreover, throughout this conversation, Larry exasperates
Clyde by repeatedly calling him Charles in order to obliquely out him as a
poseur. When Larry finally gets his shot with casting director Sid Weinberg,

he asserts his Jewishness even as he says he would be willing to change his name to Frank Riley if it would help him get the part. Weinberg and Larry end up bonding on Jewish mother aversion to an acting career, and he does ultimately get the part using his real name while Clyde Baxter's presumptuous attitude prevents him from even completing his screen test. Larry's performance of authenticity—his almost subconscious styling of himself as a male Fanny Brice/Barbra Streisand figure, a funny guy who does things his way—advances rather than impedes his career.

As in *The Way We Were*, Jews do not have a monopoly on assimilation. Bernstein, one of the first gay Black characters in film, makes use of 1950s Black-Jewish scripts in constructing an origin story for himself. He presents himself as the son of a cleaning woman who worked for a Jewish family, hence the first name of Bernstein. However, late in the film, in a moment of despair over yet another failed love relationship, he outs himself as the fatherless Floyd Lewis, born in Macon, Georgia, to a mother who died when he was three. As he puts it, "My life is a fiction; no cleaning woman, no family named Bernstein, only the gay is real; brutalized physically and mentally." Ironically, a Jewish connection that the Clyde Baxters are assiduously leaving behind for the fiction of Waspy whiteness has purchase for the racially, geographically, and sexually othered Floyd. Bernstein's fiction not only underscores the Black-Jewish penchant for self-fashioning endemic to the 1950s and beyond but also highlights the queer gender-bending associated with Jewishness. When Mrs. Lapinsky is introduced to Bernstein, she quizzically asks, "You're Jewish?" and he responds with "No, I'm gay," a scene of self-outing included in *The Celluloid Closet*, a classic documentary on gay cinematic history. Later, this gay-Jewish connection is echoed and revised when Sid Weinberg asks if Larry's residing in the Village means that he's a "faygele." Larry responds, "No, I'm Jewish." This repeated slippage between gay and Jewish suggests that this film is making Jewish men at odds with the image of dominant heterosexual masculinity.

Relatedly, through the character of Robert, played by a then relatively unknown Christopher Walken, *Next Stop, Greenwich Village* unveils and critiques WASP masculinity as did *The Way We Were* through Robert Redford's Hubbell. Like Hubbell, Robert is a writer and a pretty boy sophisticate. However, in sharp contrast to Hubbell, he is not conflicted, and there is nothing even remotely or potentially daring about him. A narcissistic manipulator, he sleeps with Sarah, Larry's girlfriend. When confronted, he dispassionately disavows love as he explains that he ran away from home at fifteen and wants to sleep with lots of women; as he cavalierly puts it, "What can I tell you—people get hurt." To this, Larry delivers the judgment that "underneath that pose is just more pose—adios." While culturally positioned and positioning himself as an aesthetic center, Robert is revealed as lacking the very substance and life force that Larry brings with him from the margins of Brownsville, Brooklyn.

Once again, a Jewish cinematic sensibility turns its lens on the open secret of passing and posing, revealed to be the pernicious province of the cultural elite. A year later, in *Annie Hall*, Christopher Walken hilariously underscores the destructive potential of this type in his role as Annie's brother, whose reckless driving in the rain while fantasizing about vehicular suicide is taken for granted by his sister but terrorizes Alvy Singer, a Brooklyn Jew, played, of course, by Woody Allen himself.

In *Stars of David*, Mazursky told Abigail Pogrebin that although he's not bothered by being labeled a Jewish director, "it wouldn't be a fair description. I'm an American director, I'm an American actor, and I happen to be cultur- ally Jewish and very proud of it and I don't hide it. I've never hidden it in my work."[31] To be sure, the Jewish sensibility of this film is conveyed through New York geography (also true in Mazursky's later film *Enemies, A Love Story*), explicit wrestling with assimilation narratives and the too Jewish question, as well as the complicating of the Jewish mother complex. However, that sensi- bility is also developed in less explicit and more Jewishly coded ways. Connie, one member of Larry's Greenwich Village *mishpachah* (Yiddish for extended family), refers to everyone as *bubelah* (Yiddish endearment for sweetie); in a similar, humorous Jewish-centric vein, Larry asks the obviously Gentile Rob- ert if he was bar mitzvahed. References to the Rosenbergs are rife throughout the film. During one of many coffee shop conversations, Larry insists on the national gravity of the case and Sarah describes it as "tragic," while Robert cas- tigates her for imprecise word choice and views the execution as no more than the death of two individuals. Literary conversations and taste also contain a Jewish subtext. Seeking to play mentor to Larry, Robert invokes the modern- ist tradition and recommends Pound, the only writer cited that Larry has not read (although not mentioned in the film, Pound's fascist sympathies are well documented). Larry's familiarity with James Joyce, who in *Ulysses* gave us Leo- pold Bloom, literature's most famous Jewish non-Jew, is evident not only dur- ing the discussion with Robert but also at the rent party where Larry dons a pretzel as a Joycean monocle and waxes playfully poetic about a wasteland of gefilte fish.

Like modernism, a Jewishly coded cinema history is repeatedly referenced. High on his evolving physical relationship with Sarah, Larry uses his wait on a subway platform as an opportunity to do a mock acceptance speech for an Oscar. A police officer interrupts him; when Larry does his Brando imitation, the officer tells him it reeks of Edward G. Robinson (aka Emanuel Golden- berg, the same actor invoked in Larry's conversation with Clyde Baxter). And when Anita Cunningham, the suicidal member of the group, needs cheering up, a viewing of *Limelight* becomes the collective prescription, with all mem- bers of the group doing the Charlie Chaplin walk down the streets of Green- wich Village. With its narrative of a has-been comedian as savior of a suicidal dancer, *Limelight* is particularly relevant to Anita's situation. Notably, this 1952 film wasn't widely released in the United States until 1972 due to Chaplin's blacklisting and expulsion from the States, and many erroneously believe that Chaplin was Jewish due to *The Great Dictator* (1940), one of the first films to take on Hitler and Nazism. The Jewish inflections of *Next Stop, Greenwich Village* extend well beyond the larger-than-life Shelley Winters. This movie not only tells but also shows what it looks like to remember where you come from while not staying in place.

Next Stop is one of the films to which Mazursky feels emotionally close.[32] He also categorized it as a film that "the powers that be didn't get" and the "movie that made [him] lose [his] faith in Hollywood."[33] Mazursky recognized that if his career had started later, he would have been a low-budget indie director rather than a Hollywood player. His reputation waned after his golden period of the 1970s and 1980s, so much so that in 2001, Elvis Mitchell wrote in the *New York Times*, "In an era when almost every director to step behind a camera in the 1970's is lionized, one of the most talented and subtle has been ignored: Paul Mazursky, whose comedies had a luscious sensuality, has yet to receive tribute"; similarly, Pauline Kael, whom Mazursky cited as one who did "get" *Next Stop*, once complained that "Paul Mazursky hasn't been given his due."[34] Such not so benign neglect was partially corrected by the retrospective of his work by the Film Society of Lincoln Center in 2007, a program that included *Next Stop, Greenwich Village* (Mazursky also was honored with a star at the Hollywood Walk of Fame and a Writers Guild Lifetime Achievement Award just months before his death in 2014). While Andrew Sarris viewed the retrospective of Mazursky as representative of "the sheer depth of American mainstream movies way back (it now seems) in the days when directors—and Mr. Mazursky in particular—knew how to be funny and adult at the same time," Elvis Mitchell speculated that his work was not duly recognized because "he's hardest to imitate."[35] John Podhoretz has suggested that Judd Apatow is the only contemporary heir to Mazursky, though he is quick to proclaim Mazursky's superiority based on cinematic ambition and social precision.[36]

Mazursky's work in general and *Next Stop, Greenwich Village* in particular can be understood as film that advances the on- and offscreen cinematic work of neither hiding nor being solely defined by Jewishness; of gazing Jewishly on the sometimes overlapping, sometimes oppositional tribes of Jews and Gentiles; of critically engaging with the overlap between Jewish history and film history; of marking the diverse ways that movies and Hollywood have expressed and shaped Jewish identity. Larry Lapinsky looks back to Hollywood funny lady Barbra Streisand, even in her arguably humorless incarnation of Katie Morosky; he also looks forward to Izzy Grossman, protagonist of Joan Micklin Silver's indie gem, *Crossing Delancey*.

Crossing Delancey (1988)

For both old and new Hollywood, Jewish women were considered "double trouble," according to Joan Micklin Silver, a director who should be as well known as Babs.[37] As a woman trying to make inroads in the movie business in the 1970s with narratives considered "too ethnic" (read "too Jewish"), Micklin Silver started her career on the low-budget indie circuit that Mazursky imagined might have been his plight. Her first feature, *Hester Street* (1975), a feminist adaptation of Abraham Cahan's *Yekl*, is set on the Lower East Side with a focus on the experience of women immigrating and adjusting to the mores of a new world. When Micklin Silver got no bites from studios, her financier husband, Ray Silver, raised the funds to get the film made; getting it distributed turned out to be another hurdle, so, heeding the advice of indie guru John Cassavetes, Joan and Ray founded the Midwest Films Company to distribute it.[38] After a showing at Cannes, the film took off. With box office earnings of $5 million and an Oscar nomination for Carol Kane, *Hester Street* established Micklin Silver as "one of the few women directors on anyone's list in the seventies" and as "a symbol of hope for women on the outside wanting to get in."[39] This film that almost didn't get made because of sexist assimilationist assumptions about audience and profit margins became part of the National Film Registry of the Library of Congress in 2011.

Film production history threatened to repeat itself when Micklin Silver was trying to get *Crossing Delancey* off the ground. The screenplay, which Susan Sandler adapted from her own play that premiered at the Jewish Repertory Theatre, was redrafted multiple times to emphasize the ways in which bookstore employee Isabelle Grossman, aka Izzy (played by Amy Irving), is torn between two potential lovers: Sam, the pickle man, favored by her bubbe who has engaged the services of a matchmaker so that Izzy won't live alone "like a dog," and suave, cosmopolitan Dutch writer Anton Maes. Although in the years after the release of *Hester Street*, there were nominally more opportunities for women, Micklin Silver found that Jews were still regarded as "bad ethnic," that is, not seen as profitable cinematic material.[40] After being rejected by three major studios and fifteen distribution companies, she got Amy Irving interested in the role of Izzy and, from there, received advice from Steven Spielberg, then Irving's husband. Spielberg recommended that she send the project to Steven Ross at Warner Brothers, the studio that ultimately produced and distributed this now-classic romantic comedy that grossed $16 million.[41]

Emanuel Levy's categorization of *Crossing Delancey* as a film about "tradition versus modernity," with tradition winning out, is a common but misleading perspective on this gem of a Jewish chick flick.[42] While Izzy is horrified that her bubbe, Ida Kantor, engages matchmaker Mrs. Mandelbaum, insisting that this is "not how [she] lives," the film brilliantly depicts the porous boundaries and counterintuitive reversals between life on Delancey Street and that of Izzy's uptown. Izzy herself is a crossroads of sorts; although she works and lives uptown, she is profoundly devoted to and emotionally and physically intimate with her grandmother, as depicted in scenes in which Izzy narrates her dreams as she plucks her elder's facial hair. Long before a matchmaker and a pickle man join the Lower East Side cast of characters, Izzy crosses Delancey as part of her routine rather than making a one-way journey to or from.[43] And even at work uptown, Izzy is tied to old worlds and new: she is an assistant at one of the last surviving independent bookstores, and she proudly counts access to Yiddish writer Isaac Bashevis Singer as a sign of her professional prowess. Similarly, although Izzy studiously rejects Mrs. Mandelbaum as a romantic anachronism, she herself undertakes the role of matchmaker between her friend Marilyn and Sam; in this way, she establishes a through line from Bubbe's kitchen table to the bars of Manhattan.

Bubbe, too, is not a static stereotype stuck in the past. Yes, she saves string and brown packaging paper and leaves a place at her table for the likes of Mrs. Mandelbaum, but she also is at home in a self-defense class taught by a young Asian woman. Determined not to be a victim, she shares a commitment to independence and self-assertion with her granddaughter, even as she acknowledges that the solitary life of a widow is no picnic. Ida and Izzy seem like a case study of Jewish continuity and change rather than representatives of "two cultural worlds that are shown to be utterly dissimilar and unassimilable."[44] The casting of Reizl Bozyk as Ida reinforces the porousness of the boundaries between old worlds and new, including that of medium. A veteran of the Yiddish theater in Poland and New York, Bozyk initially resisted even considering the film part, insisting, "I'm at home in theater, but this is a strange atmosphere, a strange language and to top it off, a leading part."[45] However, Micklin Silver's letting Bozyk be herself as well as the filming of some scenes in her own neighborhood made this work in film not only doable but pleasurable. And life ended up imitating art as Bozyk and Irving became close offscreen, with Irving making regular calls to Bozyk after the film was completed.[46]

Although Izzy's suitors seem to solidify the opposition of tradition and modernity, it is they who most upend and even reverse it. At one point, Izzy heads to Sam's pickle store to see him, only to be repulsed when she glimpses him stuffing pickles into a jar. The crudeness of these motions functions as a less than subtle commentary on his potential as a lover. Yet, once Izzy—and the viewer—gets to know him, he is revealed to be a subtle, gentle, and complex man. Not surprisingly, he respects his elders and is solicitous of Ida. Virile enough to be an imposing force on the handball court, he also has hands that smell good because his father taught him to soak them in vanilla. He woos Izzy with a story about a man whose life is changed by a new hat that enables his face to be seen; he follows up this tale about the shifting perspective of subject and viewer with a gift of a literal hat. When Sam briefly attends a soiree at Izzy's bookstore, it is clear that he knows and is in awe of the assembled literary talent. And he keeps a journal and works through life's conundrums—including how to engage with Izzy—through writing. Slowly but surely, this pickle man is revealed to be more of a suitable partner for a book woman than he first appeared. Although Izzy assumes that he is merely a nice guy, he's more savvy about the world than she gives him credit for. When he offers Nick, the married bohemian with whom Izzy occasionally hooks up, a place to stay, Izzy is touched by the gesture, whereas both Sam and the audience are keenly aware that the pickle man wants to keep Nick out of Izzy's bed. Izzy stereotypes Sam as a remnant of a passé, downtown world. Yet, like Izzy, he is third generation and is engaged in Jewish revisions rather than rejectionist assimilation. As it turns out, he, too, does not live the way of Mrs. Mandelbaum; rather, the only reason he lets the matchmaker introduce him to Izzy is that he recognized her from the neighborhood and already had his eye on her.

Ironically, Nick is one of the few inside or outside the world of the film who sees the continuity between the past of the Jewish Lower East Side and the artsy present. When Nick hears about Sam's pickle store, he recognizes it as the one that featured a Milton Berle impersonator (i.e., Sam's father). In this way, a cultural line is subtly drawn between the feminist performance art, Pat Olezko's "Keep Your Hands Off Her," heralded by one of Izzy's bookstore coworkers, and the street performances that celebrated an out Jewish comic. As in the case of Bozyk, the casting of Sam underscores cultural connections. Although Peter Riegert identifies as a secular Jew, he found himself drawn to the part of this man who starts his day in prayer: "I guess I was most attracted to his comfort with who he was." And like Bozyk, Riegert has ties to the Lower East Side, having overseen an after-school program at the University Settlement House (located on Eldridge and Rivington) in the 1960s and, more recently, serving on its board.[47]

While *Crossing Delancey* revisions a pickle man as a worldly mensch, it simultaneously unveils the male chauvinism hiding out in a supposedly modern, urbane writer. Anton Maes, whose latest book, *The Cavedweller*, is being touted by the literary establishment, including Izzy's bookstore, has more than a touch of the caveman about him. In general, he views women as his handmaidens: he doesn't let Izzy finish a sentence, although he purports to respect her opinion, and he slaps his assistant/lover on the backside with less care than Sam jars a pickle. In sharp contrast to Nick's recognition of Sam, Anton literally kicks the pickle man while holding literary court at the bookstore. It takes Izzy longer than it should to realize that Anton is a heel, in part because she is seduced by his standing in the literary world. Anton as well as Izzy's response to him suggests that the sexual revolution hasn't necessarily been all that revolutionary, a lesson still being relearned by the hookup generation.

FIG. 4.2 Toasting new family structures in *Crossing Delancey* (1988)

The sequence that perhaps best represents continuity and change, signaling that this film is neither jettisoning nor blindly reaffirming tradition, is the bris held for the son of one of Izzy's friends. Ricki has chosen motherhood apart from marriage. New family structures, critiqued by Ricki's aunt (her mother isn't present) but supported by Ricki's female posse, include Jewish ritual. The officiating rabbi explains the circumcision rites with humor, thus providing religious instruction simultaneously to the diverse crowd assembled and to Jewishly illiterate viewers of the film. The cinematic as well as narrative amalgam of old worlds and new that marks *Crossing Delancey* is reinforced by the eclectic soundtrack, which features the Roches, Run-DMC, as well as Benny Goodman's "It Had to Be You," not to mention an uncanny rendition of "Some Enchanted Evening" in the famous hot dog haven Gray Papaya and Olezko's previously mentioned "Keep Your Hands Off Her." Although much of the movie is set on the Lower East Side, an evocative and symbolic old world for American Jews, here this neighborhood is represented as a multicultural space in which Hasidic boys and matchmakers share space with African Americans, more recent Caribbean immigrants, and Asian Americans. Jewishness becomes part of the multicultural mosaic rather than collapsing into a generic whiteness or being presented as a life apart.

Crossing Delancey does complex cultural work with Jewishness and gender, and Joan Micklin Silver is a female director whom film critic Leo Biga credits with "shattering cinema's glass ceiling." More recent feminist film scholarship by Shonni Enelow and Maya Montañez Smukler situates Micklin Silver squarely within an underexposed tradition of female directors.[48] Given this, it's ironic that, in some circles, the Jewishness of *Crossing Delancey* was virtually erased as the film became a poster child for the backlash against feminism. Susan Faludi deemed *Crossing DeLancey* "typical postfeminist fare" of the 1980s and stereotyped both Izzy and Sam when she wrote, "Isabella learns to 'settle'— in this case, for the pickle vendor in the old neighborhood. He's dull but solid, a good provider for the little woman."[49] Caryn James, writing for the *New York Times*, is one of several critics who erroneously assumes that Izzy marries Sam, a view that Micklin Silver strenuously rejects: "I don't think that Izzy would necessarily end up with the pickle man. They might go out for a while, but what's important is that she has learnt to appreciate someone of real worth."[50] Yet, for James, "*Crossing Delancey* carries the unambiguous message, 'Listen to your grandmother: get married before it's too late'"; ultimately, she views it as among a group of films that are "thoroughly retrograde" and "pro-marriage in an era rife with divorce and anti-intellectual at a time when women are better educated than ever before. They offer momentary, fantastic retreats from the complex reality of contemporary women's lives."[51] Joining the backlash chorus, Elayne Rapping has this to say about Izzy and *Crossing Delancey*: "Our hip heroine, like all the sillier versions, heads for the altar and permanent bliss as though lobotomized. There is no doubt that these films, by virtue of their frequency (more titles could be mentioned) and blatant antifeminism, constitute a dangerous trend."[52] Such critical trends suggest that Jewishness, unless wholly tribal and omnipresent in every shot, is in danger of being either occluded or conflated with a reviled nostalgia.

Happily, such vapid feminist responses are not the whole critical story; deemed a classic by, among others, the National Foundation for Jewish Culture, *Crossing Delancey* is often revived at Jewish film festivals across the country and beyond. In 2011, the Santa Barbara Jewish Film Festival featured the film as well as Micklin Silver as filmmaker-in-residence. It was also part of the Atlanta and Indianapolis Jewish film festivals in 2013 and 2015, respectively. Hadley Freeman, author of *Life Moves Pretty Fast: The Lessons We Learned from Eighties Movies*, provided commentary on the film when it was shown at the 2015 UK Jewish Film Festival. Janeane Garofalo includes the film among the "guilty pleasures" that she watches "all the time": in sharp contrast to those who consider it anti-intellectual, she categorizes it as a "great, heartwarming, yet intelligent film."[53]

Most recently, the influence of *Crossing Delancey*, including the vexed critical history of leaving its Jewishness behind, has manifested itself in Rebecca Miller's *Maggie's Plan* (2015), based on a short story by Karen Rinaldi. Maggie, played by Greta Gerwig, is a cross between Izzy and Ricki; seduced by the posturing and neediness of John, a narcissistic and unhappily married anthropologist, she prioritizes motherhood and uses her manipulative matchmaking skills to get him back with his equally self-involved ex-wife, Georgette (played by Julianne Moore). By the end of the film, a pickle man emerges from the shadows as a possible romantic interest for Maggie. Whereas *Crossing Delancey* skewers high literary culture, *Maggie's Plan* highlights the hypocrisy and absurdity of academic culture. Here, too, New York plays its cinematographic role as compelling setting and character. However, in the move from the Lower East Side to Greenwich Village, the Jewish flavor of both the Big Apple and *Crossing Delancey* is nowhere to be found. Ironically, even as *Maggie's Plan* pays homage to *Crossing Delancey*, it de-Jews a profoundly smart and Jewy film that in its production and narrative—and in league with some of its viewers—resisted assimilation with humor and aplomb.

Avalon (1990) and *Liberty Heights* (1999)

The Way We Were, *Next Stop, Greenwich Village*, and *Crossing Delancey* are all New York stories that chronicle the costs of, and mobilize resistance to, assimilation. Barry Levinson's Baltimore stories—in particular, *Avalon* and *Liberty Heights*—offer a different geographic take on such narratives. Levinson, who has been dubbed "the Bard of Baltimore" and who has declared Baltimore his "homeland," is acutely aware that his movies deviate from the norm of New York Jews: "The point is, there are all types of Jews. In the movies we tend to have a New York sensibility, from Woody Allen to Neil Simon, but there is a world of Jews outside New York, and these are the ones I write about: my family, my friends and the world that I know and understand best."[54]

Levinson got his start in the movies by serving as the director trainee for Mazursky's *Next Stop, Greenwich Village* and by working with Mel Brooks on *High Anxiety*.[55] Such beginnings foretold the dual focus or schizophrenia of his career: he is known for such successful commercial movies as *Rain Man*, *Wag the Dog*, and *Good Morning, Vietnam*, alongside the financially challenging labors of love represented by the personal Baltimore period films that began with *Diner* and include *Avalon*, *Tin Men*, and *Liberty Heights*.

Avalon, made possible by the commercial success of *Rain Man*, came into being through Levinson's intensive interviewing of family members.[56] It charts the rise and fall of the Krichinsky family, the surname of Levinson's maternal side. The film begins with Sam Krichinsky's arrival in America on the Fourth of July and chronicles the fracturing of this tribe through family meetings, Americanized name changes, Thanksgiving dinners, businesses founded and lost, suburbanization, and the ever-expanding encroachment of television. By the end of the film, Michael, Sam's grandson, seems to be taking over the role of storyteller, but while he is the last bulwark against the erasure of the past, his role as preserver of history is by no means assured.[57]

The working title of *Avalon* was "The Family," and Levinson's intended theme was the destruction wrought by television replacing the paterfamilias as storyteller. While the film is often talked about—and used as a teaching tool to talk about—immigration in general and sometimes Jewish immigration in particular, Levinson was at first floored that it was received this way. According to him, "It might as well be a movie I never heard about, so unlike what I thought I was ultimately doing."[58]

For some, *Avalon* has become a quintessential story of Jewishness and Judaism left behind. Writing for the *Observer*, Philip French perceives a lack of Jewishness in the film: "It is supposedly about Jewish immigrants and the assimilation, and Sam kicks up a fuss when his son changes his surname to Kaye. Yet the only specifically Jewish events in the movie are a funeral and the arrival of a long-lost brother who has survived a Nazi camp. All family events centre on Thanksgiving and the Fourth of July. Passover is never mentioned, no one goes to the synagogue, not a single Yiddish phrase is used, antisemitism does not rear its head, and despite the specific post-war context there is no reference to Israel. This is extremely puzzling."[59] Warren Rosenberg puts it more succinctly: "A cultural absence haunts *Avalon*, the element of Jewish life."[60]

The fact that *Avalon* is structured around Thanksgiving meals rather than, say, Passover might be an indicator of what Rosenberg has termed Levinson's "ethnic closet."[61] However, the Krichinsky family's ambiguous and ambivalent relationship to Thanksgiving and other American holidays is worth noting. Even as the extended Krichinsky clan gathers for turkey and all the trimmings, Eva avers that she will "never understand this holiday" and poses the question, who's "giving thanks to whom"? That gratitude is a question rather than a foregone conclusion suggests that the bounty of America might be a mixed blessing. The song "Christmastime in the City" plays as Jules, Sam's son, is mugged and stabbed. Similarly, the department store that Jules and his cousin Izzy open on the Fourth of July literally goes up in flames that very night. The American holidays that punctuate this narrative become associated with the disasters that plague this family even as part of it becomes upwardly mobile. Such narrative organization of time belies both a reading of the film as nostalgic and Stephen Whitfield's contention that America has won.[62] Rather, what we repeatedly see are the losses of the Krichinsky family.

For me, the Jewish commitments of this film reside in its chronicling and remembrance of these losses. It seems no coincidence that the only explicitly Jewish events are the funeral of Eva, Sam's wife, and the Shoah-related subplot involving Eva's survivor brother, Simka, born after Eva left Europe. Simka's story reminds viewers of the diversity of American Jewish immigration narratives. The arrival of Simka's family creates further dissension in the Krichinsky circle, since some of Sam's brothers balk at financially providing for this distant branch of the *mishpachah*. Told in untranslated Polish, Yiddish, and Russian, the story of Simka remains fragmented both for parts of the family and for viewers.[63] Ultimately, Simka's family doesn't become integrated into the

Krichinsky clan; rather, they relocate to rural New Jersey, where Simka obtains work on a farm. He is absent from Eva's funeral, as are Sam's brothers, Gabriel and Nathan. These missing mourners cause Sam to bitterly observe that "this is not a family," and add to his grief.

At this identifiably Jewish funeral, the Krichinsky family is not fully present to do the ritual work of mourning and memorializing; at the end of the film, Sam, in a nursing home and suffering from dementia, remarks, "If I knew things would no longer be, I would have tried to have remembered better." Yet Michael, Sam's grandson, begins to relate Sam's stories to his own son, whom he has named Sam, contra the Ashkenazic Jewish tradition of naming only after the dead, not the living.[64] As we watch Michael attempting to play the role of third-generation preserver in his own unorthodox way, we might remember that earlier in the film and as a boy, he had trouble mastering the grammatical difference between "may" and "can." While Michael has given himself permission to transmit family and ethnic history to his son and Sam's namesake, it remains to be seen whether his storytelling has the ability to do such memory work. However, chronicling memory loss associated with assimilation and the unmaking of Jews can be a form of resistance to it, and *Avalon* surely commits itself to that task.

While in *Avalon* the dramas of Jewish assimilation and resistance to it are somewhat coded—or at least understated—they are front and center in *Liberty Heights*, a film that, in the words of Lisa Schwarzbaum, "calls a Jew a Jew."[65] Schwarzbaum, a film critic for *Entertainment Weekly*, unwittingly became the catalyst for Levinson making this explicitly Jewish film that encompasses "race, religion, and class distinction."[66] In a review of Levinson's *Sphere*, Schwarzbaum identified a character as "unofficially Jewish." This remark got under Levinson's skin and unleased a flood of memories of his coming-of-age in the 1950s: moments that overturned his assumption that the world was Jewish, as well as the everyday antisemitism and racism that were part of the cultural fabric at that time.[67] Such memories turned into *Liberty Heights*, a film that returns to some of the themes of *Avalon* but with significant differences.

Whereas *Avalon* charts the Krichinsky family across three generations, *Liberty Heights* follows Nate Kurtzman (Joe Mantegna), a bookie who operates his illegal gambling enterprise under the cover of a waning burlesque club, and his two sons during the course of a year. Here the passage of time is marked not by the Fourth of July or Thanksgiving but by Rosh Hashanah. During this year, Van (Adrien Brody), the older son and a college boy, works his way through the Philip Rothian malaise of an obsession with a Gentile woman; Ben (Ben Foster), a high school senior, comes of age through his friendship with, and romantic attraction to, the only Black girl in his school. At the end of the film, Nate, on his way to prison, reminds his sons of their educational and ethical responsibilities. In sharp contrast to Sam's anguished cry after Eva's funeral that "this is not a family," Nate embraces his sons as he tells them, "We're a family, and nothing can interfere with that." Underscoring the echoing of and distinctions from *Avalon*, Ben's closing voice-over is about memory and the words of "a relative who once said, 'if I knew things would no longer be I would have tried to remember better." While *Avalon* does the memory work associated with cultural losses, *Liberty Heights* remembers the role that antisemitism and Black-Jewish relations played in the making, unmaking, and remaking of Jews.

"No Jews, Dogs, or Coloreds," the words on a sign at a local swimming spot, demonstrate that social antisemitism is alive and well in the Baltimore of 1954. Such exclusion from Gentiles, dubbed "the other kind" by Jews who normalize themselves, elicits diverse responses from those coming into Jewish manhood (as a review in the *Forward* notes, young Jewish women are missing in action in this coming-of-age film).[68] As in Mazursky's *Next Stop, Greenwich Village*, one of the film sets on which Levinson cut his teeth, the attempt to pass is presented but mocked. When Van and his friends go to an upscale Halloween party on Gentile turf, they are quizzed on where they live. Yussl (David Krumholtz) feebly attempts to pass as someone who's concerned about his neighborhood being overrun by Jews: "More . . . moving in, it's getting that way." His refusal to declare himself a Jew gets him badly beaten; the next time he enters Gentile territory, he dyes his hair blond, renames himself Yates, and presents himself as Scandinavian.

Van views such strategies of passing as laughingly pathetic; however, his own assimilation drama takes the form of falling for Dubby, a blond beauty decked out for Halloween as a fairy godmother and the on-again, off-again girlfriend of Trey, a WASP bad boy whose family "must have come over on the *Mayflower*." When Trey gets into a serious car accident, Van gets his chance with Dubby, only to discover that her cultural and economic privilege belies her profound unhappiness and destructive inclinations. Van's fantasy night with Dubby ends rather unerotically with weeping and retching. As in *The Way We Were*, assimilation desires reveal the fissures in and artifice of dominant culture and identity. Put another way, Gentile emperors have no clothes. Cured of his Gentile romantic fever, Van does become friends with Trey, who uses his prestigious lawyer father's connections to provide information about the Justice Department's case against Nate. Trey also confirms institutionalized antisemitism and racism, saying, "They love to go after the Jew and the coloreds. Shit, they still have an adrenaline rush from the Rosenberg executions." Here, rather than the unmaking of a Jew, is the making of an ally. Notably, this happens on- and offscreen. Justin Chambers, who plays Trey and hails from small-town Ohio, says that although he "didn't know much about what it meant to be a Jew before," the film raised his consciousness about Jewish life and history.[69]

While Van flirts with "the other kind," Ben positions himself in relation to other "others" and remakes himself as an off-white Jew through his interracial relationship with Sylvia (Rebekah Johnson). Ben's relationship to Jewishness is complicated and contradictory. Through Ben's Lenny Bruce–like voice-over at the start of the film, we learn that encountering an excess of whiteness—white milk, white bread, mayonnaise—at the home of a boyhood friend taught him his first lessons about Jewish difference from Gentiles, "the other kind." Prior to this, his world was one of undifferentiated Jewishness. Although such whiteness is anything but appealing, he also seeks to distance himself from a tribalism that divides the world into Jews and Gentiles. His chosen icons are Samson—from the 1949 film *Samson and Delilah*—and Frank Sinatra, but his iconoclasm goes too far when he dresses up as Hitler for Halloween, a stunt that Levinson's cousin Eddie, to whom the film is dedicated, actually performed.

Ben's budding relationship with Sylvia is viewed by many—especially his and her parents—as similarly beyond the pale, but it is in relation to her that Ben begins to more thoughtfully define himself as both a Jew and a man. Ben's interest in Sylvia is sparked by her intense focus during the homeroom recitation of Psalm 23, the Lord's Prayer. Notably, when she turns his question about what Psalm 23 means to her back on him, she identifies him as a Jew; later, when he wants to walk home with her, she makes it clear that her father, a prominent doctor, would not want her to be seen with a white boy. Although Ben is woke enough to mock his friends' racist views of hypersexualized Blacks, Sylvia raises his racial consciousness by challenging his assumption that she must live downtown (she doesn't) and by exposing the absurdity of his questions about which famous African Americans her dad knows. Broadening his horizons on music beyond the "regular" radio, Sylvia provides Ben with a racial cultural education: she introduces him to Black musical traditions and comedy, including Redd Foxx on passing, which is relevant not only to Blacks but also to Jews such as Yussl.

The racial boundary crossing that is central to *Liberty Heights* hearkens back to a short sequence in *Avalon*. In that earlier film, one of Sam's stories, enacted onscreen, relates to the club he owned that featured Black performers. It is there that he learned of Jules's marriage to Ann (Elizabeth Perkins); the marriage certificate betrays his name change from Krichinsky to Kaye. The club, with its interracial dancing, becomes the setting for what Sam terms the "best wedding reception ever." This glimpse of interracial possibility is recalled and expanded considerably in *Liberty Heights*, most notably when Sylvia gets Ben tickets for a James Brown concert. Although Ben and his friend Sheldon are the only whites at the concert, Ben does not experience white self-consciousness. Rather, like the rest of the crowd, he is energized by the aesthetic brilliance and energy of an emerging musical revolution.

To be sure, the music industry has been a site of cultural appropriation and exploitation as well as coalition-building in the history of Black-Jewish relations.[70] The potential for life-changing alliances between African Americans and white Jews is made manifest after the concert when Little Melvin, a small-time drug dealer whose big gambling winnings have embroiled him in Nate's numbers business, decides to take Ben hostage. Both Sylvia and Ben display remarkable courage and loyalty during this episode. Although Melvin is only interested in holding Ben, Sylvia refuses to leave. While waiting for Nate to ransom his son with the money the bookie owes Melvin but doesn't have, Melvin invokes the history of slavery and does not respond well—or knowledgeably—to Ben's assertions that Jews, too, were slaves in Egypt.

Intrigued and disturbed by Ben's relationship with Sylvia, Melvin seems both relieved and miffed that this white boy is not "plugging" Sylvia. When Ben admits that he does find Sylvia attractive, Melvin decides to engage in some sadistic and historically overdetermined entertainment: he tells Ben to "touch her titty." When Ben refuses to do this, Melvin repeats his order, adding "The gun says yes," as he points his weapon at Ben's head. Clearly terrified but also resolute, Ben insists that there's "nothing to think about" and delivers another, stronger, resounding *"no."* At least one reviewer finds Melvin's behavior in this scene confusing and incoherent.[71] It seems to me, however, that Melvin wants to both confirm the attractiveness and desirability of the Black female and position Ben as embodying the legacy of white slaveholders who sexually assaulted Black women. Such positioning is in keeping with Melvin's viewing of Ben as a white boy and the denial of any commonalities between Black and white Jewish experience. However, Ben refuses to position himself and Sylvia in this racist, misogynist script.

For Ben, Jewishness becomes the lever that catapults him out of both tribalism—evidenced by "the other kind" rhetoric—and assimilation strategies of passing or fetishizing Gentile fairy godmothers. Ben's desire and determination to transgress the boundaries of Jew and Gentile, as well as those of Black and white, are solidified when he kisses Sylvia goodbye after graduation, much to the dismay of both sets of parents. And in a truly stupendous coming-out-as-a-Jew scene, accompanied by the soundtrack of the Jewish radio hour, Ben and his friends return to the off-limits swimming hole and dump the sign disallowing "Jews, Dogs, and Coloreds" into a garbage can. After trashing that which excludes not only his kind but also Sylvia's, the boys remove their shirts and use letters imprinted on their chests to spell out "Jew." With this act, Ben completes a journey from self-fashioning himself as Hitler to becoming an off-white Jew and a small-time civil rights activist. In *Liberty Heights*, calling a Jew a Jew also entails broadening the cultural mosaic through remembering the 1950s cultural and educational revolutions associated with James Brown and *Brown v. Board of Education*. Such a broadening was reflected in the multicultural audience in attendance for the Baltimore world premiere of the film.

In *Liberty Heights*, Levinson partially re-creates and re-presents how he was made as a Jew. "With 'Liberty Heights,' the house we used was four doors away from where my cousin Eddie lived and a block from where I lived. I found myself during breaks walking the streets, and all these images would come up—conversations that were long gone would all of the sudden resonate again."[72] Baltimore, his Jewish homeland, is on full display: the Rosh Hashanah synagogue scenes that frame the film were shot in the Shaarei Tfiloh Synagogue and feature the facade of Beth Am.[73] The film has also been praised for the "fabulous re-creation of Baltimore's now-gone center of commercial life, Pennsylvania Avenue," which was the heart of the city's Black community.[74] Not only *whether* but also *what* one remembers is part of the significance of this film.

Of course, *how* Levinson remembers Jewishness, Blackness, and their intersections is also important. As was true for *Avalon*, whether or not *Liberty Heights* passes a Jewish litmus test is a critical debate. While Warren Rosenberg recognizes the boundary-crossing work of this film, he deems it as having "as little actual Jewish content as any of the previous Levinson films" and as being "clearly uninformed by the practice or study of Judaism," a critical opinion that should beg the question of what constitutes Jewish content and whether that is defined too narrowly.[75] Or, as Levinson smartly but snarkily asks, "Do they have to wear yarmulkes in all the scenes? How many religious artifacts have to be in the film?"[76] Notably, not only critics but also the actors themselves disagree on whether this is a Jewish film. Orlando Jones, who played Little Melvin, considers it "offensive" to label this a Jewish film, since its themes are universal. He particularly identifies with Ben's sense that the whole world was Jewish: "I thought the world was completely black." Chambers, who plays Trey, disagrees: "I think it is very much a Jewish film." Whereas Jones apparently thinks that a Jewish movie is for Jews only, Chambers considers *Liberty Heights* "a Jewish film that speaks to everyone."[77] Levinson's perspective on the reception of the film supports Chambers's more expansive view of the potential audience for Jewish movies: "Jews have a tendency to assume that they will love it [a Jewish movie], but that no one else will and that is simply not the case. I've gotten a strong response to this film . . . from both the black middle class and the Gentile world."[78]

For some, *Liberty Heights* is little more than an exercise in nostalgia, replete with stereotypes. Stephen Hunter, writing for the *Washington Post*, declares, "For a movie apparently driven (according to press interviews) by Levinson's need to confront antisemitism as he first discovered it, the movie is frighteningly full of stereotypes."[79] Lisa Schwarzbaum, whose own writing caused *Liberty Heights* to come into being, concurs with Hunter: "Levinson's storytelling here relies heavily on stereotype."[80] However, with his commitment to portraying diversity within Black and Jewish communities, Levinson can and has been read as engaged in stereotype-busting. Ben Foster, who plays Ben, points out that the narrative counters the usual representation of class in Black-white Jewish relationships: "The girl of my affections is African American and of a higher class than mine. I liked that." He continues, "There's still a lot of stereotyping going on in entertainment and I liked the absence of that in this movie."[81] In an article titled "'Liberty Heights' Defies Racial Stereotypes," Kay Bourne, writing for the *Bay State Banner*, a Black newspaper, deems "black characters realistically visible" in the film, noting especially the "quality performances all around with the black actors for a change rewarded with worthwhile roles that have equity with the other characters who are not African American."[82] Like the Jewishness of a film, stereotypes may well reside in the eye of the beholder; it's also worth remembering that stereotypes, as Jewish film scholar Nathan Abrams has compellingly argued, can be invoked in the service of subverting them.[83] For Bourne, "The story gets high points for its observations on how young friendships can transcend the poison of prejudices and stereotyping." While stereotyping is well represented in *Liberty Heights*, it is rendered self-consciously and not allowed the final word.

Levinson is acutely aware that the historical work encapsulated by that "No Jews, Dogs, or Coloreds" sign is revelatory for and shocking to some of his viewers. However, although this film is set in the 1950s (like *Avalon*, *The Way We Were*, and *Next Stop, Greenwich Village*), he viewed it as neither merely historical nor nostalgic, but still relevant in 1999, with its emphasis on "race, religion, and class distinction." Given the resurgence of antisemitism, the revival of mostly unproductive questions about the whiteness of Jews, and the related anxiety about whether and how Jews should assert their distinctiveness in an increasingly unwelcoming culture, *Liberty Heights* and other films that depict assimilation and its discontents resonate in Trump's America. Taken together, *The Way We Were*, *Next Stop, Greenwich Village*, *Crossing Delancey*, *Avalon*, and *Liberty Heights* might usefully be seen as a resource and tradition that address the angst and the possibilities of the present moment.

5

Assertively Jewish Onscreen

•••••••••••••••••••••

Produced from the 1970s through the late 1980s, films such as *The Way We Were, Next Stop, Greenwich Village, Crossing Delancey, Avalon,* and *Liberty Heights* work through assimilation scripts and end by embracing diverse ways of being Jewish. But there's a postassimilation cinematic story as well, this one represented by more recent films such as Woody Allen's *Whatever Works* (2009), John Turturro's *Fading Gigolo* (2013), Eve Annenberg's *Romeo and Juliet in Yiddish* (2010), Scott Marshall's *Keeping Up with the Steins* (2006), and Zach Braff's *Wish I Was Here* (2014). In many ways, these films begin where the "assimilation and its discontents" films end. Within these assertively Jewy films, Jewishness is taken for granted, and sometimes assimilation goes in the opposite direction, that is, Gentiles assimilate to Jewish mores.[1] Dominant culture is not only critiqued by a Jewish gaze but also transformed by it. Notably, these films are directed by members of the tribe, as well as by those who know the tribe well but are not themselves of it.

Although Jewish humor abounds in these films, Judaism and its rituals are unapologetically represented as more than a joke or a yoke of oppression; rather, it is a sustained way of life that smart, funny people wrestle with, choose, and make their own. Intra-Jewish difference—that is, diversity among Jews from the ritually secular to the sometimes or strictly observant to those for whom Yiddish is their first language—is on full display. At times, we have images of dissension between Jews giving way to respectful coexistence, a potent way these films contribute to a usable tradition.

These films are certainly in keeping with the New Jews whom Nathan Abrams regards as the post-1990s norm. However, the production and reception stories of these films suggest that old assumptions sometimes accompany these New Jews offscreen. What we watch seems to render the "too-Jewish" question moot; however, that question is resurrected when it comes to financing these films or predicting who will be the audience for them. The making of responsible, respectful depictions of observant Jews requires native informant consultants, a reminder that certain forms of Jewish literacy are not yet normalized. Directors and actors sometimes have their own assumptions challenged and find themselves remade as Jews or as allies. And those who are already Jewishly identified relish the relatively uncommon experience of seeing connections between their life and their art. Just as important, the reception of these films indicates that at least some critics prefer their movie-made Jews rendered ironically, even caustically. Parts of the reception story of these films might cause one to wonder whether the oft-used terms "sentimental" and "nostalgic" (not to mention "privileged") have become code for "too Jewish." More charitably, these films suggest that self-critical but nonetheless affirming representations of diverse Jewish ways of being are, if not exceptions, hardly the norm either.

Whatever Works (2009)

Lenny Bruce famously said, "If you live in New York, you're Jewish." Of course, he wasn't spreading fake demographic news; rather, he was acknowledging that Jews, though still a minority, are a critical mass in the Big Apple and, as a result, Jewishness is part of the cosmopolitan cultural fabric of the city. When thinking about Woody Allen, especially vintage Woody Allen (e.g., *Annie Hall* and *Manhattan*), one would be hard-pressed to separate the New Yorker from the neurotic, nebbishy Jewish man. Allen's *Whatever Works* (2009), a film initially written in the 1970s but updated for the Obama era, imagines a very different resolution to the culture wars that arguably led to the Trump era.[2] Here Christian southerners are remade in the image of Jewish cosmopolitans.

Boris Yellnikoff, a quintessential Woody Allen type, is played by brother Brooklynite Larry David, who calls upon his *Curb Your Enthusiasm* trademark. A mean misanthrope, Boris is the survivor of a suicide attempt (unlike Professor Levy in *Crimes and Misdemeanors*, he hit the canopy as he went out the window). After a career as an almost Nobel Prize–winning physicist and a Columbia professor, he now teaches chess to children who endure his venomous insults. His initial direct address to the audience, a technique used throughout the film that hearkens back to *Annie Hall*, pulls no punches: he assertively introduces himself as "not a likeable guy" and preemptively reviews the film as "not the feel-good movie of the year." His would-be foil soon appears at his door: the young and importunate Melody St. Ann Celestine (Evan Rachel Wood), a runaway beauty pageant contestant from Mississippi, worms her way into his apartment and his life. Playing Eliza Doolittle to Boris's nihilistic Henry Higgins, Melody develops a crush on Boris. Summarizing a counterintuitive trend in Woody Allen's cinematic world and beyond, Melody asserts, "I don't like normal healthy men, I like you." They marry, and Boris has, as he puts it, "not the worst year of my life."

However, the plot thickens as fate knocks on Boris's door in the form of Melody's Southern Gothic family. Her mother, Marietta, admirably played by Patricia Clarkson, caterwauls about Jesus before fainting at the sight of her daughter's senior "secular humanist" husband. Her father, John, who had left Marietta for her best friend, arrives with the proclamation, "Lord, I've sinned," to which Boris moans, "Why do religious psychotics end up praying at my doorstep?"

This meeting of Mississippi and New York could easily turn into the story that Boris, in character, pessimistically predicts: "death by culture shock." But in a film that one critic has smartly characterized as "Manhattanmagical realism," New York Jewish cosmopolitanism works its magic on Melody's clan.[3] Marietta's Polaroid images of her family catch the eye of a lascivious NYU philosophy professor; shepherded by him and a gallery owner he knows, Marietta ends up not only happily ensconced in a ménage à trois but also exhibiting her "homage to lust," a collage—in old New York black and white, of course!—of nude body parts. And John designs his own romantic homage to lust by partnering with Howard Cummings, née Kaminsky (the repetition of "née Kaminsky" whenever Howard is named serves to underscore a queer Jewish connection). As Boris quips, John is "not only sleeping with a man but soon will be celebrating Purim."

With its proliferation of reversals, this "Manhattanmagical realism" might well be viewed as a Purim play onscreen. *Whatever Works* ends on New Year's Eve with an unlikely minyan congregating at Boris's apartment: one of Boris's friends from the neighborhood; Marietta and her two beaus; John and Howard; Melody and her new beau, the more age-appropriate and attractive Brit Randy Lee Jones; and Boris and Elena, the psychic whose own body served as the canopy for Boris's second suicide attempt.

Such reversals often elicit the ire of film critics, who accuse Woody of trafficking in southern stereotypes. In "Off the Rails," a review whose title says it all, Anthony Lane writes, "There is something both majestic and sad in Allen's abiding conviction that anyone from outside the tristate area is either an airhead or a chronic hick, and that a dose of Manhattan is the last and best chance for a cure."[4] Gordon Haber, writing for the *Forward*, reads the film as reproducing "the usual liberal stereotypes about Southerners to flatter Allen's urban audience."[5] Ann Hornaday, in the *Washington Post*, refers to Melody's parents as "that painfully stereotyped couple—portrayed as Bible-thumping nitwits whose way of life is irrevocably threatened by the lures of New York sophistication."[6] Even a more positive review assumes a geography of reception: Frank Scheck's take is that the film "features enough genuine laughs to give it decent commercial traction, at least in the big cities."[7]

Yet while some critics see only self-serving stereotypes, they jettison the fact that this story strongly resonates with some of the principal players in the film. For Patricia Clarkson, this role was less of a stretch than some critics might imagine: "I was born and raised in New Orleans, I'm a Southern girl through and through. I had a similar trajectory. I was a nice Southern girl, from a more progressive family than Marietta, but I do know that lady well, from being in the South for a long time. I just understood it in ways. At 19 I came to New York to pursue my art, and I arrived with very big hair that wouldn't fit through a door. Slowly it collapsed, and slowly the clothing became black. That's what happened to me, albeit at 19, not middle aged. But whatever works, right?"[8] Evan Rachel Wood echoes Clarkson's offscreen assimilation story: "I did what Melody did, and I moved to New York when I turned 18, and I was filming *Across the Universe*. I was filming on the streets of New York for the first time and singing Beatles songs, and it changed my entire life. I don't know what I would have done if I hadn't made that movie. I spent a year here, and I felt like I knew who I was finally. This city really does something to you."[9]

After shooting a cluster of films in Europe, Allen returned to New York to film *Whatever Works*. The premiere at the Tribeca Film Festival added another layer to this homecoming. "I fell in love with New York through Woody Allen's movies, and I am excited we are opening this year's festival with Sony Pictures Classics for the world premiere of Woody's *Whatever Works*," Tribeca's cofounder Jane Rosenthal said. "*Whatever Works* is a uniquely funny addition to his body of work."[10] However, "New York" and its iconic imagery are hardly homogeneous, and the Big Apple of *Whatever Works* deviates from Allen's usual white, upper-crust, East Side existence. Says Allen, "The New York that I grew up loving was, ironically enough, the New York of Hollywood movies."[11] Yet, Boris Yellnikoff's story is one of leaving Beekman Place (the Waspy enclave that Katie Morosky disdains in *The Way We Were*) and relocating to the Lower East Side, which, according to Mark Harris, "is for New York Jews . . . the old country—the original Zip Code of existential gloom."[12] The New York to which Boris introduces Melody is first and foremost ethnic New York. These walkers in the city encounter the hanging poultry of Chinatown and one of the remaining relics of Old Jewish New York, Yonah Schimmel Knish Bakery. Predictably, Melody has no idea what a knish is (at one point, she refers to it as a "kwish"), and although Boris corrects her pronunciation, this supposedly brilliant physicist cannot explain the matter of knishery. Emphasizing the Jewish geography of Boris and the New York of this movie is the sequence in which this intercultural odd couple walks out of the frame while the camera lingers lovingly on the Yonah Schimmel storefront.

Boris's quips on national and world history complicate the visual argument of ethnic New York being a source of transformational magic. The contradictions of Obama's contemporary America are aptly communicated through Boris's one-liner, "A Black man got into the White House, but he still can't get a cab in New York." When Melody sees the Statue of Liberty for the first time and recites Emma Lazarus's stirring words, Boris refutes them: "Immigrants were never welcomed; as soon as they came over, each ethnic group was met with violence and hostility; each one had to claw and fight their way in. People always hated foreigners. It's the American way." Even more piercing and prescient from the perspective of 2020 is Boris's suggestion that concentration camps should be one of the specialized camps to which responsible parents send their children so that the latter would "understand reality" and "understand what the human race is capable of." Yet, Melody, who has internalized the lessons of beauty pageant culture, counters, "We tried to focus on positive things about America," and she brings her mother to the United Nations.

When Marietta asks to be taken someplace fun, Boris communicates his usual disdain for such frivolity by suggesting the Holocaust Museum, but Melody opts for Madame Tussauds Wax Museum. In this kitschy space, "the merry culture wars" at the heart of this film are brilliantly staged. "The God racket" that Boris rails against at the outset of the film is well represented by the figure of Billy Graham, a top attraction for the Marietta who has not yet been assimilated to cosmopolitanism. Right-wing America is also on display through shots of George Bush and Ronald Reagan, though Hillary and Bill Clinton are in the background. In a scene even more resonant today than in 2009, Marietta stops at the wax figure of Donald Trump and exclaims, "*This* is the kind of man you should be married to—not that Communist who sings 'Happy Birthday' every time he washes his hands." Here a competition between real estate magnate Trump and Larry David as a stand-in and updated version of Woody Allen/Alvy Singer of *Annie Hall*/Isaac David of *Manhattan* is set up. Marietta's designation of Boris as a neurotic Communist is a thinly veiled reference to his Jewishness; it is also a potent reminder that, even as Boris's paranoia about the size of the Jewish penis becomes a questionable cinematic gag, antisemitic ideas about Jewish men not being real men still have cultural currency.

Melody ultimately ends up with neither the waxen Trump nor the neurotic Boris. However, the film doesn't shy away from the judgment that assimilating to New York Jewish cosmopolitanism and to an ideology of "whatever works as long as you don't hurt anybody" is a better individual and cultural choice than allegiance to a Christian religious right that's happy to "define for you what's appropriate." Notably, the so-called Jewish science of psychoanalysis becomes the lingua franca of the Celestine family, with Marietta talking about "sublimating my own creative needs and forcing them on my daughter" and John gleaning from his therapist that his obsession with guns was a "manifestation of sexual inadequacy." Rather than an expression of "cultural elites" dismissing "a basket of deplorables," *Whatever Works* works its magical realism by imagining that the likes of Boris can learn to like grits, while the likes of John, Marietta, and Melody can peaceably learn to dissociate sexuality from sin and guns and be happy for the "first time in [their] adult lives." Call me old-fashioned, but that works for me. And during a period when Jewish reporters have been body-slammed by elected officials, when "cuck" has become a slur of choice, and when legislators at the state and national level are busy defining appropriate bathroom use, such secular Jewish humanist imaginings might well be a light unto the nation.

Fading Gigolo (2013)

Like *Whatever Works*, John Turturro's *Fading Gigolo* is a film about fairy-tale-like New York transformations. However, here a Hasidic widow rather than secular Jewish cosmopolitanism is the transformational force. Too often dismissed as a "vanity project" because honorary Jew John Turturro not only directed the film but also cast himself as the title character, *Fading Gigolo* is a humorous and poignant film with unexpected feminist elements. It manages to address the Jewish question of Woody Allen in a narrative that respectfully situates Hasidic life in a New York multicultural mosaic. In *Fading Gigolo*, seemingly insular traditional Jewish life is shown not only as a close double but also as a tutor to secular libertine culture in need of sensual connection.

In a rare performance in a film not of his making, Woody Allen plays Murray Schwarz, a bookseller who is forced to close his doors and then reinvents himself as Dan Bongo, pimp to his friend, former employee, and reluctant "ho," Fioravante, aka Virgil Howard (John Turturro). An unhappily married female dermatologist (Sharon Stone) looking for a ménage à trois is the predictable client Murray lines up for Fioravante; more inventively, Murray tries to create some chemistry between Virgil and Avigal, a widow from the Hasidic community who delouses the brood to whom he is "Uncle Mo" (Murray lives with them and their mother, Ophelia—played by Tonya Perkins—in an interracial household that serves as a microcosm of the ethnically and racially diverse New York streets that Turturro lovingly captures on film). Murray presents Virgil to Avigal as a healing massage therapist and fudges the question of religious difference by claiming that Virgil is a Sephardic Jew.

In an early sequence, a car crash that is a metaphor for the collision between Hasidic and non-Hasidic worlds offers a conventional view of black-hatted Jews: an enraged driver emerges from his vehicle shouting, "What's the matter with you people? . . . Speak English. You're in Brooklyn. . . . You're not in the old country no more." Notably, Dovi (Liev Schreiber), suitor of Avigal and a member of the shomrim, a Hasidic community patrol, intervenes. Whereas this scene sets the stage for Hasids perceived as the eternal, provincial "other," the film rejects this reductive narrative. Instead, it knowledgeably depicts a community that lives a life apart but yet intersects with and parallels the lives of more typical New Yorkers. Such a depiction owes much to Turturro's sensibility and research. His masquerading as a Jew here is emblematic of much of his film career: he played Barton Fink in Ethan and Joel Coen's film of that name as well as Bernie Birnbaum in *Miller's Crossing*, Herbie Stempel in *Quiz Show*, and Primo Levi in *The Truce*. In the final exchange between Dovi and Fioravante, the Hasid who has won Avigal posits that his rival is "not really Jewish." Fioravante's response, "I'm not sure," functions as a metacinematic moment.

Murray's and, by extension, Woody Allen's Jewishness are also up for debate in this film. In one sequence, Woody Allen is kidnapped by the shomrim and brought before a rabbinic court because he is perceived as distancing Avigal from her religious commitments. When Murray is identified as "one who has wandered far from his tribe," we have yet another metacinematic moment. Allen's encounter here with observant "Jewish brethren" is full of fabulous one-liners. When he is first hustled into the patrol car, he insists that they've "got the wrong guy," since he's "already been circumcised"; then he queries, "What did I do—break the dietary laws?" The interrogation at the rabbinic court begins with trying to establish the extent of his Jewish identification, an issue much debated by film critics over the years. To the question "Are you proud to be a Jew?" Murray responds, "Proud and also scared." When asked if he observes "holy Shabbos," he responds, "I would love to but a guy's got to make a living." Throughout, Murray comically demonstrates his knowledge of but also his noncompliance with Jewish religious obligations. Avigal herself interrupts this Jewish slapstick. Rather than be the object of discussion, she speaks for herself. Professing guilt of "breach of modesty," she recounts not only the scene in which Fioravante removes her wig, but also their first meeting during which she cries as he touches her bare back. While the rabbis assume that her sobs are "for shame," she quietly and with great dignity corrects their misinterpretation: "No, from loneliness."

Avigal is no Melody or Marietta. At points, the camerawork suggests conventionalized narratives of the Hasidic woman who is trapped and seeks to escape the burdens of a religious life. In one scene, as she stares in a shop window, her face is reflected onto a mannequin wearing stylish but immodest clothing; in others, she is shown against a wall, walking along a gate, or in front of a glass door with barred windowpanes as if she were in prison. However, she refuses to be seduced by secular Jew-ish cosmopolitanism or to be cowed by Judaic patriarchy. Just as she talks back to the rabbis, so does she talk back to

Dovi. As she ventures outside the neighborhood, he tells her to be home by dark; her response is to ask, "Why?" and continues, "It's not Shabbos." In this way, she defines what communal boundaries she will cross and which ones she continues to hold sacred.

Fioravante awakens Avigal to touch and connection—an awakening that will ultimately but in her own time lead her to Dovi. Yet, even Fioravante's courting of her affirms rather than invalidates Jewish ritual and observance. One of the most erotic sequences of the film involves the two of them sharing a meal that he has prepared for her. We see him unpacking kosher salt as well as a new cutting board, signs that he assimilates to her food practices. And her filleting of a fish is a form of foreplay as she teaches him to "lift flesh away from the skeleton," "to grab the tail and like a zipper, pull it up," and to take the spoon that holds the delicacy of the fish's cheek from her hand. Tutored by her, Fioravante finds himself unable to perform when the ménage à trois finally comes to pass, a cause-and-effect relationship underscored by the crosscutting between the scene in the dermatologist's apartment and Avigal first alone in the synagogue balcony and then speaking before the rabbinic court.

The realistic rather than cartoonish depiction of Hasidic Jews owes much to Turturro's directorial commitments. As Miriam Moster reports, *Fading Gigolo*, like other recent films, made use of a Hasidic consultant. In this case, Isaac Schonfeld had Turturro spend time with ex-Hasids and those on the fringes of the Haredi community to illuminate Haredi customs and practices. Malky Lipshitz worked with Vanessa Paradis (Avigal), while Liev Schreiber used recordings to develop the cadences of Hasidic speech.[13] While Turturro wrote the script, he credits Woody Allen with providing critical (in all senses of the word) feedback, including the suggestion to center the narrative more on Avigal,[14] and to read Isaac Bashevis Singer for context and the texture of lives lived communally.[15]

Although raised in an Italian Catholic immigrant household, Turturro married a Jewish woman; together they have raised a son who attended Hebrew school, and Turturro is well acquainted with and quite comfortable in the world of Reform Jewry.[16] Thus the assertive Jewishness of *Fading Gigolo* is founded on his experiences as actor, director, husband, and father, and he kvelled about *Fading Gigolo* being a favorite on the Jewish film festival circuit.[17] Elliot Gertel, who is notoriously critical of most onscreen depictions of Jewish life, proposed an honorary Jewish director award for Turturro:

> If I could suggest a special Oscar category, it would be for a film director from outside the Jewish community who successfully makes movies appreciative of Jewish life and Jewish values. In such a category, the best picture would be John Turturro's *Fading Gigolo*. Turturro essentially succeeded at reinventing the Woody Allen genre with a humor that is respectful of Jewish values and of

Orthodox Jews. While the film has its flaws and improbabilities, it is a very worthy, even noble effort.[18]

Yet even such glowing words understate the Jewish significance of this film. Rather than merely respecting Haredi life but keeping it in its separate place, Turturro's cinematic vision situates Haredi life within cultural debates about erotic and ethical values. Moreover, observant Jewishness is part of the multi-cultural mix. In a wonderful sequence, Woody Allen brings Avigal's Haredi children to play baseball with Ophelia's African American kids. When one of the children suggests that they should divide up into Black and white teams, Murray responds, "No, not going to happen. Not a good idea—this is how fascism gets a toehold. Break this up—get a little rainbow coalition here." As in *Whatever Works*, *Fading Gigolo* moves Allen out of a whitewashed Upper East Side and into a more colorful, diverse New York.

Fading Gigolo came out just as an adult Dylan Farrow renewed her sexual abuse charges against Allen in the pages of the *New York Times*. Many reviewers wrestled with their ambivalence about Woody Allen, especially given the timing of Allen playing a pimp as real-world accusations against him gained ground. As Ezra Glinter wrote for the *Forward*, "Right now Woody Allen is a problem for us all. And I don't know what the solution to that problem is."[19] But the Woody Allen "problem" should not overshadow Turturro's vision here, one in which a fading gigolo, a lovesick shomer, and a rabbinic court are shamed by and assimilate to the spiritual and sensual desires of a Hasidic widow.

Romeo and Juliet in Yiddish (2010)

At one point during the car accident sequence in *Fading Gigolo*, the Hasidic driver addresses Dovi in unsubtitled Yiddish; apoplectic, the non-Hasidic driver screams "Speak English. You're in Brooklyn!" The shift from Yiddish to English has been generationally a move of assimilation and acculturation, and Yiddish tends to be dominant today only in Haredi communities. However, it's worth remembering that a Yiddish cinema flourished between the two world wars in the United States (as well as Poland and Russia); this cinematic movement was self-consciously an attempt to resist assimilation. While Hollywood and its Jewish-run studios were widely perceived as a vehicle of assimilation, the Yiddish cinema based in New York parodied Hollywood and produced narratives that prescribed tragedy for those who were seduced by the New World. To understand this Yiddish cinematic difference, one need only compare *The Jazz Singer* (1927) with *Overture to Glory* (1940): in the former, the faux jazz singer gets the girl and his mother's love as he assimilates into whiteness through blackface; in the latter, an opera singer who has forsaken a cantorial career loses his son and ultimately dies.[20] The Shoah decimated Yiddish culture and Yiddish speakers, effectively putting an end to Yiddish cinema. However, in recent years, there has been a resurgence of interest in Yiddish. The restoration and distribution of classic Yiddish films by the National Center for Jewish Film is certainly an important part of this revival (and these restored films are often part of retrospective offerings at Jewish film festivals); however, even more astonishing are contemporary U.S.-produced films that are Yiddish-centered. Such films function as a revisionist reversal of linguistic assimilation and, as Rebecca Margolis has argued, "create a community—if virtual, or imagined—of audiences of Yiddish listeners."[21]

To be sure, the Coen Brothers's Yiddish prologue to their 2009 film *A Serious Man* (discussed in chapter 3) might be seen as a seed for this new cinematic development. Notably, the credits to Eve Annenberg's *Romeo and Juliet in Yiddish* (2010) include a special thanks to the Coen Brothers (Annenberg considers the credits a "love letter").[22] And the only professional actor in Annenberg's film is Yelena Shmulenson (Lady Capulet), who appeared in the prologue. While Yiddishkeit functions as the ambiguous frame to the Coens's modern Jobian tale, writer/director Eve Annenberg rightly suggests that although "other Yiddish films will come down the pike . . . I think people might say 'Romeo and Juliet' was the first to use this much colloquial Yiddish in modern narrative in more than 50 years."[23]

Shot in thirty days on a scant $175,000 budget, *Romeo and Juliet in Yiddish* is a Chagallesque mumblecore, an indie subgenre that features nonprofessional actors, improvised scripting, and a focus on young adults. The protagonist of the frame narrative is a graduate student at Brooklyn College (in the not so subtly subtitled "Normal Brooklyn") who supports herself as a nurse. In order to keep her scholarship, Ava (Eve Annenberg) is required to translate *Romeo and Juliet* into Yiddish, a task at odds with her aversion to Haredi culture. Although Ava tries to justify this aversion by claiming that "everyone hates the Orthodox," she is haunted by her born-again Jewish youth, during which she bore and then was forced to abandon a daughter when she fled her Haredi community. Due to her linguistic inadequacy, she needs help translating and updating the play. To this end, she hires Hasidic youths who are struggling—and scamming—to survive in exile from a community much like the one she left. As she and they learn about one another, the play within the movie develops and is intermittently enacted onscreen, thus suggesting connections between the lives of the translators/producers and those of the decidedly unconventional Shakespearean characters (played by the Hasidic youths and Ava). Writing themselves into a classic love story forbidden to them by their yeshiva education, the Hasids recast the Montagues and Capulets into the Satmars and Chabadniks at war with one another in a Brooklyn seemingly at odds with the "normal" one in which Ava studies. Romeo and Juliet first meet not at a ball but at a Purim party, a fire escape supplants the famous balcony, and

Rabbi Lawrence is the not-so-close double of Friar Laurence. Those who play the warring Hasidic sects are, in real life, off the derech, that is, have themselves left the Orthodox communities into which they were born. Thus the offscreen lives of the translators/Shakespearean actors significantly overlap with what appears onscreen. In this way, *Romeo and Juliet in Yiddish* extends the tradition of Yiddish crossing boundaries to include that of fiction film and documentary.[24]

The question of who needs to assimilate to whom dominates the film. On the one hand, the Hasidic youths in exile know nothing about Shakespeare or romantic love, and their English belies the fact they were born and bred in Brooklyn. At one point, Lazar (who doubles as Romeo and is played by Lazar Weiss) shares his dream of losing his accent. Yet, they are also the ones with deep and valuable Jewish knowledge, including Yiddish. Prior to Ava's hiring of the Hasidic youths, she tries to learn Yiddish on her own. In a remarkable montage of study, we see Ava wrestle with a Yiddish-English dictionary, Miriam Weinstein's *A Nation of Words, Yiddish for Dummies*, as well as *The Complete Idiot's Guide to Learning Yiddish*. Bleary-eyed and frustrated, she tries to discern Yiddish text, and the sentence "You are an inadequate Jew and You Will Never Get This" appears before her. Here she inhabits the spectator position of Yiddish-challenged audience members. In another sequence, after Ava responds with condescension to the Hasidic youths' lack of knowledge about Shakespeare, she expresses her astonishment that the Orthodox "would fight among themselves." Lazar adroitly turns her own condescending words back on her: "You didn't know this. Gee, you don't know anything." The tension escalates as Ava declares that she has been doing real work, not "sitting on my ass studying bullshit." To which Lazar responds to Mendy, the most observant of the group and often shown laying tefillin, "If she studied bullshit, she could do her homework herself rather than hire homeless Hasids." Even as the film refuses to romanticize Haredi communities, it also refuses to endorse a secularized hierarchy of knowledge.

Even Shakespeare is assimilated to these Hasidic youths who choose life. After almost dying from a heroin overdose, Lazar tells Ava, "We need a better story. Let's fix it. . . . Why the fuck are people killing themselves? It's not smart." Like Lazar, Yiddish Romeo does not die at the end, thanks to a canny dilution of drugs.

Adapting Shakespeare's *Romeo and Juliet* is a negotiation with one of Western culture's ur-tales of tribal warfare. This film aptly uses this canonical tale to illuminate and renegotiate fault lines within Jewish communities. While the Yiddish play reimagines the Montagues and Capulets as warring observant sects, Lazar's desperate life is shaped by his father excommunicating him for leaving home and cutting off his earlocks. And the acrimony between Ava and the homeless Hasidic youths she has hired is a result of their inhabiting "two different Judaisms," defined by sexual and educational distinctions. As a drunk and avowedly secular Ava humorously puts it at a Shabbat dinner, "putting out is a cultural imperative" and "Jews are people of the book" who are "commanded to go to graduate school."

Yet the opposition between Ava and her hired Hasids is not as extensive as it first appears. Yes, Ava does not observe kashrut, made abundantly clear when the only food she has to offer the hungry Hasidic youths consists of leftover Chinese: shrimp with broccoli, crab rangoon, and spare rib tips. Yet, when her colleague and friend Melody (Melody Beal, Annenberg's neighbor and best friend) brings Ava her required free-trade coffee with soy milk, this Black, Jewishly literate nurse smartly observes that "with these many rules, you might as well keep kosher." At one point, Ava tells one of the Shabbat guests who has evinced romantic interest in her: "I don't just dislike your culture, I hate your culture." However, both Ava's past and present are deeply intertwined with Orthodoxy, emphasized with shots of Ava hanging out in a Haredi neighborhood every Sabbath in hopes of glimpsing the daughter she left behind. When Lazar and company are getting ready to leave, she is forced to admit that she does not hate them, a sentiment underscored when she literally saves Lazar's life and reassures him, "We're not fighting, sweetheart. There's nothing to fight about."

Ava's transformation is, in some ways, a recounting of Annenberg's own. In one interview, Annenberg admits, "I was not a fan of the ultra-Orthodox . . . and that's changed."[25] She explicitly acknowledges, "I'm expressing that Jew-on-Jew hostility that I'd certainly like to see less of, and I see the movie as a rapprochement between the two camps. . . . If ever a bunch of people didn't understand each other that well, it's the ultra-secular and the ultra-Orthodox."[26] Ultimately, Shakespeare's words "my only love sprung from my only hate" and "all these woes shall serve for sweet discourse in our time to come" undergird the crossing of Jewish boundaries at the heart of this film.

As numerous directors indicate, Jewish film is perceived as risky business; that is doubly true for Yiddish-language film. Anxiety about the potential audience for Yiddish art is embedded in the narrative of *Romeo and Juliet in Yiddish*. When Ava is first given the project to "contemporize" a 1939 YIVO translation of *Romeo and Juliet*, she balks, classifying Yiddish as the "world's most irrelevant language." Arguing against the value of this work, she asserts, "Who cares? No one's going to read it. Religious people aren't allowed to, and everyone else who speaks Yiddish is over ninety." Notably, this was Annenberg's own view of Yiddish prior to meeting the Hasidic exiles and being enchanted by young people speaking the language and "wanting to showcase it dramatically."[27] Doubts about audience also make their way into even admiring reviews of the film. Sue Fishkoff lauds *Romeo and Juliet in Yiddish* for its normalizing of Haredi culture and Yiddish but then ponders the impact of not providing more glossing in the movie: "That all begs the question: Will this play outside New York, and maybe L.A.?"[28]

The reception history of the film indicates the answer to that question is a resounding yes. The film premiered at the Berlin Jewish Film Festival, winning the Audience Favorite award there. The possibility of lessening intra-Jewish hostility, Annenberg's vision for this film, was represented by the audience at the UK Jewish Film Festival: half of those attending were Hasidic, not a usual occurrence for the festival. While many left during the sex scene between Romeo and Juliet filmed to a rendering of the haunting High Holiday prayer Avinu Malkeinu, they returned to watch the rest of the film.[29] Ultimately, Weiss's expectations were upended: "I thought they would disrespect it, but they very much appreciated the film."[30] Perhaps not as surprisingly, *Romeo and Juliet* was a sellout hit at the New York Jewish Film Festival and then returned later in the year for screenings at the Lincoln Center Film Society. The *Forward* included this film that uses Shakespeare to remake relations between secular and Haredi Jews among its five best picks for 2011.[31]

Keeping Up with the Steins (2006)

Fishkoff's question about *Romeo and Juliet in Yiddish*—"Will this play outside New York, and maybe L.A.?"—reminds us of the geography of American Jewish identity. As different as they are, *Whatever Works, Fading Gigolo*, and *Romeo and Juliet in Yiddish* are all set in New York. However, *Keeping Up with the Steins* (2006), a film that takes on the bar mitzvah industry through an intergenerational story about fathers and sons relearning what it means to become a Jewish man, is set in that other arguably Jewish coastal city, Los Angeles.

Like *Fading Gigolo, Keeping Up with the Steins* is directed by an honorary Jew, Scott Marshall, who invoked his Jewish wife and children to convince the producers that he had the cultural know-how to be at the helm of this film.[32] According to his father, actor and director Garry Marshall, Scott had bar mitzvah envy as an adolescent growing up in Hollywood, so *Keeping Up with the Steins* was the cinematic fulfillment of his desire to assimilate to Jewishness.[33]

Keeping Up with the Steins is the story of Benjamin Fiedler (Daryl Sabara), a reluctant bar mitzvah boy. In addition to the predictable anxieties of having to chant his haftarah in Hebrew in front of a congregation, Benjamin must also contend with his father viewing the party that attends the Jewish coming-of-age ritual as competitive sport. According to Adam Fiedler (Jeremy Piven), "It doesn't matter what happens at the temple, it's the party that counts." Adam, a movie producer turned agent, is determined to outdo the Steins's lavish *Titanic*-themed party; he is also overcompensating for his own modest bar mitzvah bash overseen by Irwin Fiedler (Garry Marshall), the father who ultimately abandoned him and his mother (Doris Roberts). Attempting to distract his father from his obsession to throw "the biggest bar mitzvah in the history of bar mitzvahs," Benjamin invites his grandpa Irwin to the event two weeks early, with the result that the run-up to the bar mitzvah and the day itself become "a special Jewish edition of the Jerry Springer show."

To be sure, the bar mitzvah industry, one among many emblems of a U.S. culture of conspicuous consumption and an American Jewish success story, is lambasted here. While coming-of-age rituals should be the gateway to Jewish continuity, here they represent a *Titanic* of Jewish life. This sinking ship is aided and abetted not only by a pushy party planner but also by a rabbi who is too busy hawking his book *The Passion of the Jews* on the O'Reilly show to provide spiritual guidance to the next generation. Customs of rote memorization that result in the boy-becoming-a-man chanting the haftarah without having a clue as to its literal or figurative meaning also contribute to the potential spiritual emptiness of this life cycle event.

However, while parts of *Keeping Up with the Steins* are reminiscent of *A Serious Man*, its register ranges from the satirical to the Jewishly earnest. At one point, the hipster Irwin (who has arrived at the Fiedler household in an RV and with a nubile Native American wannabee partner) is trying to help Benjamin sort out his confusion and complicated feelings about the bar mitzvah by asking, "What's your favorite thing about being Jewish?" He responds to Benjamin's "bagels and lox" answer with a gentle challenge: "Not a terrible answer, but maybe there should be a little more." It is Irwin who ultimately speaks truth to power to the rabbi: with unflinching honesty, he tells this faux spiritual leader that the bar mitzvah preparation is not making the ritual and text "come alive" and that the rabbi is "letting the kids down."

By the end of the film, Benjamin not only successfully chants his haftarah portion but also does the work of *tikkun olam*—repairing the world—by reconciling his father and grandfather. As he sagely informs the two during a particularly bitter bickering session, "The day I become a man, you're not supposed to act like children." During the candle lighting ceremony, Adam vows "to bust my tuchis to be as much of a mensch as my son Benjamin."

This is a boy/man-centered story—most evident in the scene when the Torah is passed from the rabbi to Irwin to Adam to Benjamin, with Joanne, Benjamin's mom (Jami Gertz), and Rose, Benjamin's grandmother, literally standing behind them. However, Jewish women's wisdom on Jewish masculinity and its discontents is evident at key moments.[34] When the countercultural Irwin explains to Rose that he abandoned her and Adam because he "couldn't be one of those schmucks" who was a commuting breadwinner, Rose corrects him: "Those schmucks were fathers, Irwin, those schmucks were husbands." Rose's grandmotherly observation that Benjamin is "a boy, is a man, it's confusing" becomes a refrain in his d'var Torah—and he cites her rather than simply appropriating her words. And it is Joanne who tells Adam to grow up and get over the anger at his father that is sabotaging his son's process of becoming a man: "Look at your life now, look at your beautiful, charmed life. Get over it." Just as the *Titanic* theme of the Steins's excessive party functions as a metaphor for what seems destined to sink contemporary American Jewish life, so do Joanne's words remind Adam—and the film's audience—that an American Jewish present need not be destroyed by overcompensation for past privations.

Just as important, Benjamin reshapes the bar mitzvah party so that his celebration of becoming a man puts feminized family traditions front and center. While Adam planned an event catered by Wolfgang Puck at Dodger Stadium, Benjamin revisions the party as an at-home affair, with a buffet featuring Grandma Rose's brisket, his mom's matzo ball soup, Grampa Irwin's stuffed derma, and Sacred's soy gluten kasha. Thanks to Rose, Neil Diamond makes a special guest appearance (she knows his mother from her canasta-playing days in the old neighborhood). However, instead of singing the national anthem at Dodger stadium as Adam had planned, Diamond sings "Hava Nagilah" as Irwin, Benjamin, and Adam are hoisted on chairs for the hora (notably, Adam only participates when Joanne tells him to "get in the frigging chair").

One critic found this Diamond-centered ending to be "a little much."[35] But Diamond himself says that "'Hava Naglia' was something I always wanted to do. . . . I've never played a bar mitzvah, so it's the closest I'll get."[36] And those who remember their American Jewish film history understand this as a post-assimilationist metacinematic moment. In the 1980s remake of *The Jazz Singer*, Neil Diamond eschews becoming a cantor and instead comes out as a pop star singing "Coming to America." In the course of two decades, the jazz singer has willingly returned to his Jewy roots, thanks in part to an intermarried director and his bar mitzvah envy.

Notably, this film was a Jewish homecoming for more than Neil Diamond and Scott Marshall. Although Grandpa Irwin was played by Garry Marshall (who has often been misidentified as Jewish due to his Bronx upbringing and Borscht Belt experience) after Jewish patriarchs Mel Brooks and Carl Reiner turned down the part, much of the rest of the cast and the production team are assertively Jewish. Many viewed their participation in the film as a welcome expression of their own commitments. As Scott Marshall reports, "The writer was Jewish, both producers were Jewish, and the executive producer was orthodox Jewish, and she was very concerned with everything being correct and not making too much fun."[37] Jami Gertz, who proudly defines herself as a Jewish professional, viewed the character of Joanne as in keeping with her own life: "I'm probably the only Jewish actress who in her contract has put in that I will not work on Yom Kippur and I will not work on Rosh Hashana, which I'm very proud of. . . . It's just a deal breaker for me. . . . Sometimes we're scared to have our convictions and see them through because we're afraid we'll be penalized or someone will judge us."[38] Doris Roberts also proudly identifies as

FIG. 5.1 "Hava Nagilah" courtesy of Neil Diamond in *Keeping Up with the Steins* (2006)

Jewish and relishes that she "was able to be in a movie about Jews that wasn't sad." According to her, "We have humor, we sing and dance, and we live great lives. . . . It's about time there was a movie [on Jews] like that."[39] Tellingly, many of those involved with the film and its production relate their own bar mitzvah stories to that of Benjamin's, and the script by Mark Zakarin was semi-autobiographical and his second attempt at writing a bar mitzvah–oriented screenplay.[40] Even the party that took place after the film's premiere at the Tribeca Film Festival exuded the ethos of the film: the venue was the Upper West Side institution Barney Greengrass, and the swag included yarmulkes imprinted with "Keeping Up with the Steins 5-2-2006."[41]

Although Jeremy Piven also claims that the film represents his Jewish identification, his offscreen behavior suggests that he still has much to learn about being a Jewish ethical man. Piven reports that *Keeping Up with the Steins* seemed to fulfill his rabbi's prediction that "Judaism was going to be like a time bomb . . . and someday it would explode." About the film, he says, "I think it's important to show the world Jewish culture in a way that is respectful, but also, it's a comedy, so we're taking shots at materialism as well as [showing] the beauty in the rite of passage in a bar or bat mitzvah."[42] However, accusations of sexual misconduct by at least eight women have caused Piven to shift from film and television to stand-up comedy (Piven denies these allegations).[43] While bar mitzvah jokes continue to be part of his shtick, Piven's recent onstage regret that homophobic epithets are off-limits suggests that the fictional Benjamin Fiedler is considerably more mature and menschy than both his onscreen father and the Jewish man who plays him.[44] Like Woody Allen, Piven reminds us that not all movie-made Jews are equal, nor should they be equally celebrated, even as their work remains Jewishly significant.

While the box office returns on *Keeping Up with the Steins* were larger than expected, critical reception was uneven. As is too often the case with films that treat Jewishness and Judaism seriously—and not just for laughs—the adjectives "sentimental" and "schmaltzy" were often used. Many reviews lauded the satirical aspects of the film and rued the deviation from that register. Writing for the *A.V. Club*, Nathan Rabin opines, "In its terrific first half, *Steins* devastatingly but affectionately lampoons the arrogance and self-absorption of upwardly mobile Jews with dead-on bits like a preening rabbi. . . . Then the film takes a turn toward the soft and squishy and never fully recovers."[45] Stephen Hunter of the *Washington Post* regrets that the screenplay wasn't more Philip Rothian.[46] Peter Howell, writing for the *Toronto Star*, is of the opinion that "buried beneath the borscht is the satire this could have been."[47] And Stephen Holden of the *New York Times* writes, "*Keeping Up with the Steins* begins as a growling, razor-toothed satire of carnivorous consumption in Hollywood. But after the first half-hour, those growls subside into whimpers, and the movie becomes a family comedy oozing good vibes, generational reconciliation and (far-fetched as it may seem) a spirit of humility." He concludes that it "would have been a much better film if it had waited twice as long before retracting its fangs."[48] Such critical valuation suggests the bias toward irony in general and ironic distance from Jewish life in particular. Marshall and company's hybrid approach of critique and respect, comedy interspersed with spirited—and spiritual—debate about Jewish values, was seen as a lack by parts of the critical establishment, though others found it "refreshing to see a film satirizing upper-middle class Jewish suburbia without taking too many cheap shots at it."[49] Without falling into prescriptive criticism about what Jewish movies should be and do, we might reflect on critical trends that canonize films and filmmakers that satirize Jews and dismiss those that include but also move beyond Jewish funny business.

Keeping Up with the Steins used grassroots marketing strategies, including outreach to Jewish professionals. This tendency led to its own brand of Jewish comedy. Per Michael Fox, "The most amusing aspect of the whole enterprise is the effusive statement in the press kit from Zakarin's Pacific Palisades cantor. 'In the future,' the cantor writes, the film 'will be required viewing for each of my b'nai mitzvah families as they begin to plan their ceremony and party.' The good news? After that, learning the Haftarah won't seem nearly as painful."[50] However, more than a decade after the film's premiere, the joke is perhaps on Fox. In 2017, the Conservative Movement's Park Slope Jewish Center included the film as part of its Shaarei Mitzvah—Gates of Mitzvah—program for b'nai mitzvah students and families, and the film is regularly referenced in articles about the bar mitzvah industry and the need to resist it.[51] Ultimately, *Keeping*

Up with the Steins suggests that assertively Jewish movies can be an intercultural project and play a role in the making of the next Jewish generation and its ritual life.

Wish I Was Here (2014)

Like *Keeping Up with the Steins*, Zach Braff's 2014 *Wish I Was Here* illuminates the challenges and the possibilities of making not only Jews but also Jewy movies. The production history of this film is arguably more well-known than the film itself, though the Jewishness of that history is too often overlooked. Braff, the director of the 2004 indie hit *Garden State* and the star of the long-running TV show *Scrubs*, wanted to make a "thematic" rather than a literal sequel to *Garden State*.[52] While *Garden State* focused on the angst of twenty-somethings trying to find their way in the world, *Wish I Was Here* moves into the next decade of life. This film focuses on a still-aspiring actor—Aidan Bloom (played by Braff)—whose professional dreams are at odds with the needs of a family, which includes wife Sarah (Kate Hudson) and two children whose attendance at Jewish day school is subsidized by a dying observant grandfather (Gabe Bloom, played by Mandy Patinkin).

Braff's vision for this film was to explicitly engage the spiritual questions of those who were raised as traditional Jews but were trying to find their own spiritual paths as proud but overwhelmingly secular Jews. According to Braff, he and his brother Adam called upon their own experience in cowriting the script: "My parents force-fed me this religion, and there's aspects of it [that] I love, but what is my spirituality right now? What do I believe? How can I reconcile my belief in science with faith? And gosh, once I start having children, what the hell am I going to teach them? We just thought that was a really interesting thing to write about, because no one else seemed to be making a movie about it."[53] However, when this successful director/actor tried to get the financing for such a script, he found that the Jewiness of it was an insuperable impediment: "There was definitely the implication that the Judaism should be toned way down because it wouldn't appeal to a broad audience."[54] Expanding on this point, Braff comments, "The studio system isn't going to make a movie about a Jewish family. . . . A financier wasn't going to make a movie about a Jewish family. It's very, very hard to get—we're 2 percent and shrinking—a movie about Jewish people made. If I made this in the studio system, they'd be like 'ix-nay on the ewish-jay.' I'd have to [dial] it down."[55] Rather than dial or tone down the Jewishness, he took the suggestion of producer Stacey Sher and opted to supplement his personal financial stake of $2 million with a Kickstarter campaign. Much to his surprise and delight, this "giant social experiment" of crowd-funding financing was wildly successful, with 46,250 people kicking in a total of more than $3 million. While this financing strategy provided Braff with the "creative freedom" he needed to make his vision of the film, it also created a public relations nightmare that impacted the critical reception of the film.[56]

According to his critics, Zach Braff's decision to use Kickstarter funds was the ultimate exercise of white privilege. Writing for *Bitch*, Lucy Vernasco identifies Braff as "not a struggling artist who can't find the support of a traditional film studio, like many interesting and forward-thinking movies that turn to Kickstarter to get off the ground." Rather, she classifies him as "a thirty-something white dude living in LA . . . [who] used all that support to follow his true passion of creating a movie that's all about a thirty-something white dude living in LA following his dream."[57] Devin Faraci echoes Vernasco, accusing Braff of making "whitesploitation films": "We all understand that you pay for these things the way movies are always paid for, not using the funding model for people who are outside of the system, people who face actual adversity when trying to get their vision accomplished. People who, basically, don't have nine seasons of sitcom royalties. . . . He could get his movie made in the standard system—he just couldn't get it made the way he wanted to get it made. . . . This is privilege. This is the face of privilege."[58] Interestingly enough, these two reviewers never use the "J" word; with that key omission, they conflate Jewishness and whiteness, while effectively denying that a specifically Jewish vision has any sort of legitimacy or claim to diversity.

However, the Kickstarter funds, along with the $2 million Braff himself put into the film, prevented the "privilege" of whitewashing Jewishness from Braff's vision, which was picked up by Focus Features after a premiere at Sundance. There's plenty of Jewish shtick here, including a dog called Kugel and a grizzled rabbi who rides a Segway in hospital corridors, bumping into walls as he seeks to fulfill his pastoral duties. Yet, there is also serious Jewish wrestling, notably represented when Aidan seeks out a younger rabbi for spiritual guidance. This sequence cuts from Aidan's space superhero fantasies, his more customary cosmic wanderings, to his entrance into a Jewish space. Struggling to come to terms with the impending death of his father as well as the gap between his Jewish-school-educated children (aka his "indoctrinated matzo balls") and his own lapsed Jewish commitments, Aidan witnesses schoolboys singing "Oseh Shalom" in harmony. He then banters and reckons with a rabbi whom Braff has categorized "as the sort of fantasy rabbi I've never met." Aidan tells the rabbi that he kept kosher until his bar mitzvah and that his becoming a man meant that his father allowed him to go his own way and eat a bacon cheeseburger. To the rabbi's question about his current spiritual connections, Aidan responds with ideas of infinity represented by the sky. The rabbi sagely counsels him to "try not to get caught up in the God who wants you to be kosher and study the Torah. Start with the God of the infinite universe and imagine that force is trying to guide you through the most challenging part of your life, even if it has to appear to you in the form of a spaceman." This "fantasy rabbi" meets Aidan where he is spiritually. As a result, Aidan figures out what he can teach his children: he recites poetry in the desert (certainly a space of Jewish wandering!) and, while he and his children are repairing the world of their backyard, identifies such recitation as "a prayer you're not expecting anyone to answer."

Like *Keeping Up with the Steins*, *Wish I Was Here* is, in part, a meditation on what it means to be and to become a Jewish man. As a father, Gabe is a castigator-in-chief: he harangues his sons for their failures, which results in Noah (Josh Gad) not talking to his father for a year and almost not showing up at his deathbed; as he puts it, when you're "old and sick, everyone's supposed to forget you're an asshole." And although Aidan, unlike Irwin in *Keeping Up with the Steins*, does not physically abandon his family, his continued commitment to an acting career going nowhere often makes him an absentee parent and partner: while he's off trying to fulfill his dream, his wife, Sarah, works a stultifying job that includes sexual harassment to support the family and has no time to consider what her own dreams might be. When Gabe can no longer pay the tuition for the Jewish day school his grandchildren—Tucker (Pierce Gagnon) and Grace (Joey King)—attend, Aidan goes to the ancient Rabbi Pearlman and asks for tzedakah, a word that Grace has taught him. Rabbi Pearlman subtly derides Aidan by identifying him as "the actor—wife provides for the family while you act" and as one who has made choices rather than "someone who needs assistance." When Aidan opportunistically asks whether God believes "in [his] pursuit of happiness," Pearlman points out that Aidan's proof text is the Declaration of Independence and that God wants him to provide milk and honey for his family. While the judgmental patriarch Gabe is hardly a male role model, both Pearlman and Sarah advocate for a model of masculinity that respects familial and communal responsibility rather than a narcissistic American dream of masculine self-fulfillment. By the end of the film, Aidan finds his calling and a modest salary in teaching theater to kids, making him neither Irwin nor Adam Fiedler.

Although, as I've already indicated, women's contributions are part of the narrative of *Keeping Up with the Steins*, women's roles in the family, in Jewish tradition, and in the workplace are more pronounced and provocative in *Wish I Was Here*. Like Joanne, Sarah helps to mend father-son relations and to make the men in her life act like mensches. As Gabe is dying, Sarah reminds him that he has "raised two incredible boys" who, despite not having "awards on their mantles" or even mantles themselves, have "big sensitive hearts," and whose last days with a father who either withholds or shares his love for them "will shape who they are as men." As a shaper of Jewish manhood herself, Sarah, whom Gabe previously derided as "a half Jew," is now identified by him as "going to make a great matriarch one day." Reflecting on his words, Sarah, played by real "half Jew," Kate Hudson (Goldie Hawn is her mother), comes back with "I already am a great matriarch, Gabe. At least I'm working on it."

Notably, this self-made matriarch puts up with sexual harassment in the form of a jerk named Jerry who likes to talk about his "half boners" and play ventriloquist for his penis. When Sarah, with dignity and discretion, reports this behavior to her boss, he tells her to "lighten up, no one's trying to touch you, no one's trying to make their penis talk like a rapper." Although he does move Jerry out of their shared cubicle and instructs him "to tone it down a notch," he also tells Sarah that she "need[s] to promise to smile a little more" and reminds her that she's "got something everyone else wants—a job." This subplot in a pre–#MeToo era film brilliantly shows what it means to report sexual harassment and be doubly victimized as well as none too subtly threatened with unemployment. I can't help but wonder if such real talk about sexual harassment would, like Jewishness, have been toned down had Braff used his studio "privilege" rather than his own money and Kickstarter funds to realize his vision.

While Sarah is acknowledged as a matriarch in the making, it is the precocious Grace who steals the Jewish show in this film. In sharp contrast to her brother, Tucker, Grace is fully at home in the world of the Jewish day school. Her observance is neither rote nor forced; rather, it is reflective and authentic. She is the one who teaches her father about basic Jewish concepts and practices, such as tzedakah and the practice of women wearing a sheitel after they are married. When her mother offers to update her conventionally modest wardrobe once Jewish day school becomes beyond the family's financial reach, Grace responds, "God is testing my faith right now, and I probably shouldn't make any drastic changes." Her empathy is on full display throughout the film, from her prayerful acknowledgment that her mom is not happy to her telling the observant Gabe that she "davens the healing prayer for him three times a day." With a goodness that is girlish/womanly, Grace is able both to silence and to comfort Gabe: she interrupts one of his tirades with a gift of welder's goggles, which she provides so that "when you go into the white light you won't have to squint so that you can find grandma." And it is Grace who helps to bring Noah to his father's deathbed by listening to his fear and sadness, which he had been masking with his justified anger, and by telling him, "Listen, I know you don't believe in God but maybe you can believe in family." Like Benjamin in *Keeping Up with the Steins*, Grace turns the generational tables. However, even more so than Benjamin, she embodies Jewish wisdom and knowledge and, like the fantasy rabbi, embraces a continuum of Jewish expression.

Grace is represented not only as the product of a Jewish day school but also as a movie-made Jew. When Aidan follows in his father's footsteps and teasingly emasculates Tucker by calling him "Yentl" as he struggles to put on his tzitzit, Grace refuses to see the film as a joke. Rather, this Jewish movie matters because it gives voice to her feeling that "boys get to do all the cool things to honor Hashem and I won't get to do anything remotely cool until I buy my

FIG. 5.2 An observant granddaughter comforts her dying grandfather in *Wish I Was Here* (2014)

sheitel." That moment comes sooner than expected: in order to be more Jewishly visible as she is being separated from her intellectual and spiritual community, she shaves her head and then, courtesy of her father, ends up with a vivid hot pink wig. This quirky *frum* adolescent may be the film's most innovative contribution to the indie canon.

The making of this film not only represented but also extended the Jewish expressiveness and identification of many involved. Josh Gad, who plays Aidan's brother Noah and is perhaps best known for his role in *Frozen*, is the grandson of Holocaust survivors. He found that the themes of *Wish I Was Here* resonated with both his commitments to tradition and his wrestling with faith. For Gad, the film was "an interesting ride,"[59] as it "called into account what [his] relationship is with Judaism, with God," which is "always evolving."[60] Braff, whose brother had a dismal experience at a yeshiva and who himself views Woody Allen movies as services for High Holidays, discovered a very different world of Modern Orthodoxy during the making of the film: "It wasn't until shooting this movie, in the yeshiva we actually shot in, that I saw a Modern Orthodox school. It was a wonderful school, and the rabbis that I talked to were really charming guys and we actually had some interesting conversations about religion, and the kids were all happy and having a wonderful time."[61] In interviews, Mandy Patinkin insists on the universality of the film and denies that its Jewish themes attracted him to the role.[62] Nonetheless, he marked the completion of the film, which occurred shortly before Rosh Hashanah, with the sounding of a shofar. According to Braff, Patinkin "blew a tekiah gedolah. No doubt the non-Jewish crew members were left wondering if all Jewish films end on just such a note."[63]

Ultimately, both the narrative and the production history of *Wish I Was Here* take Jewishness and Judaism seriously in a way rarely seen in Hollywood. An encounter between Grace and a non-Jewish peer serves as indirect commentary on this phenomenon. In that humorous scene, Grace is explaining to Jesse that she is going to be homeschooled because her family can no longer afford private school. When he assumes that the choice to be homeschooled indicates that they're Amish, she corrects him and tells him that they're Jewish. To his stereotypical response, "I thought Jews ran Hollywood," she quips, "I thought so, too; maybe we're the wrong tribe or something." In the cinematic world, "the wrong tribe" still seems to be the one perceived as "too Jewish." As the production and reception histories of *Wish I Was Here* and the other assertively Jewish films covered in this chapter demonstrate, the assumption persists that Jewishness needs to be dialed down for the box office. Yet, as Braff makes clear, a committed cinematic audience along with directors, producers, and actors sharing a vision can change that calculus: "I was allowed to make a Jewish movie because of my fans."[64] In the days of Kickstarter, those making Jewish movies go way beyond the usual suspects.

6

Queering the Jewish Gaze

•••••••••••••••••••

Film history contains repeated parallels and intersections of the gay and the Jewish question. The anti-antisemitism film *Crossfire* (1947) set the stage for one paradigmatic, though troubling, relationship between gays and Jews in cinema. The film, about the murder of a Jewish man by an antisemitic U.S. soldier and the ensuing investigation, was the cinematic companion to *Gentleman's Agreement*: both films were credited with indicting U.S. antisemitism as unpatriotic after the war against fascism had been fought and won in the European theater of war. However, as many scholars have noted, the fight against antisemitism in these two films comes at the cost of Jewish bodies.[1] As I discuss in chapter 2, *Gentleman's Agreement* focuses on a journalist writing an exposé on antisemitism who pretends to be a Jew to get his story. In order to teach the liberal lesson that Jews are just like everyone else, Jewishness becomes defined by antisemitism, which must be eradicated. This leaves no cinematic space for Judaic practice (synagogues are deemed Jewish churches!) or cultural particularism. *Crossfire* literalizes the disappearing Jew with the murder plot: for the vast majority of the film, Jewishness is represented only as a dead body and an offscreen victim of antisemitism.

Notably, the adaptation process of *Crossfire* offs the queer body: in Richard Brooks's *The Brick Foxhole*, the novel on which *Crossfire* is based, the murder victim is a gay man. Both the Production Code's prohibitive rules regarding sexuality and the desire to cinematically expose U.S. antisemitism in the immediate post-Holocaust era led to the substitution of Jew for gay. Years later, *Bent* (1997), a film based on Martin Sherman's play of the same name that helped to make gay Holocaust history visible, explicitly reverses the substitution at the heart of *Crossfire*. In the final scene, Max, a gay concentration camp prisoner who has been masquerading as a Jew, replaces his yellow star with a pink triangle prior to electrocuting himself on the camp fence.[2]

Such substitutions set up an analogue between the experience of gays and Jews as oppressed minorities who often have the opportunity and the burden to pass or assimilate. This analogue has a clear cinematic dimension: both Jewish and queer film history have been defined by closets, open secrets, and coded images. A comparison of two canonical documentaries about film, *The Celluloid Closet* (1995), informed by Vito Russo's book of the same name, and *Hollywoodism: Jews, Movies and the American Dream* (1998), loosely based on Neil Gabler's book *An Empire of Their Own: How the Jews Invented Hollywood*, illuminates the parallel and sometimes overlapping histories of queer and American Jewish film.[3] Both documentaries include a discussion of stock characters who function as comic relief; both talk about the professional consequences of being out, especially for actors, which meant that Jews changed their names and gays felt compelled to play it straight onscreen and off; both identify the Hays Production Code and its enforcer Joseph Breen as the official vehicle of antisemitism and homophobia, and the blacklist as backlash against the open secret of gayness and Jewishness.

Perhaps the most profound parallel between these two documentaries and thus Jewish and queer film history is the emphasis on gay and Jewish identifications and desires strategically being performed through codes, "subtext," indirection. While *Hollywoodism* presents Wild West shootouts as indirect pogrom imagery reflecting the background of Jewish studio heads and the white picket fences of the Hardy Boys as a fantasy of an America in which outsiders could become insiders, *The Celluloid Closet* turns our attention to the queer cinematic metanarrative performed by the song "Secret Love" in *Calamity Jane* (1953) and to the same-sex desire represented by gunplay in *Red River* (1948) and by the Alan Ladd photo in Sal Mineo's locker in *Rebel without a Cause* (1955). Such strategies of indirection mean that the Jewishness and the queerness of a film often reside in the eyes of the beholder, and the recent renaissance of Jewish film studies is, in part, indebted to the notion of Jewishly literate viewers decoding "encrypted Jewishness."[4] Henry Bial has argued that the charting of Jewish film history prior to the 1960s necessarily entails an understanding of "double-coding" dependent on "reading Jewishly."[5] Following Barbara Kirshenblatt-Gimblett's insight that "Jewish film is what happens when it encounters an audience," Alisa Lebow prioritizes reception and the necessity of "watching Jewishly" in her work on Jewish autoethnography, including queer Jewish autoethnography.[6]

At points Friedman and Epstein's *The Celluloid Closet* suggests the affinity and potential intersections between gays and Jews. A highlighted scene from the transformational film *The Boys in the Band* (1970) features Harold, played by Leonard Frey, explicitly identifying himself as a "Jew fairy."[7] And *The Celluloid Closet* includes the scene (discussed in chapter 4) from Paul Mazursky's *Next Stop Greenwich Village* (1976) in which white Jewish mother Shelley Winters asks Black Antonio Fargas if he's Jewish, and he responds, "No, I'm gay." The slippage between Jewish and gay in that scene in particular and in the cinematic interchange/paralleling between gays and Jews in film history in general gestures toward what is now a well-documented open secret history of Jewish queerness: the sense that circumcised men who prove their manliness through study in homosocial spaces or through business rather than through physical strength or production of goods are feminized and thus not real men according to dominant, heteronormative definitions of masculinity.[8] And Jewish women, those stereotypically mouthy beings who worked in the public sphere while their men studied and prayed, similarly do not conform to dominant, heteronormative models of femininity.

This open secret of Jewish queerness impacts the cultural performances of all Jews, whether they identify as straight, gay or lesbian, or queer.[9] In particular, it has meant that narratives of Jewish assimilation, perforce, include gender and sexual assimilation.[10] Such assimilation patterns, in tandem with prohibitions against homosexuality embedded in halakhah (Jewish law), often foreclose or complicate rich and explicit performances of the queerJew (I use this term to avoid one identity category being relegated to the adjectival, condiment position). Put another way, too often Jewish gays and lesbians are explicitly represented—or represent themselves—as belonging primarily to either the Jewish or the gay camp.[11] One identity category might substitute for, suggest, or parallel the other; however, as Janet Jakobsen notes, such analogizing "tends to create two distinctive groups" or "tends to make the first term the center of analysis while marginalizing (if including at all) any analysis of the second term."[12] The queerJew risks being relegated to a specifically Jewish closet or exiled from Jewish life. Perniciously, queer Jews are in danger of being straightened out while Jewish queers are potentially de-Jewed. In other words, Jewish queers have too often had to choose between two essential parts of their being: Jewish *or* queer rather than Jewish *and* queer.

This chapter focuses on the continuing challenges and possibilities— onscreen and off—to be assertively Jewish and queer, to refuse to give up an essential part of oneself. I begin by focusing on two fiction films—*I Now Pronounce You Chuck and Larry* and *Kissing Jessica Stein*—that do important antihomophobic work but nonetheless fail to fully realize a vision of sustained queer Jewishness. A comparison of Rob Epstein's documentary *The Times of Harvey Milk* and Gus Van Sant's biopic *Milk* shows how the cultural Jewishness of this iconic queer politician has been cinematically conveyed and whitewashed. While Lebow's title *Treyf* indicates that queer Jews find themselves simultaneously at odds and in keeping with diverse forms of

Jewish tradition, *Trembling Before G-d* and *Hineini* put into sharp focus the specifically religious struggles that observant queer Jews encounter as they demand to be seen. These films, including their production and reception histories, feature the making, unmaking, and remaking of queerJews. Taken together, they demonstrate the difference that American Jewish movies can make.

I Now Pronounce You Chuck and Larry (2007) and *Kissing Jessica Stein* (2001)

Ironically, some relatively recent films that normalize Jews and strive to do anti-homophobic work continue to separate the Jewish from the gay body. *I Now Pronounce You Chuck and Larry* and *Kissing Jessica Stein* might be thought of as a cinematic odd couple. *Chuck and Larry* is a crude Adam Sandler comedy, while *Kissing Jessica Stein* is a Woody Allenesque arty romantic dramedy. Despite fairly pronounced tonal differences, both of these films entertain the possibility of Jewish queer subjects but ultimately do quite a bit of work to straighten them out in the end.

The title characters of *I Now Pronounce You Chuck and Larry* are firemen played, respectively, by Adam Sandler and Kevin James. Larry Valentine's wife has died, and he has been too grief-stricken to meet the deadline of a cumbersome bureaucratic pension process that would financially protect his children if anything happened to him; Chuck Levine is a fearless firefighter who finds his pleasure in porn and one-night stands. After Larry saves Chuck's life on the job, the widowed father of two convinces his best friend to file for domestic partnership so that Chuck can be the beneficiary of Larry's pension funds and take care of his kids in the event of his death. When Chuck and Larry are investigated for fraud, they must prove that they are a couple (such exploits are familiar from films that feature a foreign national trying to get a green card through marriage). This gay farce goes to the altar and then beyond to a hearing. When the investigator insists that Chuck and Larry show their affection for one another publicly before the law, the film becomes a bromance that stops short of kissing between men.

Beyond the obvious Jewish associations that Adam "Chanukah Song" Sandler brings with him, Chuck explicitly identifies himself as a Jew during the wedding sequence and insists that he and Larry don yarmulkes as they exchange vows in Canada.[13] The fact that Chuck is the only one that Larry trusts with his children's future in the event of his demise calls upon stereotypical narratives of the Jewish man as a good provider and serious family man, if also a pervert. And much to his chagrin, Chuck is always assumed to be the "woman" in his relationship with Larry, a sign that Jewish manhood is still considered queer-ish (culturally bent, if you will), even in its most virulently misogynist and heterosexually pornographic performances (Sandler's role here is not for the prudish).

While the film has fun with and even celebrates the Jewish man who plays with being queer, there seems to be no room for the Jewish man whose sexual orientation is unambiguously gay, whose brotherly love extends into the bedroom. To be sure, Chuck helps Larry's son, who yearns to be a dancer rather than a ball player, to come into his own as a gender bender, and the faux gay antics of Chuck and Larry facilitate the coming-out process of a virile Black firefighter, played by Ving Rhames. However, the gay men's room remains without Jews, as the overtly antihomophobic closing underscores. Chuck instructs his gay-baiting, firefighting bros that the use of the term "faggot" is not OK; as he explains, that word is as offensive as "kike." Epithets for gay and Jew are parallels, analogues. While the Jewish bad boy can develop into an ally, he apparently can't ultimately be cast as a Jewish gay boy. Such gay development is left here to the hypermasculinized Black man.

According to Jennifer Westfeldt, cowriter and costar of *Kissing Jessica Stein*, independent films are a different sort of cinematic animal: they "explor[e] issues that Hollywood won't explore and give a quirkier kind of entertainment where not everyone is drop-dead beautiful and where not everything works out neatly. I think . . . the role and job of independent film [is] to tell stories that maybe [have] something riskier to say and maybe to show actors who don't normally get to work."[14] However, as *Kissing Jessica Stein* shows, the boundaries between indywood and Hollywood can be porous, especially when it comes to assertively gay and lesbian Jews—or the cinematic lack thereof.

Kissing Jessica Stein has its origin in the Catskills. At a theater workshop in that legendary Jewish comic capital, Westfeldt met cowriter and costar Heather Juergensen. Realizing that they were both engaged in writing about "Mars Venus dating hell," they cowrote a play titled *Lipschtick*, which had a six-day run far off Broadway.[15] A studio bought the film rights to the play. However, the project seemed unable to get out of development, so Westfeldt and Juergensen bought back the rights and developed a script that reflected their interests in what a female Alvy Singer—the male lead character in Woody Allen's *Annie Hall*—would look like.[16] According to their vision, Jessica Stein, frustrated by the impoverished choices for the male romantic lead in her life, becomes involved with Waspy Helen Cooper (played by Juergensen), only to realize that she isn't lesbian after all.

To be sure, *Kissing Jessica Stein*, like *I Now Pronounce You Chuck and Larry*, does considerable antihomophobic cultural work. Helen and Jessica are shepherded through their new world of same-sex relationships by a committed, loving male couple; both the cross-gender mentoring and the representation of a stable gay male relationship are significant in a representational world that tends to depict gay men as from Mars and lesbians from Venus. Westfeldt and

Juergensen, who both identify as straight, did considerable research for their screenplay and interviewed many lesbians, including some couples belonging to Westfeldt's shul, about their relationships.[17] The film's director, Charles Herman-Wurmfeld, reports that he "basically lived Helen's part" and that his "coming-out story was very similar but certainly not as funny as the movie version."[18] Helen does end up with a new girlfriend, so lesbian romance is certainly not erased from this film that earned a Gay and Lesbian Alliance Anti-Defamation (GLAAD) Media Award.

Kissing Jessica Stein also does important cultural work in revisioning the Jewish family. The film begins with an Allenesque parody of both the Jewish mother and Judaic practice. Jessica is in synagogue with her mother and grandmother on Yom Kippur; on this holiest day of the year, in the midst of the Viddui, Jewish mother Judy Stein is matchmaking in the pews. Mother and grandmother argue about the suitability of available prospects (mom advocates for not being a perfectionist lest her daughter end up alone, but grandma thinks that Jessica shouldn't settle for someone without a chin or sex appeal). In a fit of frustration, Jessica yells at her mother, "Shut up, I'm atoning," a High Holiday service–buster line if ever there were one.

However, in sharp distinction with a Woody Allen film (with the possible exception of *Crimes and Misdemeanors*, discussed in chapter 3), *Kissing Jessica Stein* doesn't treat Jewish life merely as a joke factory. While Jewish life cycle events and Jewish ritual do provide their fair share of humor, they also become occasions for the important cultural work of making the Jewish family queer-friendly. When Jessica brings Helen to her brother's wedding, a group of elder Jewish yentas energetically engage the new couple on religious and reproductive issues, much to Helen's Waspy chagrin. Predictably and stereotypically, the yentas' first question is whether Helen is Jewish, though unpredictably, the yentas are satisfied enough with Helen's feeble answer that she has attended a seder. Even more unpredictably, this Jewish women's chorus offers advice to the couple about expanding the tribe through artificial insemination. The message seems clear: lesbians who bear *kinder* (children) will be welcome additions to the *mishpachah*.

A less humorous, more poignant, and far more significant moment occurs between Jessica and her mother, played by Tovah Feldshuh, the night before the wedding. Trying to save a clearly distracted and distraught Jessica from a painful coming-out declaration, Mrs. Stein's subtle and subdued "Helen is a very nice girl" speaks volumes. This mother, who at the beginning of the film is represented as a walking stereotype, is clearly struggling with her daughter's romantic trajectory. Yet she has accurately read Jessica's relationship with Helen and has chosen the path of a wise and welcoming cosmopolitan who only wants her *shaynah maideleh*, her beautiful daughter, to be happy. This unconditional embrace of a Jewish lesbian daughter by Feldshuh, who has played Golda Meir, mother of the Jewish nation, in both the Broadway play *Golda's Balcony* and *O Jerusalem*, should not be underestimated.

Indeed, this scene might even constitute a cinematic revolution. Traditionally, the overbearing Jewish mother has been associated with compulsory heterosexuality or heteronormativity. No same-sex funny business for the stereotypical Jewish mother: her job is to ensure that her sons and daughters make good matches with Jewish members of the "opposite sex" so that they can be fruitful and multiply. As Harvey Fierstein's *Torch Song Trilogy* (1988) dramatically represents, when those *kinder* dare to queer their own lives, notions of the respectable Jewish family, and Jewish ritual, so-called family values can end up being complicit with hate crimes. In *Torch Song Trilogy* Anne Bancroft, the mother of protagonist Arnold Beckstein (played by Fierstein), is cast as the ultimate Jewish policewoman for the heteronormative family. Beckstein has lost his lover, Alan (played by straight man Matthew Broderick), to a homophobic hate crime. When Arnold accompanies his mother to the cemetery where his father is buried, she is horrified when her son begins to recite Kaddish for Alan; she objects to this perceived sacrilege at top volume (the default volume for the stereotypical Jewish mother). A comparison of this sequence to Mrs. Stein's recognition of Jessica and Helen's relationship enables us to more fully appreciate the ways in which *Kissing Jessica Stein* revises representations of the Jewish mother and the possibility of queering the Jewish family.

However, much to the disappointment of many of its viewers, Jessica's lesbian love story is not to be. By the end of the movie, there's coffee rather than pillow talk between Jessica and Helen, as the latter prepares to tell all about her new girlfriend and Jessica reveals the formerly unrealized soulmate potential of Josh, Jessica's ex-boyfriend and boss. Significantly, this soulmate potential is first realized at a Sabbath dinner at her birth family's home. When Josh's usual sardonic performance gives way to a sincere and erotic—at least for Jessica—rendering of *Motzi*, the blessing over bread, she looks anew at him. Film scholar Nathan Abrams has rightly pointed out that, in a cinematic tradition that rarely shows Jews falling in love with other Jews, we should celebrate Jessica and Josh's coupling.[19] While I agree that there's something Jewishly touching here—what's not to like when a Jew becomes sexy by making *Motzi*?—I do wish that such Jewish and Judaic positivity wasn't tied to a counter-coming-out story. Although the film contemplates and seems willing to unconditionally embrace a Jewish lesbian subject position, that embrace is not narratively sustained.[20] At least one article in the Jewish press wants to make sure that we know that Jessica's romantic plot also applies to Westfeldt: "Her own sexuality is an open-and-shut case—she's straight as is Juergensen—although she has admitted to 'girl crushes' when a student at Yale."[21] Rather than reflexively celebrating the normalizing of Judaic representation, we need to reflect upon the diverse and sometimes contradictory plots and politics that such normalization can promote.

We also should not forget to ask whether and for whom such normalization takes place. Given that the film ultimately seems to remove the lesbian from the Jew, it seems ironic that the Jew is removed from even the potential lesbian by some reviewers. In *Off Our Backs*, Karla Mantilla and Jennie Ruby reduce Jewishness to whiteness when they comment, "The characters were interesting and not stereotypical (other than the obligatory thin white leading women)."[22] Tamar Jeffers McDonald views the film as "marginalizing the very sexuality it was meant to showcase" by focusing on Jessica rather than Helen.[23] Yet her analysis erases Jessica's Jewishness from critical consideration. Given that the Jewishness of *Kissing Jessica Stein* is hardly coded—even if you gloss over the Stein of the title, it *does* begin in a synagogue and includes a Jewish wedding as well as a Shabbat dinner—one has to wonder what it takes for some to see a movie-made Jew.

The Times of Harvey Milk (1984) and Milk (2008)

While the lesbian ends up missing in action in the Jewish coupling of Jessica Stein, the Jewish dimension of Harvey Milk is oddly underexposed and ironically even closeted in Gus Van Sant's magisterial biopic of the queer political icon. That irony is heightened when we consider that Rob Epstein's *The Times of Harvey Milk*, the Oscar-winning documentary that is a source text for *Milk* and that appeared almost a quarter of a century earlier, adroitly represents Harvey's "kosher-style" activist being. A Jewishly inflected analysis of the two major films devoted to this iconic gay activist reminds us that American Jewish film history is a narrative of continuity and change rather than one of unremitting progress. And both the status of Milk for gay and lesbian Jews and the response of the Jewish community to the biopic make *Milk* a limit case for the very definition of a Jewish film.

A history of Jewish queerness (which includes but is not limited to genderbending) might be and has been mobilized to *actively* resist heteronormativity. Jewish overrepresentation in feminist and queer activist, aesthetic, and academic spheres suggests this mobilization—think, for example, of Bella Abzug, Adrienne Rich, Judith Butler, Eve Kosofsky Sedgwick, Leslie Feinberg, Larry Kramer, Tony Kushner, and, of course, Harvey Milk. By naming names, I am engaging in a very particular form of Jewhooing, defined by David Kaufman as "the naming and claiming of famous 'members of the tribe'—and the consequent projection of group identity onto them."[24] Kaufman argues that "the main motive of Jewhooing today remains the construction of Jewish identity and the related countering of assimilation—an unconscious attempt to reverse the very processes of social integration and de-Judaization that touch most every Jew in the modern world."[25] The naming and claiming of specifically queer Jews becomes a form of resistance to both ethnoreligious and gender/sexual assimilation; queer Jewhooing—what I will henceforth refer to as "Jewqhooing"—affirms and simultaneously constructs queerJewishness, especially along ethnic rather than religious lines. Jewqhooing needs to be understood as a refusal to have Jewishness or queerness substitute for, parallel, or suggest the other; those who Jewqhoo profess faith in the plenitude of both/and while seeking to avoid the impoverishment of either/or. Jewqhooing is an assertion of being twice blessed rather than doubly abjected and constitutes a communal refusal to reside in one closet or another. Rather than winking and nodding at the potential for grounding a queer life in Jewishness, Jewqhooing celebrates, realizes, and extends that potential. Unsurprisingly, a prominent "Jew fairy" politician such as Harvey Milk is a prime candidate for Jewqhooing, and Rob Epstein's *The Times of Harvey Milk* cinematically elects him to that office.

No gay decoding is necessary when it comes to the life and death of Harvey Milk, the San Francisco supervisor who was instrumental in defeating Proposition 6, also known as the Briggs Initiative (John Briggs, California state senator, was the sponsor of this proposition that would have made it illegal for gays and lesbians to work in California public schools). Milk and San Francisco mayor George Moscone were murdered by Dan White in 1978. An openly gay politician known for his tireless activism and his skills at coalition-building, Milk opted to be an out politician and activist, even though he anticipated assassination. And just as Milk's position in gay history is assured, so does *The Times of Harvey Milk* hold a central place in gay film history. Thomas Waugh deems Epstein's documentary "a breakthrough in the homo history genre because of its wealth of audiovisual documentation of newly visible gay public life in the late seventies and early eighties, especially mainstream electoral politics" and argues that its winning the 1985 Oscar for Best Documentary "symbolized once and for all the real end of famine."[26] B. Ruby Rich regards *The Times of Harvey Milk* as "one of the landmark films of the gay documentary movement by anybody's standards."[27] This film—along with *Word Is Out, Common Threads*, and *Paragraph 175*—represents Epstein's use of documentary to unlock the historical closet for spectators across the spectrum of sexual orientation. Moreover, the grassroots and coalition politics successfully practiced by Harvey Milk and foregrounded in Epstein's documentary not only was crucial for his own times but also functioned as a model and a call to arms for the AIDS-ravaged times in which the film was released and feted.

Here I extend the significance of *The Times of Harvey Milk* by including its underappreciated but seminal role in the Jewqhooing of Milk. Unquestionably, Milk is a doubly iconic figure for gay and lesbian Jews; this was true during his life, and it has become even more pronounced in the years following his death.

As one might expect, Milk is an oft-Jewqhooed figure. During the fight against the Briggs Initiative, a gay Jewish group called the Lost Tribe cited Milk as its leader.[28] Lesléa Newman, a prolific writer in multiple genres who is probably best known for her children's book *Heather Has Two Mommies*, Jewqhooed Milk in her prize-winning short story "A Letter to Harvey Milk."[29] This text does the Jewish memory/historical work that Kaufman identifies as central to Jewhooing by charting a continuum of queer Jewishness that extends from the Shoah to the contemporary moment.[30] Kaufman argues that cultural group Jewhooing is often done in institutional sites such as museums, and he specifically cites the relatively new National Museum of American Jewish History in Philadelphia.[31] Significantly, when in 2011 journalist Mark Segal took the newly opened museum to task for neglecting the LGBTQ Jewish experience, he Jewqhooed Milk as an emblematic figure who needed to be featured.[32] Keshet, a Boston-based Jewish LGBTQ organization, includes Milk in its heroes poster series that serves as an exemplar of the Jewqhooing phenomenon.[33]

In Jewqhooing Milk, Epstein not only contributed to an inclusive documentarian signature that both preceded and came after *The Times of Harvey Milk* but also extended the specifically Jewish memorialization that he did for Milk offscreen. Epstein, a gay Jew who knew Milk from the Castro neighborhood and as a local politician, was keenly aware of Milk's heritage after he was killed; indeed, he and a friend "felt there should be a Jewish service as well [as the famous candlelight march]."[34] According to Epstein, "We contacted Temple Emanu-El, the big Reform synagogue in San Francisco. That set in motion the Jewish service that took place soon afterwards."[35]

Early in the film, narrator Harvey Fierstein informs us that Milk was born to Long Island Jewish parents; in this way, Milk's Jewish lineage is established at the outset of the documentary. Such an introduction to Milk's Jewishness brilliantly and accurately represents the complexities related to his own Jewish identification. Milk has been categorized variously as a non-Jewish Jew, a secular Jew, a Jew estranged from Judaism in particular and from institutionalized, homophobic religion in general.[36] According to Naphtali Offen, who knew Milk, "He had really strong feelings about the role that organized religion was playing in oppressing gay people. He felt alienated from Jewish religion."[37] In the famous recording he made to be played in the event of his assassination, he explicitly requested that no religious services be held, and it is notable that, antithetical to Judaic death rites, he was cremated, with his ashes being scattered in the Pacific.[38]

However, Milk's estrangement from Judaism is only one part of his Jewish story. Despite having rejected Judaism as an adolescent, he sought out a rabbi as he struggled with what was then the secret of his homosexuality and never forgot the sage words he was offered: "You shouldn't be concerned about how you live your life, as long as you feel you're living it right."[39] During one winter break, he helped a friend hang Christmas lights by constructing a Star of David with his allotment of bulbs.[40] In categorizing his late uncle, Stuart Milk avers that "Harvey absolutely identified himself as a Jew," although he "was not religious or observant."[41] He was a New York Jew; for that particular hypervisible Jewish type, geographic distinctiveness and ethnoreligious identity are not easily separated. As Lenny Bruce memorably quipped, "If you live in New York or any other big city, you are Jewish."[42] Unpacking Bruce's Jewish coding schema, New York in particular and urban life in general are aligned with a Jewish sensibility. Sharyn Saslafsky, a political friend who used to visit Milk at his famous camera store on Castro Street to share some Yiddish talk, suggests that New York pride and Jewish pride were intermingled for Milk: "He wasn't a religious Jew, but he was always proud of being Jewish. . . . He always had a sense of pride that he came from New York."[43]

Moreover, Saslafsky suggests that Milk's politics were informed by his Jewish sensibility: "We would also talk about Yiddishkayt, about what Judaism stresses. . . . That was clearly very important to Harvey. I believe his concern for justice, fairness, equality and ethical behavior came from his Jewish background."[44] Milk's nephew supports that reading: "Jewish sensitivity to civil rights absolutely had an impact on Harvey. In fact, he was the one who told me about how much support Jewish organizations and Jewish individuals gave to minorities. He often said that Jews feel they cannot allow another group to suffer discrimination, if for no other reason than that they might be on that list someday."[45] Even in his first flawed and failed campaign, Milk strove to articulate what would eventually become his winning coalitional vision and identified himself as both gay and Jewish: "I will strive to bring the government to the people, be they intellectuals or fellow homosexuals, be they blacks or fellow Jews, be they the tax-starved elderly or fellow small-shop owners."[46] Saslafsky, affiliated with Sha'ar Zahav (a gay synagogue founded in San Francisco in 1977, just a year before Milk's untimely death), also has memories of Milk occasionally attending that synagogue's services.[47] Allen Bennett, the gay rabbi of the congregation at that time, recalls, "He wasn't there to pray, he was there to get votes. . . . So he certainly understood there was a Jewish community he could relate to."[48]

The choice of Harvey Fierstein as the narrator of *The Times of Harvey Milk* ensures that the New York Jewishness of Milk is present throughout the film and that the progressive politics associated with his secular ethnic sensibility is associated with his times, that is, the gay civil rights movement. Fierstein's New York Jewish speech echoes Harvey Milk's own; moreover, Fierstein's palpable grief over Milk's murder reminds us that he was *mishpachah* (Yiddish for extended family) in more ways than one. Fierstein's *Torch Song Trilogy* (1988), which gave voice to the challenges and absolute necessity of refusing to choose between being gay and being Jewish, would only strengthen identification between Harvey Fierstein and Harvey Milk and the former's Jewqhooing of the latter.[49] Aptly, Jon Else refers to Fierstein's narrative voice as that of "a tribal elder."[50]

For Epstein, the challenge of the documentary was "to tell a story retrospectively but have it play in the present tense for the audience."[51] Notably, the challenges and possibilities associated with this historical narrative of gay liberation echo those associated with the ur–liberation story of Exodus recounted each year at diverse Passover seders: Jews are exhorted to merge past and present as if they, themselves, were being freed from Egypt.[52] Thematically, an exodus narrative is reinforced within the film when we are told that Milk "emigrated" to San Francisco; at one point, Milk is referred to as a "gay immigrant," an identity marker reinforced by an iconic image of him from the 1978 Gay Freedom Day Parade holding a sign that reads "I'm from Woodmere, NY." Here Milk's geographic origins and identifications, allied to his ethnoreligious origins, are on full display, as an immigration narrative is used to foster the times that he represents. Although the archival image used in the film literally only calls upon the Jewish geography of Woodmere, New York, Stuart Milk recalls that Harvey's signage at marches would proclaim "I'm from Woodmere. I'm Jewish. I'm gay."[53] Whether technically accurate or not, Stuart Milk's memory aptly summarizes the Jewqhooing work of this image in combination with Fierstein's voice chronicling Milk's physical and political journeys.

We know from the historic record that Milk's Jewish consciousness was inseparable from his consciousness of the Holocaust. When dining with a German friend of his lover Joe Campbell in 1958, Milk challenged the notion that ordinary Germans were ignorant of the death camps with such vehemence that Campbell saw Milk as suffering from a persecution complex, and Milk saw Campbell as an antisemite.[54] Milk's political consciousness and strategizing were derived from his knowledge of the Warsaw ghetto uprising, and he often invoked the Holocaust and Nazis to illuminate the horrors of homophobia and the need for coalition politics as well as sustained vigilance to all forms of injustice and discrimination. When battling Briggs, Milk routinely accused the senator of "making wild inflammatory remarks that, to anyone who knows the facts, sounds as if it were the KKK talking about blacks or Hitler about Jews."[55] Of course, in comparing Briggs to Hitler, Milk was also invoking Nazi discourse on and action against gays. When we try to discern whether the political invocation to remember Nazi Germany functions to keep gays and Jews in parallel planes or to establish these two groups—and Milk himself—as embodying the overlapping orbits of the Jewish queer, we return to the possibility of double-coding and the ways in which Jewqhooing can be accomplished through directorial choices and spectatorship.

Epstein's documentary features voice recordings from Milk's successful fight against Proposition 6 that include Holocaust comparisons, an established part of his political rhetoric: "Look what happened in Germany. Anita Bryant [who actively promoted antigay measures in Florida and served as a model/catalyst for Briggs] already says Jews and Moslems are going to Hell. You know she's got a shopping list." In accord with the coalitional and intergenerational political vision that marked Milk's political career (one that at least some have coded as Jewish)[56] and in spite of his distrust of institutionalized religion, he cites religious minorities, including but not solely Jews, as needing to be in league against contemporary forces of homophobia. Very early in the documentary, right after the opening archival footage of Dianne Feinstein announcing Milk's death and before Fierstein's narration begins, we see footage of a celebratory Milk at the 1978 Gay Freedom Day Parade and glimpse a pink triangle on his black armband.[57] Later in the film, that same sequence is repeated and expanded: we see the previously mentioned shot of Milk holding the sign bearing the Jewish marker "I'm from Woodmere, NY," then the footage used at the opening of the film without the sign. This footage is also part of the documentary's final sequence. There we see the black armband from the front (but not the pink triangle); at the very edge of the frame, we see part of the Woodmere sign. Taken together, Holocaust allusions and comparisons in *The Times of Harvey Milk* tend to reference both historic and contemporary Jewish and gay subjects, with Milk himself as a coded crossroads.

Epstein also includes an explicit reminder of not only Milk's Jewishness but also the awareness of that part of his identity by his cohort when political consultant and friend Tory Hartmann recollects Milk's encounter with Ruth Carter Stapleton, the evangelical sister of Jimmy Carter.[58] As Hartmann tells it on camera, Milk's Jewishness didn't stop Carter Stapleton from promising this gay man that "if he committed himself to Jesus, his homosexuality would disappear." Without missing a beat, Milk expressed surprise that she would shake his hand; to her confusion at this response, Milk delivered the punch line that literally stunned Carter Stapleton into silence: "You never know where that hand has been." Here, Milk uses his sharp and queerly playful wit to counter this two-pronged religious/sexual conversion script. In one frame of footage from a Castro Street fair, a sign advertising "all beef kosher style hot dogs" can be seen in the background. Directly and indirectly, Epstein seems to have captured Milk's "kosher style" without overstating or misrepresenting Milk's performances of and commitments to Jewishness.

Without question, Gus Van Sant's biopic *Milk* (2008), which deservedly earned two Oscars of its own, pays homage to its documentary predecessor. The film's credits begin with "Special thanks to the Academy Award winning film *The Times of Harvey Milk* for its enormous contribution to the making of this movie and to Rob Epstein." Van Sant's and screenwriter Dustin Lance Black's personal and activist admiration for the documentary inspired their desire to bring Milk's story to an even larger and mainstream audience.[59] The activists/

politicos featured in Epstein's documentary who were still alive served as historical consultants for *Milk*, with a number of them having cameos in the feature film.[60] Epstein granted Van Sant permission to use footage of the candlelight vigil from the documentary, and he shared oral histories that were part of the documentary's preproduction process not only with cast members of *Milk* but also with the director and screenwriter.[61] Film critic R. Ruby Rich has suggested that the influence of the documentary on *Milk* might be captured by the phrase "adapted screenplay."[62] Certainly, the film's dramatization of several archival scenes in *The Times of Harvey Milk* contributes to this sense of adaptation from one genre to another. However, the differences between the films are equally noteworthy, some of which are attributable to genre as well as the more than two decades that separate the cinematic events. While Epstein's documentary project was to view Harvey Milk as representing a political epoch (after all, only one half of the phrase "the life and times" makes it into the title), Van Sant provides us with a docudrama of an activist politician's life. While Milk's lovers are present in the post–*Brokeback Mountain* biopic, the trial of Dan White and the White Night Riots are relegated to historical footnotes.[63] Given the Jewqhooing embedded in Epstein's documentary, the ways in which Van Sant and Black Jewishly deracinate Milk even as they provide a much larger audience with a spectacular and more intimate portrait of him merits analysis.

The only explicit reference to Milk's Jewishness is made very early in this biopic when Milk introduces himself to a homophobic Castro business owner: "I'm not an interloper, a Jew perhaps, but I hope you'll forgive that." Even if we read, as I do, Milk's asking for forgiveness for "perhaps" being a Jew as strategic, rhetorical, and subtly ironic, it's hardly enough to Jewishly define the film or its protagonist, notwithstanding Milk's privately pronouncing the man a "schmuck." I should also note that this lone moment of explicit Jewish identification was barely audible when I first saw the movie in a theater. Rich reports that when *Milk* initially came out, she both appreciated the movie and was a bit disappointed. Some of that disappointment related to the disconnect between Sean Penn and the Jewish geography question of the historical Harvey Milk. Writes Rich, "Had I turned into a purist who wanted to see a New York Jew, as Harvey was, play the part? I'd never been such a literalist before."[64] While Harvey Fierstein's narration reinforced that part of Milk's legacy in Epstein's documentary, the Jewish dimension of Harvey Milk is oddly underexposed in Gus Van Sant's biopic.[65]

To be sure, *Milk* includes some of the Jewish-coded markers included in the documentary that preceded it. Woodmere is mentioned twice: when Milk likens his Castro Street Camera Store to the shop of Morris and Minnie Milk of Woodmere and among a list of places in which gay youth needing hope reside. However, he never explicitly claims Woodmere as the site of his origins.[66] Likewise, some Holocaust comparisons and references are included.

Most significantly, Sean Penn as Milk is shown on a small-screen television speaking the overwhelmingly archival words, "Look what happened in Germany. Bryant has already said Jews and Moslems are going to Hell. You know she has a shopping list." While accurately conveying the use of the Holocaust in his political rhetoric, this is a moment in the film when Milk seems smaller than life, and the connection between the Jews of this speech and Milk himself is lessened by the lack of direct and indirect Jewish identifications threaded throughout the documentary. Iconic shots from the 1978 Gay Freedom Day Parade are re-created in *Milk*; notably, although the pink triangle on Penn's black armband is much more prominent than in the archival footage included in *The Times of Harvey Milk*, the sign that self-identifies Milk as originating from Woodmere, New York, is absent. A line of marchers holds banners, one of which depicts an image of Hitler. The words "Once the Jews" are seen just behind and above another banner imprinted with an image of Anita Bryant, suggesting that gays are the new Jews of a potentially fascist state. Here the Jewish/gay relationship tends to be one of parallelism and even substitution, and Milk is not Jewishly identified enough to serve as connecting tissue for those not already inclined to view Jewishly.

Like the historical Milk, Dustin Lance Black was well schooled in the anti-gay tendencies of organized religion. Growing up Mormon in San Antonio, Texas, Black credits Milk as he encountered him through Epstein's documentary with giving him hope and the courage to come out. He continues to experience religious and familial exile. In his moving Oscar acceptance speech, Black stated, "If Harvey had not been taken from us 30 years ago, I think he'd want me to say to all of the gay and lesbian kids out there tonight who have been told that they are less than, by their churches, by the government, or by their families, that you are beautiful, wonderful creatures of value and that no matter what anyone tells you, God does love you."[67] Black received kudos from the media machine for this speech as well as letters from young gays indicating that his film and his words at the Oscars caused their families to talk to them about being gay for the first time. However, he also told an interviewer, in a subdued voice, that his Oscar talk resulted in "one letter from a cousin . . . expressing the great shame I've brought to our family. . . . I was disappointed by that."[68]

Notably, one of the few creative liberties Black took as he moved from the historical, documentary record into the realm of a historically based but fictionalized biopic involved cultural/religious representation. Although the historical record indicates that Milk attended a baby shower at the Whites's home, Black's Milk is shown at the baptism of Dan White's son in a Roman Catholic church. When Milk first accepts White's invitation to the christening, he tells his aghast staff, "I would let him christen me if he would vote for the gay rights ordinance; we need allies." With this line, Milk's Jewishness, represented by that early "perhaps," becomes an even more disposable commodity. The baptism

FIG. 6.1 A counterhistorical baptism in *Milk* (2008)

sequence is a relatively long one. During the ceremony, Milk smiles and waves at Dan, wanting to ensure that his presence is registered. When White's wife interrupts their political talk later in the sequence, Dan apologizes for "shop talk," which Milk identifies more specifically as the gay rights ordinance. When Mrs. White suggests that such a subject is "inappropriate" at her son's christening, Milk quips, "Don't knock it till you've tried it," thus representing the queer sense of humor that the historic Milk evinced during conversion talk with Ruth Carter Stapleton. In Epstein's documentary, Milk's ironic resistance to Christian homophobia served to reinforce his status as a queer Jew; here, however, he is presented as holding his ground as a gay activist immediately after he has professed, albeit jokingly, a willingness to sell his Jewish soul for a straight ally. According to Black, the minor transformation from historic baby shower to fictional christening was intended to convey White's religious orientation "more vividly."[69] Without being a purist and without underestimating or devaluing how much this movie matters just the way it is, I can't help wishing that Black had also chosen to portray Milk's historic New York Jewish sensibilities more vividly.

Despite the lack of Jewish inflection to Van Sant and Black's *Milk*, the film has furthered the tradition of Jewqhooing that iconic figure. Following Milk's untimely and tragic death, a Jewish memorial service was held not only at Temple Emanu-El, a major Reform synagogue in San Francisco (organized by Epstein), but also at Sha'ar Zahav, the previously mentioned gay San Francisco synagogue that Milk occasionally attended. Mourning and memorialization can become prime expressions of Jewhooing and Jewqhooing, and this has certainly been true for Milk, whose assassination positioned him as a queer Jewish martyr. In 1998, Sha'ar Zahav marked the twentieth anniversary of Milk's death with a special yahrzeit (memorial) program. In emphasizing Milk's legacy, Rabbi Jane Litman advocated "looking to the heroes of our community for moral guidance. Our social action fund is named after Harvey Milk. He is a bright star in our firmament."[70] Litman's language, in particular her repetition of the plural possessive "our," exemplifies the naming and citing of Milk in order to do the "group identity" work that Kaufman associates with Jewhooing. In memory of the sleepless night that followed Milk's murder and in honor of this gay Jewish martyr, the congregation held a *tikkun leyl*, an all-night study session more usually associated with Shavuot, the holiday that marks the giving of the Torah to the Israelites.[71] In this queer Jewish space, Harvey Milk becomes symbolically akin to Torah that, tradition teaches, needs to be studied, remembered, and transmitted from generation to generation. While Jews in general are People of the Book, queerJews are potentially People of Milk.

In 2008, two decades after that all-night yahrzeit program, Sha'ar Zahav and the San Francisco Jewish Film Festival[72] cosponsored a screening of Van Sant's *Milk* organized by the San Francisco Jewish Community Federation.[73] Saslafsky, who traded Yiddishisms with Harvey at his camera store, as well as Avi Rose, a member of the Lost Tribe, reminisced before the screening about Harvey and his times.[74] Sharon Papo and spouse Amber Weiss attested to the importance of the film, especially after the anti–gay marriage Proposition 8 was passed even as Barack Obama was elected for the first time. Said Papo, "I've felt devastated since Prop. 8 passed, but the film rejuvenated and reinspired me. And to see it with Jews from all walks of life makes me very proud of my Jewish community."[75] So, although Van Sant and Black served primarily queer Milk, at least some of the film's viewers savored queerJewish Milk. Even the most critical of film critics should not underestimate the sweetness of an "LGBT megahit" based on this queerJew icon.[76] Nor should they underestimate the excitement that a much Jewqhooed figure had arrived on the national big screen as an emblem of mourning for the past and Prop 8 present, as well as a harbinger of hope for the future.

Both Epstein's and Van Sant's films have participated in the cultural work of Jewqhooing Harvey Milk and merit inclusion in the American Jewish cinematic canon. However, *The Times of Harvey Milk* does some of that work within the documentary itself, while *Milk* leaves much of that work to the realm of reception, that is, to viewers who are literate in the still often coded intersections of queerness and Jewishness in life, art, and history.[77] Taken together, the two films devoted to the life and times of Harvey Milk, made almost a quarter of a century apart, beg the question of whether a Jewish movie is made by its director, its screenwriter, its actors, or its audience. In Talmudic fashion and in keeping with the work of such scholars as Henry Bial, Barbara Kirshenblatt-Gimblett, Alisa Lebow, and Nathan Abrams, I want to preserve and honor all these possibilities. I also want to resist the seductive narrative that genre is ethnic and ethical destiny. To be sure, the biopic has historically been a conservative genre heralding the values of liberal individualism and whitewashing ethnic identity in general and Jewish difference in particular (*The Life of Emile Zola*, anyone?).[78] Yet, before we accept genre determinism on the Jewish question, we might also remember that *Funny Girl*, a biopic of Fanny Brice (and, arguably and indirectly, of Barbra Streisand) is credited with making the explicitly Jewish mouthy woman sexy, at least in some quarters.[79] And the centrality of the propaganda film *The Triumph of the Will* to the history of documentary should temper the temptation to laud that genre for its essential ethical commitments.[80]

Ultimately, for me, the subtle but important shift from *The Times of Harvey Milk* to *Milk* raises the question of whether the double-coding of Jewishness in film has been relegated to the past. According to a progressive narrative of Jewish cinematic expression, proffered by Bial, Abrams, and Goldman, the explicit representation of Jewishness has been largely normalized and diversified.[81] Put another way, Jewishness has come out of the cinematic closet, and viewers no longer require a decoder ring to recognize, as Bial puts it, that "a Jew without a beard is still a Jew."[82] Ironically, however, a 2008 film devoted to not only the times but also the life of one of the most iconic queerJews relegated a Jewish angle of vision to the provisional realm. Van Sant's, Black's, and Sean Penn's *Milk* is indeed only "perhaps" a Jew; a more Jewish-positive identification remains dependent on critical spectatorship that includes knowledge not only of the historical Milk but also of the intersections of Jewish and queer cinematic history. Both *The Times of Harvey Milk* and *Milk* should be considered part of that busy crossroads.

Treyf (1998)

Jewqhooing, a practice central to viewing Van Sant's *Milk* as a Jewish film, is humorously anticipated by Alisa Lebow, codirector with Cynthia Madansky of *Treyf*. In an early sequence of this first-person or autoethnographic film, Lebow tells us that her mother has sent her a book titled *Hollywood Lesbians*: "Mom plays 'name the lesbian' like she plays 'name the Jew.' Soon she's going to be playing 'name the Jewish lesbian.'" Yet the very title of this film conveys the challenges of bringing together historically paralleled identities. The film self-consciously extends the definition of *treyf*, traditionally used to describe those foodstuffs such as shrimp and pork that are beyond the kosher pale: "may also be used in reference to lesbians or unorthodox political and social views."

A fragmented narrative in which image and voice-over often contradict one another, *Treyf* begins with a recounting of Alisa and Cynthia's meeting at an alternative queer seder and their diversely Jewish upbringing—secular Zionism and suburban Modern Orthodoxy, respectively. Examples of *treyf* range from Katz's kosher-style deli on the Lower East Side to their sense, after being at the peace rally where Prime Minister Rabin was assassinated and filming illegal settlements, that Israel is no longer a place for them. For Lebow and Madansky, *treyf* is the mark of being simultaneously inside and outside tradition given that an insider's understanding of *treyf* is required to identify yourself as or with it.

At the center of *Treyf* is a Jewish lesbian filming fest: Alisa and Cynthia put out a call about the film they are making and invite Jewish lesbians to make themselves visible, to eat, and to dance. Alisa and Cynthia prepare trays of Jewish food as they listen to phone messages from the invitees to this simcha (Jewish celebration). One woman's RSVP—"While I'm a Jew and a lesbian, I've never really seen myself as a Jewish lesbian"—points to the identity construction work that this film undertakes. The culmination of this event is a joyful dancing of the hora to the culturally adaptable Israeli folk song "Hava Nagila."

One reviewer, taken with the dance scene, wonders "why Lebow and Madansky didn't end with this sequence; it's by far the most engaging in the film. . . . In the movie's best shot the camera loops and swirls as a powerful line of Nikes, Doc Martens, and biker boots pound the floor in an exuberant, whip-fast hora. In that moment you can feel Madansky and Lebow get what they're after. Together with their friends they define and celebrate their own tradition."[83] However, in her own commentary on *Treyf*, Lebow, ever the self-conscious filmmaker and film theorist, critiques the dancing sequence as a fictionalized, inauthentic community; as she tells it, the Jewish lesbian collective that came together for that part of the film never convened again.[84]

Yet whether or not that celebratory scene ever became ritualized, the fact remains that, through and in *Treyf*, it became a visual possibility and actuality, if only a fleeting one. Caryn Aviv's response to the film shows the importance of such seemingly ephemeral images:

> I loved this film. I was so nourished that I wanted to invite Lebow and
> Madansky for coffee and a schmooze. When my parents asked me what
> I thought of the film, I told them it was the first time I had seen so many parts
> of my own story on screen. They said they had never realized how difficult (but
> rewarding) it can be to embrace being "out" as a Jew and a lesbian. Their
> comment spoke volumes about the consciousness-raising that needs to be done.
> I, for one, am deeply grateful to the filmmakers for making their "treyf" lives
> visible.[85]

In a cinematic tradition that does not often give Jewish queers hope that they need not give up one vital part of their being to embrace another part, the power of such fleeting images should not be underestimated. What's produced onscreen as well as discussion about it helps to make queerJews and their allies.

Treyf received funding from the National Foundation for Jewish Culture and premiered on the Sundance Channel in a series titled "She Said."[86] It was part of the chai celebration of the San Francisco Jewish Film Festival and the center of a night focused on "Queer Jews Creating Change." According to Jan Plotkin, in the early days of the festival at the Roxie, "The audience was largely lesbians who lived in the neighborhood. . . . Many were coming to terms with both their sexual orientation and their Jewishness. . . . At 18, we feel like the festival has been reinvigorated with life. . . . We're coming full circle now by acknowledging the gay and lesbian community."[87] The Jewish film festival that became the model for the multitude of festivals that feature Jewish movies that make Jews owes its very existence and continuity to *treyf* Jews. And just as *Treyf* represented continuity and change in 1998, so, too, does it resonate at the contemporary moment. While both queerJews and profound ambivalence about Israeli politics are less unorthodox now than they were when this film was first conceived, wrestling with Zion still adds to the challenges of finding a home as a Jewish lesbian. At one point in the film Alisa states that "anti-Zionism still seems like a dangerous cover for antisemitism." Clashes over Jewish pride flags at Dyke Marches demonstrate that the struggle to be simultaneously visible as a Jew and as a lesbian continues.[88] Given such struggles, queer movie-made Jews do significant cultural work.

Trembling Before G-d (2001)

In *Treyf*, Alisa Lebow is obsessed with Orthodoxy, much to Cynthia Madansky's chagrin.[89] For Madansky, Orthodoxy was an essential part of her upbringing and being until she realized that her identity as a woman and as a lesbian put her at odds with that world. Although she does not eat *treyf*, she positions herself as *treyf* and decidedly unorthodox. However, Sandi Dubowski regards the Orthodox world as a site for queer Jewish activism, onscreen and off, so that Jews like Madansky can be not only queer and Jewish but also queer and Orthodox. Dubowski's documentary *Trembling Before G-d* (2001) and its offspring *Trembling on the Road* became a testament of continuity and change in the Orthodox world as well as the role of movies in making and remaking Jews. The production and reception history of *Trembling Before G-d* demonstrates that moving images can shift even seemingly static worlds.

The film's apparent simplicity contributes to its power. Diverse subjects speak their Jewish pain at trying and often failing to reconcile same-sex love and Judaic commitments. David chronicles his useless but traumatic attempts to convert to heterosexuality. The rubber bands that he was told to flick against his wrists whenever he felt attracted to a man succeeded only in adding physical pain to the spiritual and emotional agony that was already his lot. Morose and overweight Michelle takes the filmmakers through the beloved community from which she is exiled. Malka and Leah celebrate their love and Shabbat—complete with footage of challah making at its braided best— even as Malka endures strained nonconversations with her parents and fears about her and Leah's fate in the world to come. Israel expansively chronicles his family's abandonment of him, his abandonment of an observant life, and the pathos of being a grown man who craves the comforts of Daddy and a Jewish life that is now off-limits to him. Although dying of AIDS, Mark, a British Jew, seems to have made peace with his whole being. Having left the world of the yeshiva, he still maintains an effusively affectionate relationship with his *abba* and *imma* (Hebrew for father and mother) and dons a gender-bending apron inscribed with "Yiddishe-Momme" to cook a communal meal for other Jewishly committed queer outcasts. Secure in the blessings and goodness of Hashem, Mark proclaims the gift of Jewishness. His joy and rebellion suggest possibilities that seem denied to those represented only in silhouette to protect their identities. Such silhouettes formally and cinematically represent a Jewish closet ordained by halakhah and minhag, law and custom.

Yet, as chronicled in *Trembling on the Road*, a DVD "featurette" that documents the movie becoming a movement, Dubowski's 2001 film has done much to unlock and even open the closet door in Orthodox circles and beyond. The film enabled Malka to resume contact with her brother, from whom she had been estranged; her nieces and nephews are now part of her life. Leah appears directly onscreen rather than in silhouette as she had previously; Michelle, 130 pounds lighter, now represents herself as a happy, articulate, proud queer Jew; Israel, acknowledging that there has been no "Hollywood ending" for his relationship with his father, since "some fathers are not very nice people," nonetheless reports that he has reconciled with himself. A young queer Jew, Mordechai, reads the film as the beginning of "our history": gay observant Jews are now known as "tremblers," and a sex educator for Ramaz, a Modern Orthodox day school in New York, vows that he will teach Leviticus and Jewish perspectives on homosexuality differently after seeing the film. Numerous Orthodox synagogues have hosted screenings of the film, and at the first of these, in Riverdale, New York, 500 people attended, causing Dubowski to liken the event to High Holidays. Dubowski also likens the film to a prayer to G-d, rabbis, and the community that "had to be heard." According to Ruby Lerner, president of the Creative Capital Foundation, an arts foundation based in New York that provided funding for *Trembling*, the film reached its potential in the world and not just on the screen thanks to Dubowski's vision: "You have to have an artist who is absolutely passionate about the issue, someone who is skilled at organizing, and someone willing to take the long view and make a commitment... He didn't just move on to his next film."[90] The *Forward* included Dubowski in its list of Jewish leaders in the arts for 2001, and Steven Spielberg's Righteous Persons Foundation has supported educational outreach efforts related to *Trembling*.[91]

While *Trembling Before G-d* is undoubtedly a success story, its long and difficult gestation process makes its momentum all the more notable. The prohibitions on and invisibility of homosexuality in the Orthodox world made it very difficult for Dubowski to identify people willing to go on camera for the documentary. He reports that, early on in the process, when he told people that he was making a film about Orthodox and Hasidic gay Jews, their response was to laugh at the idea that such a species of Jews actually existed.[92] While getting gay *frum* Jews to talk was hard, getting their parents on film was even harder: Dubowski spent six years trying to get observant Jews to open up about their gay offspring, to no avail.[93] In *Trembling on the Road*, psychotherapist Shlomo Ashkinazy, who appeared in the 2001 documentary, ruefully remembers telling Dubowski that he shouldn't make the film and that no one would watch it.[94]

Of course, such naysaying was woefully misguided. *Trembling* made considerable waves at the 2001 Sundance Film Festival, where it premiered. Along with Henry Bean's *The Believer*, it helped to turn that Sundance festival into a mini–Jewish film festival, complete with a Mormon-Jewish gay interfaith dialogue as well as a Havdalah ceremony cosponsored by CLAL, the National Jewish Center for Learning and Leadership.[95] Its run at the Film Forum in New York was accompanied by an Orthodox community dialogue. When it showed at the San Francisco Jewish Film Festival in the Castro, Harvey Milk's old stomping ground, Rabbi Langer appeared onstage with one of the film's subjects, David, and publicly apologized to him for the inadequacy of his counsel years before.[96] Langer later made good on his offer to host a Friday night Shabbaton in the Castro so that diverse Jews could begin to bridge their differences through the "joys of Shabbat."

To be sure, not everyone embraced *Trembling* or newly out tremblers. Screenings in Baltimore—a city with a critical mass of Orthodox Jews—were especially controversial. As Dubowski quipped, a particular kind of interfaith work took place there: Orthodox Jews and evangelical Christians joined forces to protest the film, and they got air time on Fox News. Making use of material from Agudath Israel, an Orthodox organization whose position was summarized by the article title "Dissembling before G-d," protesters advocated for Jews Offering New Alternatives to Homosexuality (JONAH) and critiqued the film for not featuring Orthodox Jews who had assimilated successfully to heterosexuality and remained halachically correct according to the most rigid interpretation of Jewish law.[97] Rabbi Steven Greenberg, who appears in the film and is the first openly gay Orthodox rabbi, attended the screening at the Charles Theater; his entrance initiated a heated exchange at odds with the commitments to dialogue that the film had otherwise engendered.[98]

Baltimore continued to be a *Trembling* hot spot. To mark the anniversary of the first showing of *Trembling* at an Orthodox synagogue (Riverdale's Hebrew Institute in New York), Rabbi Yakov Chaitovsky arranged, at the suggestion of Rabbi Gershon Sonnenschein, to show the film at his own Modern Orthodox congregation, Baltimore's Beth Tfiloh Synagogue. According to protester Mark Hart, the shame of such programming had a geographic dimension: "Baltimore is not New York.... I'm really disappointed in these Orthodox rabbis who have decided to show this movie in an Orthodox synagogue. It's atrocious to even think about it." However, Rabbi Chaitovsky affirmed the Jewish integrity of the screening and the after-film discussion with Dubowski and Greenberg: "It was not a struggle for me to decide to show the film.... As soon as I saw it, I realized the film was moving and important. It paints a real-life drama, warts and all, that is important to be shown. And what other venue should it be shown in than one that is bound-aried by Torah and Torah sensibilities? To show it in a movie theater is not the same."[99] With that perspective, Chaitovsky not only affirmed the Judaic value of *Trembling* but also the role that Jewish film can and does play in the evolution of Jewish life, identity, law, and custom.

Trembling has become a reference point for intra-Jewish debates and anxieties. For years, the Conservative movement—the Jewish orientation of Dubowski's upbringing—deliberated on whether or not to sanction the ordination of gays and lesbians as well as same-sex commitment ceremonies. *Trembling* is widely regarded as providing the "tipping point" for the historic 2006 decision to allow both of these.[100] When Yeshiva of Flatbush refused to allow a gay alum to bring his partner to a reunion, *Jewish Week*'s Debra Nussbaum Cohen noted that "the controversy comes more than six years after *Trembling Before G-d*... increased awareness of homosexuality in the Orthodox world."[101] Interestingly enough, both liberal Jews who support gay rights in the religious and secular realms and those traditional Jews who regard Levitical prohibitions on men lying with men as with a woman as the last possible word on homosexuality worried that the Jewish voices in *Trembling* would be heard as representing all Jews. Such concerns suggest that anxieties surrounding public images of Jews generally and cinematic Jewishness in particular are, for better or worse, not a thing of the past.

Reception of the documentary by non-Orthodox viewers is frequently featured in reviews. While one mainstream secular reviewer regards *Trembling* as ultimately revealing "a private world of distress about which a non-Orthodox audience can do little more than murmur, how awful," a reviewer writing for the Jewish feminist magazine *Lilith* posits that *Trembling* provides "non-Orthodox viewers a sense of the force and embrace of that community, the loss of which offers liberation to some but an empty void to others."[102] Writing for *In the Family*, a queer magazine, Ellen Elgart finds her secularist perspective challenged by the film: "*Trembling Before G-d* is a powerful film and has allowed me to rekindle my compassion for people who will not be run out of their religions. . . . maybe it's not so simple to give up on your religion just because it's given up on you. In fact, perhaps finding a way to affirm your gay identity and your religion, both, requires the greatest faith of all."[103] Implicit in much of the praise and protest about the film is the age-old question, "Is it good for the Jews?" or an even more particularist version of that question, "Is it good for the Orthodox?" Of course, there can be no single answer to such questions, but it's worth noting that, much to Dubowski's surprise, the making of this film has made him more religious, and he has described himself as "feeling . . . nourished by Orthodoxy."[104] Clearly, this film was good for the box office. According to *Variety*, *Trembling* "set the opening-day record at New York's Film Forum, grossing $5,502 on Oct. 24. The film went on to earn $31,130 on that one screen in its first five days."[105] Not bad for a documentary about a Jewish group presumed to be nonexistent prior to a movie and the movement that it spawned.

Hineini: Coming Out in a Jewish High School (2005)

Irena Fayngold's *Hineini: Coming Out in a Jewish High School* (2005) is a successor to *Trembling Before G-d*. This documentary chronicles the story of Shulamit Izen and her struggle to start a gay-straight student alliance at the New Jewish High School in Boston, now known as the Gann Academy. The school was the brainchild of its then headmaster, Daniel Lehmann, who was determined to educate students to live productively and respectfully within the tensions of different forms and expressions of Judaism. However, he and the diverse Jewish educational community he founded were challenged not only by Shulamit's coming out but also by her seeking institutional recognition of the lived experience of gay and lesbian Jews. In production for well over three years, *Hineini*—Hebrew for "Here I Am," Abraham's response to God's calling him by name—focuses on a Jewish lesbian wrestling with tradition and the limits of pluralism.

The film was initially conceived as a short profile of Izen underwritten by a closeted Jewish businessman. He had heard her speak at an informal gathering sponsored by Keshet, an activist and advocacy group for queer Jews, and decided that her voice needed to be amplified.[106] However, Fayngold and executive producer Idit Klein quickly understood that this story was not only about Izen but also about the transformation of a community.[107] Setting out to make that film, Fayngold, like Dubowski, encountered what seemed like insuperable impediments. After an initial day of shooting, the board of the school withdrew its permission to allow her to film on the premises or to interview Lehmann. Fayngold proceeded with the project by making do with interviews

FIG. 6.2 Shulamit refusing to choose between Jewish and queer in *Hineini* (2005)

conducted off campus as well as footage supplied by student filmmaker Arnon Shorr. At the same time, she continued the battle to get access to the school and to Lehmann, which she received very late in the production process.[108]

The early part of the film depicts Izen's struggle to find her place within Jewish tradition, to find a way to be a holy lesbian Jew. This part of her struggle is aptly represented by a Talmud teacher who, teaching Izen about the alien fire that consumes Nadav and Avihu, sends her mixed messages about being gay. An exquisite sequence in which an image of Shulamit davening is superimposed on Hebrew text in motion suggests that she can navigate this part of her journey. However, she still must struggle with her immediate Jewish context, that of her school. Ready and able to wrestle with God and Torah, she wants to do that Jewish work within a safe and supportive community. However, such Jewish space has to be made, and the film devotes much of its narrative to that arduous construction work.

Part of that work consists of Jewish queers saying "Hineini" to one another, face-to-face. A lesbian teacher at the school, Gina Fried, retrospectively understands that her rainbow key chain would only be noticed by a "like soul." This reciprocal coming-out process is shown in a series of crosscuts. While Izen recounts telling Fried that she liked her key chain and that Fried "understood what she meant," Fried confirms her recognition that Izen was silently communicating, "I see you; are you going to let me see you? Are you going to see me back?" The answer to these questions about Jewish queer seeing was an irrevocable yes. Once they recognized one another, they determined the need for a gay-straight alliance so that they could be seen by the wider New Jewish community.

Being recognized and embraced by the larger community was a process, a key part of which was the organizing of a Beit Midrash, a school-wide assembly, that discussed sexual orientation as a serious issue within the context of Jewish tradition. The program included two rabbis, Izen, and, after much soul-searching on the part of teachers, Jessica Keimowitz, a popular history teacher and the softball coach. The Beit Midrash sequence is framed with a montage of student responses and questions that range from the invoking of Jewish evolution as the key to Jewish survival to the view that homosexuality "almost inherently conflicted with the religious doctrines of . . . Orthodox Jews," to questioning whether pluralism "mean[s] compromise" and assuming that pluralism involves an "underlying value of respect, . . . how far does that respect extend?" Notably, the pluralistic sensibility central to the mission of the school and this program was viewed as a potential impediment to this discussion. Rabbi Lehmann feared that the "strong emotions" associated with Izen and Keimowitz might "shut down conversation" by making "it impossible for people who oppose homosexuality . . . to express their views openly." It is this odd but certainly not queer concern about "not creat[ing] . . . pressure to adopt the position that homosexuality is perfectly OK" that led to the founding of New Jew's Open House, a support group named after the Jerusalem organization that nonetheless disavows advocacy for or celebration of Jewish queer life.

While the institutional response to the Beit Midrash was quite limited, the rousing applause Keimowitz and Izen received made Shulamit feel that for "the first time New Jew was my community." The simple note that she received from Rabbi Lehmann, which read, "Yasher Koach, Shulamit—I'm so proud of you," went a long way toward healing the hurt that she felt when she first came out to him and he responded, "I don't want to hear about your sex life." Lehmann acknowledges in the film that he was engaged in his "own struggle," that his "own relationship to Judaism's understanding of homosexuality and how . . . modern Jews should confront this was something that [he] was really grappling with." On the tenth anniversary of the film, Lehmann reaffirmed the surprising transformation that he underwent: "I never imagined as a person rooted in my Orthodox identity I would be engaging in LGBT issues and providing a core example of a school dealing with it."[109] Lehmann's transformation is one of many documented in *Hineini*. Torah teacher Tanchel indicates that it was very hard not to be out at the Beit Midrash; she quietly but consciously came out to her students subsequent to this catalyzing event. One of her Orthodox students shared his evolving response. While, at first, he thought, "She's gay and she's teaching me Tanakh and that just didn't work with me," he ultimately decided that he would "not shun people for being gay just as I wouldn't shun people for being Reform or not keeping kosher." At least for this student, pluralistic respect extended to sexual orientation.

Just as the Beit Midrash and the founding of Open House at the New Jewish High School remade Jewish queers and straights alike, so did the production and viewing of the film play their part in the making and remaking of Jews. Director Irena Fayngold reports that she was inspired by Izen's insistence on claiming her place in Judaism rather than distancing herself from it as Fayngold had when she first encountered Judaism's seemingly intractable patriarchal, misogynist bent.[110] Given Fayngold's own history, it is particularly poignant that she was such a formidable force in making a film that, like Dubowski's *Trembling Before G-d*, has become a resource for Jewish communal conversations about the need to create safe and inclusive spaces for queer members of the tribe.

For many of the film's viewers, *Hineini* was hardly just a movie; rather, it expressed and made visible their own Jewish wrestlings. According to Stuart Kurlander, who pioneered a JCC gay and lesbian outreach program and organized a screening of *Hineini* at the Washington Film Festival as its coming-out event, Izen's struggle to be Jewish, gay, and holy "resonated with a lot of people here because a lot of us grew up in Jewish households and went to Jewish schools. . . . While everyone has their own story, there are pieces that are representative of everyone's story."[111]

The film not only represents the experience of queer Jewish spectators but also helps to make Jewish allies. Late in the film, Tanchel relates that when another student came out to her, she was "terrified." However, her desire to be "helpful and supportive and nurturing" resulted in her responding with a heartfelt "mazel tov." Thanks to watching the film, a rabbi at a Solomon Schechter school reported that, when a student came out to her, she knew the right thing to say: "Mazel tov."[112] For this rabbi, life imitates documentary art. And just as *Trembling Before G-d* was not for Jews only, so has *Hineini* been mobilized to represent and advocate for the larger queer community. In Massachusetts, Representative Jay Kaufman organized a showing of the film to mark the second anniversary of Massachusetts becoming the first state to issue marriage licenses to same-sex couples and to lobby against a state constitutional amendment banning gay marriage. For Kaufman, "Being part of the legislature that affirmed same-sex marriage, it was very important to me that people understand that this isn't just a legal change, but has very deep meaning to our neighbors and friends and family. . . . This was one powerful story that reflected the power of a larger story."[113] Movie-made American Jews play a role in the larger U.S. body politic, and a cinematic tradition that includes such diverse films as *I Now Pronounce You Chuck and Larry*, *Kissing Jessica Stein*, *The Times of Harvey Milk*, *Milk*, *Treyf*, *Trembling Before G-d*, and *Hineini* is a potent reminder of that.

7

Cinematic Alliances

•••••••••••••••••••••

Throughout *Movie-Made Jews*, I've argued that American Jewish film not only makes Jews but also makes Jewish allies onscreen and off. In this chapter, I zero in on a set of films that represents and makes Jews in relation to other groups. These films focus on relationships between Black Gentiles and white Jews, as well as between Muslims and Jews; they explore the promise of alliances but also the challenges to making and sustaining them.[1] Films such as *Heart of Stone*, *Crime after Crime*, and *Zebrahead* recognize the racial privilege of white Jews; they also recognize that white Jews have historically had a complicated relationship to whiteness and might be usefully viewed as off-white as they play supporting roles in plots that affirm that Black lives matter. Post-9/11, American Jewish alliance films such as *Arranged* and *David* challenge the assumption that politics abroad make American Jews and American Muslims born enemies. Taken together, these movies show that American Jewish cinema is often simultaneously multicultural cinema.

Black/Jewish relations are a complicated cinematic social problem. One origin story of this vexed cinematic relationship is that of Al Jolson blacking up in the motion picture that transitioned Hollywood into sound, *The Jazz Singer* (1927). Michael Rogin has argued that Jews used blackface to strengthen their tenuous hold on whiteness; if Jews can and need to black up, then that affirms their whiteness.[2] However, while that reading of the unquestionably racist tradition of blackface is well supported by Jolson's final blacked-up rendition of "Mammy," it is complicated by an odd scene too often glossed over: a black-faced Jack Robin, formerly Jakie Rabinowitz, looks in a mirror and sees the face of his Orthodox cantor father. The beard, earlocks, and skullcap as the mirror image of his blacked-up visage suggest the haunting off-whiteness of Jewishness, especially unassimilated religiously observant Jewishness. In that private primal scene, blackface becomes allied with Jewface. Is this a story of racial assimilation or a potent reminder that Jews are seen and continue to see themselves as racialized, even as they drop syllables from their names and don the masks that unambiguously white folks wear? Put another way, do Black/Jewish relations affirm affinity or difference or both simultaneously? That question is a framing one for American Jewish cinema.

Robert Rossen's *Body and Soul* (1947), not as well known as it should be, offers a counter to the narratives—onscreen and off—that have cast Jews as a model minority and as often patronizing guides for the unwhitewashed Black masses that were brought to the United States in literal chains. Watched retrospectively, it's a breath of fresh air to see a Jewish boxer, played by John Garfield, formerly the Garfinkle boy, learn the ethical ropes from a Black boxer, played by Canada Lee. A Jewish mother, a Gentile girlfriend, and a Black peer remind that boy seduced by greenbacks that body and soul need to work together rather than be torn asunder by capitalist handlers.

Spike Lee's joints contribute more grist for this vexed movie mill, from *Mo' Better Blues* (1990), with its pernicious Jewish sharks out to exploit Black musicians, to the considerably more subtle and reflective *Get on the Bus*, in which a Jewish driver feels compelled to get off the bus bound for the Million Man March. That working-class Jew can only see and hear Reverend Farrakhan's trash talk about Jews and not register the empowerment narrative for Black men at risk. Black Gentiles and white Jews part ways here, respectfully, wistfully, perhaps necessarily. However, disengagement, cinematically and otherwise, is as much a fantasy as natural alliances or natural opposition. Lee himself powerfully and brilliantly makes this point in *BlacKkKlansman* (2018), in which a Black undercover cop (John David Washington) infiltrates the Klan in Colorado Springs, with the help of Jewish Flip Zimmerman (Adam Driver). Lee wisely puts limits on his ability to resolve a historically complicated and overdetermined social issue: according to him, *BlacKkKlansman* "might start some discussions, but ask me how I can mend black-Jewish relations—I can't speak to that."[3] However, he does end the film with documentary footage of Charlottesville, including images of white nationalists carrying torches and chanting, "Jews will not replace us." This ending serves as Lee's potent reminder that Blacks and Jews are joined together by continuing to be in the crosshairs of white supremacy.

According to Debra Kaufman, who codirected with Alan Snitow the documentary *Blacks and Jews* (1997), "If we're going to have alliances, we have to acknowledge difference. . . . There was a time when understanding that we had a shared history of oppression might have been enough to bring about an alliance, but since the civil rights movement, our differences have become greater."[4] As demonstrated by the segment on *Schindler's List* and Castlemont High School, which many critics cite as the most original and compelling part of the documentary, movies and their reception not only reflect but also shape the real and perceived differences between Black Gentiles and white Jews.[5]

It was Martin Luther King Jr. Day, 1994. A well-intentioned teacher decided that his Oakland students should take a field trip to see *Schindler's List*, the new Steven Spielberg blockbuster with historical consciousness and a conscience. The movie wasn't contextualized for students with a much-needed, grade-appropriate Holocaust curriculum; most of the history classes hadn't yet studied World War II in general or the Shoah in particular. To the mostly Black students of Castlemont in the audience, *Schindler's List* was only a movie, and their theater behavior was no different than it would be for any other flick— they talked and laughed, especially as a woman fell at an odd angle when she was executed at close range. To the Jewish members of the audience, for whom *Schindler's List* functioned as a communal memorial service, such behavior was distressing and disrespectful: it signaled that Holocaust memory was fading or, worse, that attempted genocide was inconsequential to non-Jews in general and Black Americans in particular. The sixty-nine Castlemont students were expelled from the theater, and the event made national news.

Predictably, Castlemont became part of the media narrative of Black-Jewish tensions, a continuation of the tale crystallized by the tragic accidental death of Gavin Cato and the murder of Yankel Rosenbaum in Crown Heights three years earlier. With Castlemont, the Shoah became the purported fault line between the two communities. The students offered a public apology, and plans for Holocaust education were put into place, including visits from survivors as well as a joint appearance by Spielberg himself and Pete Wilson, the Republican California governor at the time. While there were literally signs of formulaic animosity—according to some news reports, one placard read, "The Holocaust Is a Lie" and another, "Spielberg Is a Zionist Jew"—the event with Spielberg and Wilson was a complicated one.[6] One student spoke out against Wilson and the state government he represented for the habitual neglect of schools and communities like Castlemont; she also took him to task for the political opportunism that brought him to the assembly that day and was castigated by school officials for her exercise of free speech. Spielberg's true confession that, as a youth, he had been thrown out of a theater for talking during *Ben Hur* won over the audience. His response to this debacle was to promote *Schindler's List* as an educational tool, which he would provide free of charge to schools.

In reviewing Kaufman and Snitow's *Blacks and Jews* for the *Forward*, Jonathan Mahler suggests that returning to well-trodden battle lines may not be the most productive strategy for reengaging Blacks and Jews. As he puts it, "New trends . . . , not fresh takes on tired stories, may well hold the key to the future of black-Jewish relations."[7] Beth Toni Kruvant's distinctive documentary *Heart of Stone* (2009) suggests there needs to be a place both for revisiting history and for documenting and shaping new trends. In particular, this film shows how Jews were historically made—and then remade as allies. The high school setting of *Heart of Stone*, which premiered and won the Audience Award at the Slamdance Film Festival, makes it a useful complement to the saga of Castlemont and *Schindler's List*.

Heart of Stone (2009)

Heart of Stone is the story of the renaissance of Weequahic High School in Newark, New Jersey, under the leadership of principal Ron Stone, whose good heart and educational chops chiseled away at the stone hearts of rival gangs. Stone's educational vision was supported by the Weequahic Alumni Foundation, composed of older Jewish and younger Black alums who benefited from the stellar education they received at Weequahic: in its heyday from the 1930s to the early 1960s, Weequahic was one of the top public secondary education institutions in the country, and its most famous alum is none other than Jewish literary bad boy Philip Roth. Notably, taking a Philip Roth tour of the city played a part in convincing director Beth Kruvant to view the high school, its history, and the alumni foundation as a worthy documentary project. Her own father also has Weequahic roots: he deemed his high school experience more rigorous than law school. Zach Braff, the director, writer, and actor (see discussion of *Wish I Was Here* in chapter 5), served as the executive producer of *Heart of Stone*; he is also the son of Hal Braff, the cofounder of the Weequahic Alumni Foundation. So this film is an intergenerational and interethnic family affair on many levels.

Like the alumni foundation, the history of Weequahic and the larger story of Black/Jewish relations support and contextualize the contemporary moment rather than dominating it. This reflects Kruvant's commitment to a vision of a Black/Jewish story in which Jews are truly supporting actors rather than the leading men (and I purposefully use gender-specific language here for reasons that will soon become obvious). Both alliance and antagonism are part of the historical story presented, with some familiar history and some surprising twists. Rabbi Michael Lerner, a Weequahic alum and founder of *Tikkun* magazine, invokes a "special affinity" between Blacks and Jews that was demonstrated by the election of an African American class president in 1960 by a largely Jewish student body. Lerner's affinity talk is, given his politics, predictable; less predictable alliance talk occurs when Amiri Baraka proclaims onscreen that "there has never been any closer ties than Blacks and Jews in terms of fighting injustice" (this is a jaw-dropper for all those who remember Baraka's infamous antisemitic post-9/11 poetic conspiracy: "who told 4000 Israelis to stay home that day").[8] A high point of Black/Jewish history is Rabbi Joachim Prinz, Shoah refugee, proclaiming the tragedy of silence at the 1963 March on Washington; the nadir is the burning of Jewish businesses during the Newark 1967 riots.

However, nostalgia and mourning for the past do not overshadow the profound challenges and possibilities of the present. The film opens with Stone preparing to make the rounds of the school and the neighborhood; to do so, he dons a bulletproof vest. As principal, he strives to mentor the young men who join gangs to protect themselves on the mean streets of Newark; for many of these students, gangs serve as surrogate families that teach members to be "men." In sharp contrast to the police captain who proclaims onscreen that "we don't work with gang members," Stone is a realist who understands that "gang culture is already too entrenched . . . so shutting them down is not an option." In partnership with committed teachers at the school, he works at "inviting them into the conversation" by conducting conflict-resolution groups so that Bloods and Crips can "sit next to one another like men." Sharif, a member of the Bloods, suggests that gang members resort to violence in part because they "don't know how to deal with emotions." He credits the conflict-resolution groups with teaching those skills. Under Stone's watch and using the formidable leadership skills of Sharif and Rayvon, a Crip, the gangs become an institution that preaches "you better stay on your books" and works to ensure that "the homies going to graduate." Rather than becoming a dead end—sometimes literally—the Bloods and the Crips are reimagined to "give brothers options."

Another key element of Stone's strategy was to provide "something for the kids to do." His brainchild was to reinvigorate the football program and unify the school through the achievement of a state championship. Football was not to be an end in itself but a means to other sorts of achievement. As he puts it, "Success is transferable." A graduation ceremony featured late in the film demonstrates Stone's wisdom: in this sequence, the school is unified in cheering on Rayvon and Sharif, leaders of rival gangs, as they receive their diplomas.

Stone's motivations for his heroic work are complex and are gradually revealed throughout the documentary. He chronicles the racist violence of Newark streets controlled by political vigilante Anthony Imperiale and being raised by a mother who graduated from college despite being involved in an abusive relationship. Men who beat up women are an ongoing concern for him, and his mentorship of male students who initially commit themselves to violence but then, with his help, find other ways of being in the world seems no coincidence. He also credits his coming from a "long line of Baptist ministers" for his unquestioning commitment to service. Very late in the film, Stone also shares that he is married to a Jewish woman and that his desire to understand Judaism and work with Jewish alums derives in part from his intermarriage. The understatement of this revelation works against the hypervisibility of interracial romantic narratives in the saga of Black Gentiles and white Jews. Five months after the graduation ceremony, Stone tragically dies of a heart attack; at a moving memorial service, Meg Charney Stone speaks onscreen for the first time. Channeling her husband's cheerleading rhetoric, she reminds the assembled students that, according to Stone, "failure is not an option," and Ricky, a Blood, commits to do his best to "fulfill his legacy."

Just as Stone's motivations for his service to Weequahic are revealed as complex, so too are those of the Jewish alums. To be sure, noble though predictable progressive sentiments are professed early on in the film. Hal Braff expresses the alums' desire to give current Weequahic students the "possibilities we had" and talks about wanting "to make a difference," which he notes, "by the way, is a very Jewish thing to do." Philip Yourish explicitly connects the work of the alums to a "mitzvah," which "all people," "not just Jewish people" are supposed to be the recipients of. In later sequences, Jewish alums highlight systemic inequality and their awareness that while suburban schools have generous athletic budgets, Weequahic has none. Aiming to literally and figuratively level the playing field, they provide support to the football team and raise more than $100,000 for college scholarships.

However, the identification between the Jewish alums and the gangbangers is less predictable and even counterintuitive. At one point, Hal Braff suggests a need to "remember who you are and where you came from." Although the Jewish alums do not conflate their youth and that of current Weequahic students—"these are street kids, we had a mother and father, we had a bed to sleep in"—athletics in general and football in particular become a point of connection within and across generations. Stories of Black Gentiles and white Jews playing on the same team and signaling plays in Yiddish and Hebrew as a strategy against the opposing Italian American–dominated team are shared in the film; the Jewish alums also fondly remember the cheer, "Mikey, Mikey, Jakey, Sam, we're the boys that eat no ham. We play football, we play soccer, we keep matzos in our locker."

Memories of forming gangs for self-defense also link Weequahic's past and present student bodies. As Richie Roberts, a criminal defense lawyer, tells it, Jewish boys of Newark were targeted by the Barbarians, an Italian street gang that reveled in the practice of "bagging a Jew." Thus the offensively named Redskins, a gang designed to protect Jewish kids from antisemitic attacks, was born. As Roberts puts it—after asking permission from the camera crew to curse—he would "go into non-Jewish areas to prove to myself and everyone else that I'm a tough motherfucking Jew." From the cheer proclaiming that Jewishness and athletic prowess go together to gang membership in the immediate post-Shoah era when Jewish boys needed to be "tattooed in pride" rather than shame, these Jewish alums were trying to understand and revise masculine options in terms that surprisingly echo those of contemporary Black male

Weequahic students. Such identification across potential generational and racialized fault lines is a productive new narrative for Black/Jewish relations. Here Jewish paternalism is not the core of the story; rather, Ron Stone takes his rightful place as a Black father figure, and Jews are remade as allies. Even Beth Kruvant, the director of the film, emphasizes that she "can only help to carry on his legacy."[9]

Given the alternative Black/Jewish narratives at the heart of this film, it's fitting that it premiered and won the Audience Award at the Slamdance Film Festival, which occurs at the same time as Sundance and styles itself as an alternative to that now iconic institution, showcasing truly independent films that Sundance has rejected. At the San Francisco Jewish Film Festival, *Heart of Stone* garnered the Curator Choice Award. Both the content and the distribution of this documentary have crossed ethnoracial lines—it has made the circuit of both Jewish and African American film festivals, and a grant from the Righteous Persons Foundation enabled Kruvant to expand the venues and audiences exposed to the documentary. Kruvant is determined to help Stone's legacy continue offscreen. In keeping with her goal that Weequahic could become a model for other impoverished urban schools that once provided a stellar education and thus have a pool of successful alums who can be called upon for support, Kruvant began Campaign Kinship. That campaign, designed to bring the film to diverse educational and ethnoracial communities as well as to activate kinship ties between Blacks and Jews that recognize both shared and distinctive histories, was launched on Martin Luther King Jr.'s birthday in 2010.[10] Quite a counterpoint to the ill-conceived Castlemont field trip to see *Schindler's List* in 1994. Cinematic tales of Blacks and Jews at Castlemont and Weequahic High School suggest that it is never only a movie, and that Jews can and must get on the bus.

Crime after Crime (2011)

Like *Heart of Stone*, Yoav Potash's award-winning documentary *Crime after Crime* (2011) remakes images of Jewish manhood with a narrative that represents counterintuitive connections between an Orthodox white lawyer and his Black Christian client. Joshua Safran, in concert with Nadia Costa, worked tirelessly and pro bono to secure the release of Deborah Peagler, a Black battered woman given a trumped-up life prison sentence for involvement in the murder of Oliver Wilson, her batterer and pimp. Safran's legal work on behalf of Peagler is a performance of his Judaism and an alliance narrative that features a different view of Orthodoxy both for principals in the true-life story and for the audience of Potash's documentary.

We first view Safran in the opening of the film: he and Costa enter the attorney's room in Central LA Women's Facility and greet Peagler with tight,

FIG. 7.1 Debbie and Joshua hug in *Crime after Crime* (2011)

effusive hugs. The back of Safran's yarmulke-covered head is prominent, so we know from the outset that this observant Jew does not shun physical contact with women who are not immediate family members. This sequence is repeated and then continued later in the film. The purpose of this prison visit is to share the game-changing news that an investigation of Peagler's original court files revealed that key evidence was suppressed, an act of judicial misconduct. The disclosure of this relevant evidence would have warranted a six-year sentence for voluntary manslaughter rather than life in prison for first-degree murder. Safran and Costa have a letter from the current district attorney, Steve Cooley, indicating that Peagler has already served more time in prison than was warranted and that she should be released. Despite Safran and Costa's "faith that this letter meant the DA would do the right thing," the DA reneges on his written plea agreement. Debbie's legal team continues its fight to free this model prisoner and to limit the influence of a corrupt DA's office, which even denies her compassionate release when she is diagnosed with stage 4 lung cancer. After finally being granted parole, Peagler considers herself blessed to spend her last months with her children and grandchildren while also working on behalf of battered women. She considers the documentary part of her afterlife and says onscreen, "Even after I pass, this film will continue on." *Crime after Crime* both preserves and is part of Debbie's legacy.

The relationship between Debbie and Joshua ultimately extended beyond that of attorney and client; rather, it was "like family." He—along with cocounsel Nadia Costa—accompanied Debbie to her first chemotherapy treatment. The day after she is released from prison, he shares a walk with her on the beach, and his young daughter, who was born just as he took on Debbie's case, joins them in this exercise of freedom. His daughter's presence—she walks between them as they are filmed from the back—is particularly meaningful to Debbie, as she indicates through a voice-over. Notably, his daughter was also part of how Joshua had always imagined Debbie's release; in that vision, Debbie's freedom would help to explain to his daughter why so many of his nights during the past seven years had been consumed by work. Here, the sacred though often exhausting obligation of social justice and alliance politics is presented as *l'dor v'dor*, from generation to generation.

As the film makes clear, Joshua's Jewishness motivated him, in part, to take on Debbie's case. In one sequence that shows him laying tefillin, part of the ritual of morning prayer for observant Jewish men, he talks about the blessing *matir asurim*, to free those who are bound. As he explains it, "One of the core principles of Judaism is that if someone is wrongfully imprisoned, we have an obligation to free them, to liberate them." A shot of Joshua's desk on which volumes of Jewish law written in Hebrew sit atop the California State Prisoners' Handbook reinforce the connection between his religious and professional commitments. Notably, at the outset of Joshua's relationship with Debbie, religious difference is recognized as a potential problem. When Nadia first brought Joshua on board as cocounsel, Debbie remembers thinking that his obvious Jewishness "should be interesting being that I'm Christian." Like Joshua's skullcap, Debbie's cross is prominent in many shots, and she is often shown in her role as a key member of the prison's gospel choir. The credits at the end of the film are accompanied by shots of Debbie and the choir singing "None of us are free if one of us is chained." Ultimately, Debbie's and Joshua's different expressions of faith become one of the many ties that bind them.

Just as religion began as a potential divider but became a point of identification and alliance, so did gender and its scripts of violence begin as a marker of difference and turn into a bond of understanding and shared experience. Debbie relates onscreen that she was "apprehensive [about talking to Joshua] because he was a man," but that when he made "eye contact with me, his eyes told me it's OK." As she soon learned, Joshua was well-versed in a life structured by the dynamics of abuse. Joshua acknowledges that whenever Debbie talked about her reactions to Oliver, it was "so familiar . . . so personal to me, and that's obviously because of my mother's and my experience . . . she and my mother metaphorically connect. Debbie's experiences in some way are an extension of what could have or would have happened had my mother and I not escaped." Given their shared knowledge of masculine scripts of violence, it becomes deeply ironic that Debbie's freedom hinged on the cinematic embodiment of such scripts turned politician, Arnold Schwarzenegger. Then governor of California, Schwarzenegger was charged with upholding or overturning the parole board's decision to release Debbie from prison. In a sequence that begins with a voice-over and then shifts to shots of Joshua driving with a Rambo cutout dangling from his windshield, this Orthodox Jewish lawyer describes his awareness of the "bizarre narrative twist, typical of this case," that "Debbie's fate rests in the hands of all people a man who before he became governor was best known for portraying a merciless robotic killing machine."

The reception of the film indicates the extent to which Joshua upends the conventional view of Orthodox Jews in general and Orthodox men in particular, held even and especially by non-Orthodox Jews. In an interview with Jewish film critic Michael Fox, Safran recognizes that positive responses to the film often betray stereotypical conceptions of observant Jews: "The one thing that has been troubling to me is a lot of [Jewish] people have given me sort of a backhanded compliment, saying essentially, 'It's amazing that you did this even though you're an Orthodox Jew.' That's really sad to me. At the same time, I understand why they're saying it. The Orthodox community in America has an image of insularity. And that's a problem." To understand this cultural and cinematic image of the inflexible, insular Orthodox patriarch, one need only remember the cantor father in *The Jazz Singer*. As a male feminist ally of a Black woman who was abused not only by her pimp but also by the state and became an activist in her own right, Joshua belies this culturally ingrained image. As he puts it, "For me, part of what being an Orthodox Jew means is having the same engagement with the secular world and the non-Jewish world that every other group of Jews does, except for essentially different reasons."[11] In this way, Safran bridges intra-Jewish tensions and difference just as he bridges interracial and interreligious tensions and difference in his relationship with Peagler.

Potash is acutely aware of Safran's potential impact as a movie-made Jew. "I think Joshua comes across in Jewish terms as such a mensch. . . . Even audiences that don't know or use that word, they kind of fall in love with him or at the very least are very impressed with him and see him as a sort of hero. And that is bonding for someone who is not Jewish and maybe hasn't seen a lot of positive depictions of Jews."[12] The exhibition and reception history of *Crime after Crime* suggests its role in a cinema of alliance. Potash's film won the Audience Award and the Golden Gate Award for Investigative Documentary at the San Francisco International Film Festival, it was an official selection of the 2011 Sundance Film Festival, and it was featured on the final day of the 2011 New York Jewish Film Festival; it also aired on the Oprah Winfrey Network. Says Potash, "I'm proud it can hold its own either in a totally Jewish context or a totally secular context. . . . That was my vision when I crafted the film. . . . I wanted it to be Jewish enough that Jewish festivals and audiences saw something of themselves in the film, and at the same time non-Jewish audiences would feel like it's not overly Jewish but that they would learn something about Jews and other issues in a positive way."[13]

Potash tried to walk that much debated line—cinematic and otherwise— between too Jewish and not Jewish enough. Yet, it's worth noting that a review of the film in *Variety* considers Peagler's race worthy of note but not Safran's Orthodoxy.[14] Some Jewish alliance films may not be widely recognized as such because some viewers and reviewers collapse Jewishness into whiteness, rendering it invisible. Such tendencies, relevant to too many films in this study, reaffirm the importance of contextualizing diverse performances of onscreen Jewishness, especially when they occur in relation to other minority and/or marginalized groups.

Zebrahead (1992)

Zebrahead (1992) is a film that performs not only the potential to render Jewishness invisible but also the challenges associated with intercultural, interethnic alliances. Like the documentary *Heart of Stone, Zebrahead* is set in an urban high school. Filmed in Detroit (it was originally conceived as taking place in Long Island, where director and writer Anthony Drazan grew up, but air traffic from JFK squelched that shooting locale), *Zebrahead* is an interracial romance.[15] Zack, a white Jewish DJ (Michael Rapaport) who has one foot in Black culture thanks to his musical tastes and his best friend Dee, becomes enamored with Dee's cousin, Nikki (N'Bushe Wright), who has recently moved to Detroit from the violent streets of East New York. Intrigued by Zack's cultural fluidity and fluency, Nikki becomes involved with him, only to reconsider that decision when she overhears him talking erotic trash about being with a Black woman. She provisionally turns her attention to the aptly named Nut (Ron Johnson), a "brother" who lays claim to her. When the attraction between Zack and Nikki gets rekindled at a school event, Nut's jealousy and possessiveness spiral out of control, Dee intervenes, and Nut shoots and kills him. While classmates and school officials respond to Dee's death by trying to redraw the color line, grief and mourning over the tragic loss of Dee reaffirm the bond between Zack and Nikki.

 Zebrahead is a fiction film; however, the impetus for it came from Anthony Drazan's experience growing up in Cedarhurst, Long Island, where his best friend was Black. Acutely aware that his white Jewishness meant that he needed to represent communities not his own with great care and knowledge, Drazan spent time doing research in a Yonkers high school. In fact, a key scene in which women of color not only talk about dating white boys but also debate who counts as white—"Italian is not white," declares one—comes from a conversation that Drazan videotaped.[16] *Zebrahead* was Drazan's first film and received the Filmmaker's Trophy award at the 1992 Sundance at which it premiered.

 Although even as savvy a critic as Janet Maslin of the *New York Times* describes Zack simply as white, his Jewishness is established early in the film.[17] We see Zack in the kitchen at his restaurant job, and one of his coworkers facetiously refers to an elderly couple as "the big spenders." Understanding the

coded antisemitism at work with such a reductive and disrespectful characterization, Zack responds, "Those are my grandparents . . . watch your mouth."
References to his bar mitzvah and to a yahrzeit candle for the mother who died
when he was quite young confirm his Jewish identity, though his lack of knowledge about the proffered memorial candle indicates that he is more secular
than religious (true for both Drazan and Rapaport). However, the most moving and evocative performance of Zack's Jewishness occurs at Dee's funeral,
when Zack recites Kaddish for his best friend.

This most Jewish of moments is simultaneously the one that cements the
crossing of racial boundaries. Traditionally, a mourner recites Kaddish publicly
for only the most intimate family members—parents, children, spouse, siblings.
Thus, this recitation is Zack's ultimate claiming of Dee as kin. While Nikki
counters those who seek to score political points and reconstitute racial
boundaries from his murder by talking about Dee being blood, her and Zack's
mutual claiming of Dee as family seems to bring them back together at the end
of the film.

Refreshingly, this movie is neither a multicultural Pollyannaish narrative nor
a hopeless tale of inevitable racial strife. To be sure, the school scenes after Dee's
death, which recall Spike Lee's use of a panoramic neighborhood chorus, are raw
and bracing. While Nikki arrives at school to find "white" painted on her locker,
Zack finds "wannabe" painted on his. In the classroom, some Black students
spout nationalist rhetoric and denounce Dee as an Uncle Tom; one of the Italian
students who apparently still needs to prove his whiteness uses the "N" epithet
and brawling to confirm his racial and racist alliances. Perhaps most disturbing
is the advice that the white, likely Jewish, principal gives to Zack: "Stick with
your tribe, that's how you know who you are." It's one thing for high school students to unreflectively spout the balkanizing rhetoric that surrounds them;
when authoritative educators promote disengagement from others to shore up
the porous boundaries of identity and identification, opposition rather than alliance is destined to be transmitted from generation to generation.

However, Zack's paternal inheritance provides him with an alternative cross-
generational script that molds his knowledge and interest in aesthetic cross-
pollination. Zack is a DJ who, with best friend, Dee, engages in the musical
practice of sampling—a production process that has hybridity at its core. That
musical trend might suggest a superficial, potentially exploitative trying out or
consumption of Black musical styles (and Black women), but it also can signify
deep forms of knowledge, engagement, and collaboration. Zack comes by his
musical knowledge through his family's record store, a legacy of his grandfather
replete with a personally lived history of jazz and hip-hop as evidenced from the
signed posters that adorn the wall. While Zack's dad faces the undesirable task
of closing the no-longer-profitable store, Zack seems to be bringing that interracial collaboration into the future. As he puts it to Nikki, "This is who I am."

Yet Zack clearly also struggles with the racist legacy of eroticizing and exoticizing (i.e., demeaning and othering) Black culture, including Black female sexuality. A party scene in which Zack reduces Nikki to "sweet juice" is as telling for his initial resistance to such racist discourse as for his ultimate fall into it. When his white Jewish bar mitzvah buddies want the lowdown on—and the vicarious thrill of—being with a Black woman, Zack initially refuses to engage in such racist vulgarity but then yields to their prompting with a predetermined line of racial titillation. With that act of complicity, he not only sabotages his romantic relationship with Nikki but also endangers his long-standing friendship with Dee.

Notably, Nikki and her family also struggle with interracial romance. Although Zack is welcomed in Dee's home, he is not embraced as a suitable beau for Nikki. And Nikki finds herself internally conflicted about her romantic choices. She refuses to be an antidote for Zack's perceived jungle fever, yet she is also restive with Nut's racialized possessiveness. Just as Zack must wrestle with predetermined and pernicious narratives about Black women's sexuality, so must Nikki wrest herself from being an object of exchange or the spoils in a patriarchal race war. This is not just Nikki's struggle, but also that of the actor who plays Nikki, N'Bushe Wright. Although in a 1992 interview, Wright asserted that she doesn't "date outside my race now," she did have an interracial relationship in high school, which met with parental disapproval. As Wright puts it, "I've been in interracial relationships and I have been in normal relationships."[18] By suggesting through her language that interracial romance is culturally abnormal, she reveals that such romance is among the most challenging and overdetermined forms of alliance.

The cinematic landscape of *Zebrahead* includes a field whose saturated oil reserves enable spontaneous combustion, metaphorically suggesting both the revolutionary and destructive possibilities historically engendered by interracial romance. The repeated shots of this fiery field also serve as a metaphor for critical responses to *Zebrahead*, which range from glowing, even gushing, admiration to outraged vilification for perpetuating racist stereotypes. Craig Smith, focusing his analysis on Nut and the students spouting Black nationalist rhetoric, argues that the hopelessly "conventional" *Zebrahead* is a film that makes Black men newly visible as hyperviolent and the "snakes in the multicultural garden." With no discussion of the white principal's counsel that I find so significant, he views the film as highlighting Black resistance to interracial relationships, which displaces the racist legacy of white antimiscegenation sentiments.[19] Lawrence King, writing for the *Philadelphia Tribune*, ups the rhetorical ante as he categorizes the film as a "neo Blaxploitation film" and one among many "pathetic, propagandistic productions of white filmmakers trying to capitalize on Hollywood's recent interest in marketing 'blackness' or should we say the rather perturbed, distorted, asinine, racist perceptions of the

African-American experience in America." For Lawrence, "*Zebrahead* was nothing more than a '90s ill-written, 'West Side Story' vehicle of a Detroit Jewish youth, who with silly, Al Jolson, Vanilla Ice–like mannerisms wins the affections of a teenage, high school African-American female."[20] In other words, Zack—and, by extension, Drazan—are trafficking in a contemporary version of blackface.

In sharp contrast, the eminent film critic Robin Wood regards *Zebrahead* as both "overlooked" and "the most intelligent Hollywood film about miscegenation . . . since Mandingo."[21] Gregory Stephens, writing for *Interrace*, asserts that "*Zebrahead* is the most realistic portrayal of contemporary interracial relations to date. It makes room for the spectrum of responses young interracial couples face." He considers Zack's family legacy of engagement with Black music as contributing to "one of the beauties of Zebrahead. . . . it illustrates that involvement with Black culture is not always a fad for non-Black youth." Stephens views Zack as "not 'frontin'—Black culture forms a central part of his worldview, but he's not trying to be somebody else either."[22] In a review that appeared in the *Los Angeles Sentinel*, Marsha Mitchell proclaims *Zebrahead* to be "the most exciting film about interracial dating since Sidney Poitier's *Guess Who's Coming to Dinner*." She specifically commends Drazan as a white director, writing, "I agree with Spike Lee in that I think it is difficult for a white director to capture the nuances of black culture, but Drazan does it, for the most part."[23]

Some discussions of *Zebrahead* collapse Jewishness into whiteness and erase a much more specific history of coalition and tension. Such a collapse was decidedly not at work at the 1992 San Francisco Jewish Film Festival, which was thematically focused on "tolerance and justice in multicultural society" and featured *Zebrahead* as the closing film. Spotlighting the film in this way certainly accords with Drazan's view that "clashes [between Blacks and Jews] . . . are not inevitable. . . . Both groups have gotten beaten up in the past. . . . If we have a shared sense of earth, we will find a way to live together."[24] For Drazan, Jews have no choice but to stay on the bus; however, whether Jews and Blacks getting it on is the best or even a possible way to make that journey together is the question of *Zebrahead* and its reception.

Arranged (2007)

Although Black-Jewish relations, tensions, and alliances get much onscreen time, intergroup encounters have gone beyond Black and white Jewish. Since 9/11, Muslim-Jewish connections have become increasingly prominent. As religious minorities in the United States, Jews and Muslims have much in common. However, given that they are assumed to be rooting for opposing kin in the Middle East, Muslims and Jews are also perceived as destined for enmity.

The contradictions of these two dominant narratives lend themselves to dramatic potential.

The enmity script is explicitly given voice—and challenged by bonds of shared faith—in Diane Crespo and Stefan C. Schaefer's indie film *Arranged* (2007). The film charts both the friendship between and parallel marriage plots of two neophyte teachers, Rochel Meshenberg (Zoe Lister-Jones), an Orthodox Jew, and Nasira Khaldi (Francis Benhamou), an observant Muslim with familial origins in Syria. An official Sundance selection as well as the recipient of audience awards at the Washington and Palm Beach Jewish film festivals, *Arranged* demonstrates that movies and their reception often reinforce one or both of those scripts.

Out of the mouths of babes come formulaic scripts of antagonism and hatred. During one classroom scene early in the film, a Black student named Justin confronts Nasira with another student's belief that "you and Miss Rachel [an Anglicized version of Rochel] can't be friends because you're different religions, like you hate one another or something." When Jimmy, the student supposedly knowledgeable about interfaith antagonism, is asked to explain his thinking, he asserts that he "*heard* that Muslims want to kill all the Jews. Aren't you Muslim?" Although the two women representing these reportedly warring groups contradict such sentiments—to Nasira's pedagogically pointed question, "Do you think I want to kill you?" Rochel responds, "No, of course not!"—what students "hear" dominates their thinking. Rebecca backs up Justin and Jimmy, saying, "I heard that, too, that Muslims want to push Israel back into the ocean." When Nasira attempts to explain the diversity of the Muslim community, the students shift into a numbers game: when one asks, "So how many of them want to kill the Jews?" another assumes the role of chorus, "Yeah, so how many?"

Even when murderous urges are not assumed, suspicion, tension, and awkwardness are depicted as the norm. When Rochel brings Nasira to her home, her mother is anything but welcoming. On a visit to Nasira's home, Mrs. Khalidi tries to be genuinely hospitable and offers food that an embarrassed Rochel must refuse due to laws of kashrut; however, Nasira's father's words of welcome are clearly forced and hollow. Crespo and Schaefer deserve credit for portraying a continuum of the subtle and crude messages that might function to keep these women apart.

Although one review terms the friendship between Rochel and Nasira a "fable," this film has factual rather than fabulistic origins. Using a pseudonym, Yuta Silverman, a Modern Orthodox woman, contacted Stefan Schaefer. After reading about the Israeli film *Ushpizin*, Silverman decided that her friendship with a Muslim woman whose disabled son she tutored merited cinematic treatment. Schaefer agreed, wrote the script, and teamed up with Crespo to direct and produce the film on a $300,000 budget and a seventeen-day shooting

FIG. 7.2 Listening to religious intolerance disguised as progressive thought in *Arranged* (2007)

schedule. Silverman's home as well as Schaefer's apartment served as sets, while Woody Allen's *Annie Hall* inspired the talking while walking scenes that portray the developing friendship between the two first-year teachers.[25]

While Rochel's and Nasira's students and families need to be tutored in the possibilities of cross-cultural, interfaith friendship, the person most in need of a multicultural, multifaith education is the school's principal, Ms. Jacoby. Although Jewish, Jacoby needs multiple lessons before she can properly pronounce "Rochel," and she assumes that Nasira wears a hijab because her father compels her to do so. She is tone-deaf to Nasira's assertion that she chooses to wear it, and Jacoby's intolerance is on full display when she praises Rochel's and Nasira's work as teachers while admonishing them to give up "this religious thing" because "we're in the twenty-first century. There was a woman's movement." Her feminist counsel is to be less serious, to buy designer clothes, and to have a drink (it is unclear whether she is ignorant of Islamic prohibitions on alcohol or whether she is advocating religious transgression). While Jacoby is a cartoonish figure, she represents the so-called educated secular elite's hostility to religion and the assumption that observant women of minority faiths must be oppressed and suffering from false consciousness. Both Nasira and Rochel are on to Jacoby, and this shared awareness of religious bigotry veiled as progressive thought helps to make them allies.

Nasira and Rochel refuse to embrace contemporary discourses that dismiss their faith and practice as antithetical to modernity. At the same time, they strive to broaden familial and communal perspectives on not only their choice of friends but also their marriage options. Both women have been put on the marriage market by their well-meaning parents, and both resist practical but romantically unappealing choices. In Rochel's case, the dates arranged by a shadchen (a matchmaker) form a painfully laughable montage of suitors; these range from a stuttering bumbler to a dominator who neither pauses to take a breath nor listens to the female human on the opposite side of the table. The writer Gary Shteyngart makes a cameo appearance as a Russian émigré who thinks of a wife as one who has the privilege to serve him. As Michael Rowin notes, this sequence is indebted to *Kissing Jessica Stein*.[26] Rowin reads this sequence as an example of *Arranged* falling into predictable and derivative territory; however, I think that it creates parallels between the secular dating scene and arranged marriage practice, suggesting the overlap between the "liberated" singleton and the observant unmarried woman, two types who are usually assumed to be polar opposites. A scene in the school cafeteria in which a teacher holds court about the engagement ring she is about to receive from her boyfriend indicates that marital arrangements are not only the province of religious minorities. When Rochel finally confronts Jacoby on her judgmental assumptions that traditional practices are "nonsense," she explicitly puts warding off the evil eye into dialogue with reading horoscopes and smartly asks, "Why is getting drunk and sleeping with some guy you don't even know a better way of finding love? How is that more liberated than how we do it?" This film that brings observant Muslims and Jews into dialogue and alliance also provides critical commentary on the mores of the mainstream. Like *The Way We Were*, *Crossing Delancey*, and *Fading Gigolo*, *Arranged* refuses an assimilationist gaze.

Notably, Eddy, a visually impaired student whom Rochel teaches, applauds her for standing up to principal Jacoby, saying admiringly that "you didn't take no shit from her" and "you did the right thing." Eddy, who in an early scene asks Rochel if he can feel her face, demonstrates a different way of seeing. Rochel's advocacy for integrating Eddy into the school as much as possible is also a worldview that can be applied to religious minorities—difference need not entail opposition, isolation, or rejection.

Such an understanding of difference, with its attendant negotiation with tradition, animates Nasira and Rochel in their own lives and in their friendship, in their rejection of tribalism without leaving the tribe, and in their assertion of romantic agency. When Rochel is frustrated by and refuses the marriage prospects on offer, she visits her cousin Leah, who has left the fold and advises Rochel that she, too, can "step out." Determined to expand Rochel's horizons, Leah takes her to a party. Overwhelmed by the scene there, Rochel is befriended by Matthew Cohen. Although he professes some understanding of her world— he has Orthodox cousins in her Ditmas Park neighborhood that he doesn't get to see much—he nonetheless tries to force her to dance and to drink. Like Jacoby and Leah, Matthew can only imagine being inside or outside, observant or secular, and assumes that Rochel must be redeemed from her anachronistic life. In sharp contrast, Nasira comforts Rochel as the latter begins to lose faith, saying, "Something will work out. God will show a way, we both still believe that, right?"

However, Nasira's support goes far beyond an unquestioning belief in God. When she realizes that there are sparks of romantic interest between Rochel and an Orthodox Jewish classmate of her brother's, she takes it upon herself to play shadchen: pretending to be a journalism student interviewing people of different faiths, she gets key information about Gideon Horowitz, affirms his suitability, and then, clad in a headscarf rather than her habitual hijab, delivers this information to the official shadchen. Nasira is assumed to be a Sephardic Jew, an indicator of the close doubling of the observant Muslim and Jew emphasized formally by the crosscutting technique that dominates the film (Nasira's onscreen masquerade had its counterpart in the production history of the film: Francis Benhamou did not let the directors know that she is Jewish until after shooting was complete).[27] While Matthew, Leah, and Jacoby can only offer an exit strategy, Rochel's Muslim ally affirms that there is another way, that she need not leave a part of herself behind, that religious and romantic desire need not be at odds.

Those involved in the film's production found that the cross-cultural education represented onscreen was mirrored in their own experiences. Yuta Silverman's family was, like Rochel's in the film, initially uncomfortable with Silverman's friendship with a Muslim. However, they ultimately allowed their own home to be used as Rochel Meshenberg's, and the public school scenes in the film were shot at the yeshiva where Silverman's father works. Although Silverman's rabbi did not approve the project, he likewise did not prohibit it.[28] Codirector Crespo, who identifies as lesbian and was raised Catholic, acknowledges:

> I knew very little about the Orthodox community before this project.... Yuta allowing us into her life and world, insisting that we come in and giving us a window into this community was amazing. We all probably have preconceived notions of the roles of women in an Orthodox community. Before I knew better it seemed oppressive and lacked any equality. As a woman, as a feminist, you always want to free women from that. But meeting Yuta and her mom I really saw the freedom, that they don't feel limited in any way, and it was nice for the women on set to see that.[29]

Similarly, Zoe Lister-Jones, although Jewish, was unfamiliar with and judgmental about the Orthodox world of her character. After making the film, she finds herself more ambivalent and conflicted: "Yuta is an amazing woman, and that has always brought me to the other side. Her friends are amazing, too. All these bad-[expletive] Jewish girls who are totally outspoken. But I still do have issues."[30] Francis Benhamou's preparation for playing Nasira included a crash course in Islam: "I realized I didn't know anything about it. It's really a very beautiful religion and I felt very inspired by it."[31]

The fact that *Arranged* won audience awards at significant Jewish film festivals suggests a responsiveness to this emerging alliance narrative. Although there aren't—yet—parallel institutions in Muslim communities, Crespo reports that attempts to reach Muslim viewers have resulted in positive reactions: "We've reached out to Muslim student communities and gotten a very good response. . . . when we've invited Muslims to the general screenings it's gone over really well."[32]

However, some professional reviews suggest that what we might term the Jacoby syndrome is far from fictional or anachronistic. Writing for the *New York Times*, Jeannette Catsoulis asserts that "both women are about to learn that happiness lies in conformity and that, whatever your beliefs, Father always knows best. . . . Packed with the stereotypes it aspires to challenge, Diane Crespo and Stefan C. Schaefer's well-meaning but oblivious film presents ostensibly modern young women who are nevertheless defined solely by their faith. . . . As unworldly as its two protagonists, *Arranged* is a doctrinaire wolf in rebel-sheep's clothing. Within its cloistered boundaries, patriarchy can't help but prevail."[33] Catsoulis's assumptions about religious "conformity" and "patriarchy" show once again that whether the production of cinematic stereotypes happens onscreen or in the mainstream reviewing process is in the eye of the beholder. As with so many of the films discussed in *Movie-Made Jews*, *Arranged* demonstrates that production and reception history matters.

David (2011)

Following in the footsteps of *Arranged*, including the involvement of Yuta Silverman as coproducer, Joel Fendelman and Patrick Daly's *David* (2011) explores the close doubling of observant Muslims and Jews in Brooklyn. This "docustyle" fiction feature film focuses on Daud (Muatasem Mishal), a young Muslim boy from an immigrant family who passes as Jewish due to a bookish comedy of errors that involves mistakenly leaving a prized family Quran at a yeshiva. Even after Daud retrieves his tradition's holy book, he continues his religious masquerade due to his developing friendship with one of the Jewish boys, Yoav (Binyomin Shtaynberger). In his own community, Daud, the son of the imam, is viewed as and expected to act as an adult: he watches his younger sister, helps his mother with laundry and grocery shopping, and mentors younger boys even as he prepares for his own recitation of the Quran. However, in the world of the yeshiva where he is known as the Sephardic David, he is tutored in the mores of American boyhood, a world of basketball and baseball cards as well as swimming and rides at Coney Island. His wrestling with his identity is cannily conveyed by an out-of-focus shot of him after his father has taken away the family Quran that his uncle had given him. Daud's older sister, Aisha (Dina Shihabi), also struggles: after being accepted to Stanford, she must decide whether committing herself to an arranged marriage is the only way to achieve her educational, intellectual, and professional ambitions. And even the imam (Maz Jobrani) wrestles with how to be a good father and religious role model to his Americanizing children. His struggle to embrace not only tradition but also his children recalls and revises the role of the authoritarian cantor in *The Jazz Singer*.

To be sure, the narratives that separate Jews from Muslims are present throughout the film. When Daud asks his father about the commonalities between Jewish tradition and the Quran, the imam first acknowledges a shared inheritance but goes on to say that Jews "don't follow the prophet. . . . God still punishes them for that." He then cautions Daud to be careful, avowing that "they don't like Arabs." The fact that the father fears Jewish antagonism is both a reversal of and an analogue to Jewish anxiety about Arab antagonism. Ironically, this warning indirectly sets into motion the confusion about Daud's identity at the yeshiva: remembering his father's cautionary words, he removes his *thawb* (the long tunic that observant Muslim men and boys often wear) and is thus assumed to be Jewish when he enters the yeshiva to retrieve his Quran. Later, when one of the yeshiva boys discovers the Quran in David's bookbag, he unmasks him with the ready-made epithet "lying Arab." Although Yoav chides Moishe for such language, his own sense of betrayal initially prevents him from listening to David's apology and explanation.

Despite such formulaic friction, it is the camaraderie and the similarities between Daud and Yoav that ground the film, as well as Yoav's impulses of generosity toward a newcomer who does not yet know the ropes. When David is brought to the cafeteria by a well-meaning rabbi, Yoav immediately shares his lunch with him; he also teaches David to play basketball and gives him valuable baseball cards. Notably, Yoav collects cards from all different teams, even the Red Sox—a reminder that sports culture can serve as a training ground for alliances as well as competition and enmity. And while within the narrative of the film Yoav's generosity is offered to one whom he assumes is a fellow Jew, his role suggests that third-generation observant Jews might function as a model for observant Muslims to both acculturate and retain their religious difference. Moreover, Daud is bullied as both a Muslim and a Jew, a potent reminder that these two religious minority groups face similar challenges, which underscores Yoav's affirmation that "we have to stick together."

The ending of the film neither forecloses nor guarantees the possibility of Muslims and Jews sticking together. Thanks to the wisdom and urging of the rabbi who initially mistook Daud for a Jew, Yoav does hear Daud out. And as he completes the school project on family history that he and Daud had been working on together—a project that makes the abstract notion of "diaspora" concrete—he chooses to include a photograph of him and David outside of the magnificent Eldridge Street Synagogue located on the Lower East Side. Fendelman conceived of the open-endedness of the film as a nod to its "realistic optimism," an invitation for dialogue to its viewers, and a refusal to "tie it up and present an easy answer to a complex question."

For Fendelman, the writing and shooting of *David* were part of his remaking himself as a Jew: "I grew up Jewish, had a bar mitzvah and didn't really look back at that aspect of my life. In the last five years or so, I have been really questioning 'what does it mean to be Jewish.'"[34] Daud's identity struggle was, in some ways, an expression of Fendelman's sense of difference as one of only a few Jews in his largely Hispanic high school in Miami. However, *David* was also conceived as a response to his post-9/11 awareness of ignorance about and stereotyping of Muslims. Prior to the making of *David*, Fendelman volunteered at the Arab American Community Association in Bay Ridge, where he tutored immigrant Muslim women in English and directed a summer youth group. Knowing little about Orthodox Jews, he also spent time in a yeshiva in Jerusalem, as well as with the Jewish community in Borough Park. The profoundly limited production budget for this film—a $25,000 "microbudget"—meant that the film was shot on location in Bay Ridge and Borough Park, two adjacent Brooklyn neighborhoods that include streets shared by identifiably observant Muslims and Orthodox Jews; such streets spatially represent possibilities for interfaith coexistence and cooperation.[35] According to Fendelman, "This special place of cross over allowed for the story of *David* to take place."[36] To ensure accuracy and fairness of representation, the production of *David* included both Muslim and Jewish advisers.[37]

For the two young nonprofessional actors, *David* was an experience in alliance-building. Fendelman recruited Muatasem Mishal from the youth group program at which he volunteered, and he discovered Binyomin Shtaynberger at a kosher café in Borough Park. While Binyomin's Yoav was largely a version of himself, Muatasem is less religious and serious than Daud. As Fendelman tells it, "He would be bouncing off the walls and then when I would say 'Action!' he would drop right into his role. It was amazing to see."[38] On the first day of filming, the cultural differences and potential tensions between the two boys and their families were on stark display: Binyomin was accompanied by his entire Orthodox Jewish nuclear family, and Muatasem's sister, clad in full hijab, accompanied her brother, who was wearing a "Free Palestine" wristband (filming began shortly after the Gaza flotilla raid).[39] Fendelman reports that despite initial discomfort, the two families were "brought together" by the film.[40] At one after-screening Q&A session, Binyomin admitted that he was initially nervous about working with the Muslim Muatasem, but he quickly got over that and they became Facebook friends, the consummate indicator of relationship for his generation.[41] As a testament to the cultural work that film-ing can accomplish, Fendelman reports that the scene in which Yoav learns that Daud is not Jewish and "where they were actually butting heads and hav-ing a conflict was actually the most out of natural experience" that occurred during production and was "one of the most difficult scenes to film."[42] In other words, the production of *David* made animosity between Muslims and Jews seem unnatural!

Reception of the film was generally positive. While *Variety* praised "its mes-sage of cultural reconciliation presented sans preachiness, melodrama, easy answers or sweeping generalities," *Time Out* noted that it was "refreshing to see a film that focuses on the similarities not the differences between Judaism and Islam."[43] Patrick Daly, the film's codirector and cowriter, noted that within one ten-day period, the film was shown and well received at an Iranian film festival, a significant Jewish film festival, and an Arab American conference.[44] *David* earned the Audience Choice Award for Best Narrative Feature at the 2011 Brooklyn International Film Festival, where it premiered, as well as the Ecumenical Award at the Montreal Film Festival.

The very act of watching the film was, for many, an interfaith and intercul-tural experience. According to Fendelman, an early private screening that included cast members was notable for its "groups of women with Hijabs and guys with black hats all coming to the same space to watch the film together." These Muslim and Jews "connected on the film, felt it was very authentic and spoke a truth to them, but everyone was also able to start a conversation after-wards."[45] Indeed, a logo for the film is "Start a Conversation: *David*." The screenings of the film at Quad Cinema in Manhattan, a hub for serious film culture, included interfaith programming that coincided with the tenth anni-versary of 9/11, and showings of the film in Italy did interfaith work for Cath-olic and non-Catholic children.[46] At Bryn Mawr College, the Muslim Students Association and Hillel collaborated to bring Fendelman to campus for a screen-ing and discussion of *David*.

Despite the "realistic optimism" with which Fendelman made the film,[47] he has indicated in numerous interviews that "the film asks the question, 'Can Daud and Yoav be friends?' As an idealist, I say yes. As a realist, I say no. The only thing left is to ask why."[48] Yet, in the Trump era and its aftermath, a post-9/11 cinematic vision of potential alliances between Muslims and Jews seems more realistic than ever. Observant Jewish groups such as Torah Trumps Hate were vocal opponents of the various versions of the Muslim ban; the Sisterhood of Salaam Shalom, designed to "grow relationships between Muslim and Jew-ish women to build bridges and fight hate, negative stereotyping and prejudice," has grown exponentially since 2016; and many Muslims and Jews have come to see antisemitism and Islamophobia as twin illiberal enemies of religious plural-ism in these more and more divided United States. The most likely association most of us now have with Charlottesville is the Unite the Right Rally during which, among many other atrocities, torch-carrying neo-Nazis chanted "Sieg Heil" as they marched past Congregation Beth Israel, a Reform synagogue. However, the reception history of *David* provides us with a divergent view of Charlottesville: in November 2011, the Virginia Film Festival realized a partnership with Jewish/Israeli Voices sponsored by the very same Congregation Beth Israel; this partnership resulted in the screening of *David* with Fendelman in attendance.[49] Think about that: a non-Jewish film festival that includes Jewish/Israeli voices by featuring a film about a fraught but powerful friendship between Muslim and Jewish boys. The Jews onscreen and off who make and are made by such alliance films are part of the resistance to antidemocratic, anti-immigrant, and anti–religious freedom trends at home and abroad. Those who would dismiss such films as *David*, *Arranged*, *Crime after Crime*, *Zebrahead*, and *Heart of Stone* as only movies underestimate the role that art might play in creating a more perfect union and in doing the work of *tikkun olam*, healing a broken world.

8

Epilogue

•••••••••••••••••••••

Cinematic Continuity and Change through a Feminist Lens

Two arguably Jewish feminist documentaries of 2018—Paula Eiselt's *93Queen* and Julie Cohen and Betsy West's *RBG*—demonstrate the narrative of cinematic continuity and change that *Movie-Made Jews* has charted. Taken together, they indicate that a Jewish gaze is sometimes explicitly behind the camera and on the screen and sometimes mostly represented by the eyes of Jewishly literate viewers. However, no matter where the Jewish gaze resides, these films—including their production and reception histories—show that American Jewish movies help to shape Jewish self-images as well as Gentile understanding of diverse forms of Jewish being, becoming, and experience.

93Queen (2018)

Like the fiction films discussed in chapter 5, the documentary *93Queen* is assertively and unapologetically Jewish. It charts the struggle to birth Ezras Nashim, a women's EMT corps that serves the Hasidic community in Borough Park, Brooklyn (93Queen is the emergency code provided to Ezras Nashim by the New York City Fire Department; the name Ezras Nashim translates as "women helping women" and, as Laura Adkins points out, also refers to the women's section of traditional synagogues that are segregated by gender).[1] Ezras Nashim came into being because the existing EMT corps, Hatzaloh, refused to allow women into its ranks. Given that contact between men and women is prohibited under usual circumstances, members of this Hasidic community recognized that women might prefer to be aided by other women during medical events, including childbirth. Led by Rachel "Ruchie" Freier, an attorney and the first Hasidic woman elected as a public official (she became a civil court judge in 2016), a group of women trained as paramedics and triumphed over the considerable backlash from Hatzaloh to found Ezras Nashim, which in 2017 earned the Basic Life Support Agency of the Year Award from the State of New York.

Like so many of the films discussed in *Movie-Made Jews*, *93Queen* had to surmount significant production impediments. Getting access to a community that is immensely distrustful of media and has historically shunned it was one challenge. The director's own Modern Orthodox identity enabled her to overcome this challenge. Eiselt's knowledge of and willingness to follow Hasidic modesty customs during filming earned the trust of Ruchie and her sister Ezras Nashim members; Ruchie was also swayed by Eiselt's arguments that representing oneself rather than being represented by outsiders can counter the overwhelmingly negative and stereotypical narratives of Hasidic Jews in general and Hasidic women in particular.[2] By convincingly arguing that movies matter and that they help to shape perceptions of observant Jews, Eiselt was able to tell the story of Ezras Nashim to a broad audience. The antagonists of Ezras Nashim— Hatzaloh and others in the community who accused Ruchie and her posse of being immodest and of enabling secular feminism to transgress the fence of a Torah-bound community—saw the making of *93Queen* as similarly impactful. As one commenter in *Yeshiva World*, an online communal venue, put it, "Now Ezras Nashim is coming out with a movie to complain about hatzolah and Chassidic community in general r"l [short for Rachmana Litzlan—May God Save Us]. It's time to put a stop to this, if these women want to break all boundaries of tznius, they shouldn't be allowed to be part of the Jewish community especially not the chassidish ones."[3] Clearly, *93Queen*, like all the movies discussed in these pages, is not just a movie.

Even as Eiselt was gaining the trust of Ruchie and other members of the fledgling Ezras Nashim crew, she found it difficult to get funding for a film that challenged predetermined scripts about Hasidic women. According to Eiselt, "Many in the industry did not want to see a film made about empowered Hasidic women. Women's organizations were sometimes the most challenging. They saw these women as either really oppressed or so privileged, that they were beyond redemption. 'Why don't they just leave? Why are they complicit in their own oppression?' . . . It became very clear to me that there was a real bias towards this type of film. . . . The industry isn't as open as you'd think it would be to certain stories, and certain communities."[4] Producer Heidi Reinberg affirms

Eiselt's view: she experienced overt hostility from industry friends because of her work on a film that didn't conform to a reductive leave-religious-patriarchy-behind narrative.[5] Even after funding came through from the Independent Television Service (ITVS), the funding arm of the Public Broadcasting Service (PBS), and then in an avalanche from Sundance, Tribeca, the International Documentary Association (IDA), and Fork Films, *93Queen* was rejected by film festivals associated with those funding streams, most notably Sundance. However, the narrative and feminist difference represented by *93Queen* did earn it a place in the Hot Docs Pitch Forum and then its First Look prize, with their favorite line being "Change isn't made by the people who leave, it's made by the people who stay."[6] The documentary's world premiere ended up being held at the Hot Docs Film Festival, and then the film had its U.S. premiere at the San Francisco Jewish Film Festival. From there, it earned a coveted theatrical run, including at New York's IFC Theater, and then aired on PBS's *Point of View* series. As is the case with so many of the films discussed here, the production and exhibition history of *93Queen* illuminates the challenges and possibilities associated with making films potentially perceived as "too Jewish."

This assertively Jewish film features the alliance politics at work in the fiction films and documentaries discussed in chapter 7. In one scene, an African American man in charge of the EMT training tells the dispirited women of Ezras Nashim that he's Black and that he's been successful because he's twice as good. In a spirit of mentorship and alliance, he predicts that strategy will work for them as well. Letitia James, at the time a New York City public advocate and now New York's first African American and woman attorney general, has ample screen time during the sequence in which Ruchie is sworn in as a judge and avers that she "know[s] a little bit about history and wanted to be in the room where we are making history here in the borough of Brooklyn." James's focus on "breaking through glass ceilings" and her view that "right women make some noise" indicate her understanding that feminism has many faces and that Ruchie is one of them, even though this Hasidic woman might not embrace a term that has negative connotations in her religious community.

Notably, Eiselt credits alliance politics for helping her to find her cinematic voice and vision. Marco Williams, a Black award-winning documentary filmmaker, was one of her mentors during her time at NYU's Tisch School of the Arts and beyond. He encouraged Eiselt to view her identity as an observant Jewish woman as a positive contribution rather than an impediment to her filmmaking career. Ultimately, the alliance politics she perceives and represents onscreen mirror those that have been central to her own development:

> African Americans have helped me in my journey more than anyone else— more than Jews. The nurturing and the generosity from my mentors happened to be people of color. I think there is a real potential reality of empathy,

FIG. 8.1 A mentor and an ally in *93Queen* (2018)

understanding, between Jews and African Americans. I think when we get it right, we get it really right. Our experiences are parallel until they diverge. I just wish more Jews would see how much help we get from other communities.[7]

93Queen proves that a film can uphold religious modesty requirements and be cosmopolitan in its vision and execution.

Although some might view Hasidic Jews as a static, anachronistic group, *93Queen* is a film about Hasidic Jews in the making. Just as the opening credits spell out *93Queen*, so are viewers presented with Ezras Nashim coming into being and Hasidic women being transformed by this project. While Hatzaloh and members of the community who oppose Ezras Nashim want to ensure that women become homemakers and mothers, Ruchie debunks the idea that lawyers and challah-makers are oxymoronic.[8] The belief that Ezras Nashim is remaking notions of Hasidic womanhood appears frequently onscreen: when the possibility arises that Ruchie's daughters might have to leave their religious school, since Ezras Nashim is "not what we encourage our girls to do"; when Ruchie's daughters and their friends are talking about their educational aspirations and one expresses concern that at twenty-two, "it already starts getting harder to date"; when Ruchie's daughters robe her at her swearing-in ceremony; and when Hadassah Ellis, an EMT recruit, attends that swearing-in ceremony and affirms that the newborn daughter in her arms now has role models to teach her that "she doesn't have to sacrifice her religious beliefs or practices in order to do the things she dreams of." A Hasidic boy is also shown more ready to believe that a women's Hatzaloh exists than some of his male elders. As *93Queen* chronicles competing gender construction projects within the Hasidic community, the next generation confirms that these times they are a-changing even as they are continuing.

In keeping with the overarching argument of this book, the making of Jews is not only part of the narrative of *93Queen* but also part of its production and reception history. Even the filmmaker had her perceptions of Hasidic Jews and her own Orthodoxy reconfigured in the making of the film. The genesis of this documentary was Eiselt reading about the founding of Ezras Nashim on an Orthodox website. The plan for this organization both raised Eiselt's awareness that Hatzaloh did not allow women EMTs and represented what she considered an extraordinary example of "Chasidic women not taking no for an answer." Moreover, according to Eiselt, "Ruchie just shattered every one of my stereotypes."[9] The director's experience at the Independent Film Project Lab allowed her to integrate her whole being, including her Orthodoxy, into her view of herself as a filmmaker. Says Eiselt, "I finally felt okay owning being a mom, an Orthodox Jew and filmmaker. I used to attempt to hide the non-filmmaker parts of myself from the industry—I didn't think I would be taken seriously and that I would be deemed too niche."[10] Even as "too niche" hearkens back to the "too Jewish" question, Eiselt reminds us that the making of assertively Jewish films is part of the process of making Jews, even and especially in the film industry. Writing for *Documentary Magazine*, Lauren Wissot identified herself as a secular Jew and admitted that "the notion of a feminist Hasid would strike me as outlandish as a hipster sporting payot. Enter Rachel 'Ruchie' Freier to upend my preconceived notions."[11] Further attesting to the ways that Jewish films matter, Simon Kilmurry, executive director of the IDA, wrote to Eiselt about the role her film played in raising his consciousness about Jewish difference: "Having lived in Brooklyn for many years, and despite considering myself an open and tolerant type, I would too often find myself stereotyping the Hasidic community. . . . Watching films like 93QUEEN helped me to recognize this."[12]

93Queen even shifted the conversation around Ezras Nashim in the Hasidic community. Some members of Hatzaloh attended screenings of the film to show solidarity with Freier. According to a Facebook post by Eiselt, "They wanted to let her know that the leadership does not speak for them and that there are dozens of other members who are supporting her. They are whispering about what they are going to do to help Ezras Nashim."[13] Even this brief and recent reception history of *93Queen* demonstrates that movie-made Jews reside onscreen and off.

The film raises questions not only about continuity and change within Hasidic communities but also about what feminism looks like in different cultural contexts. The latter issue is also explored in *Arranged*, a reminder of the overlap between documentaries and fiction film. Both *93Queen* and Ruchie herself, as shown in the film and in postfilm interviews, highlight questions of feminist identity. While in one scene Ruchie goes on a Jewish radio station to disavow feminism as a "secular concept," at the end of the film she asserts, "My connection to secular feminism is very obvious but you can't just in one sentence narrow me down to a few specific words. It just doesn't work with me." She doubles down on this theme in an interview with Wissot, saying, "Without amazing and strong women like Ruth Bader Ginsburg, I could have never been where I am today."[14] As a lawyer, a judge, and a Jew, RBG would have particular significance for Freier. And, of course, RBG is also the subject of another popular documentary of 2018, one that I want to argue functions, like *Milk*, as a limit case for American Jewish films.

RBG (2018)

That *RBG* was received as a Jewish film by members of the tribe is indisputable. The Jewish press reviewed it extensively and covered its Oscar nomination; writing for the Jewish Telegraphic Agency, Josefin Dolsten explicitly refers to Justice Ginsburg as a "Jewish jurist."[15] *RBG* not only was shown in theaters and on CNN, but also was popular on the Jewish film festival circuit, including the Rutgers Jewish Film Festival, the National Center for Jewish Film's Twenty-First Annual Film Festival, the Washington Jewish Film Festival, and the Atlanta Jewish Film Festival, which boasted about its RBG swag on social media. The Jewish Film Institute (affiliated with the San Francisco Jewish Film Festival) hosted an online member screening of the doc. A screening and discussion held at the Center for Jewish History in New York was cosponsored by the center, the American Jewish Historical Society, and the Muslim American Leadership Alliance; such cosponsorship clearly indicates the film was perceived as an opportunity for alliance politics. As a further reminder of the manifold ways that Jewish movies matter, the Miami Jewish Film Festival sponsored, prior to the midterm elections, a free screening at which a "speaker from Engage Miami, a nonpartisan group focused on engaging and educating youth voters, . . . introduce[d] the film and raise[d] awareness about voting in the Nov. 6 elections."[16]

According to the Jewish publication *Kveller*, "The film traced [RBG's] status as a Jewish feminist icon." Writing for the *New York Times*, A. O. Scott, whose mother is Jewish, commented that the film is "a reminder that the upward striving of first- and second-generation Jewish immigrants in the middle decades of the 20th century was accompanied by fervent political idealism. Justice Ginsburg's career was marked by intense intellectual ambition and also by a determination to use the law as an instrument of change."[17]

Such screenings and commentary would lead one to believe that the film talks about Ginsburg as a Jewish feminist or highlights the impact that her

Jewish immigrant heritage had on her remarkable career. Yet the film itself, which is truly marvelous and matters just the way it is, is hardly assertively Jewish. Indeed, Ginsburg's Jewishness is explicitly referenced just a few times. Early in the film, when she is stressing the importance placed on education in her family, Ginsburg talks about her father's Odessa origins and mentions that "during his growing up years, Jews were no longer admitted to Russian schools." At another point, Clara Spera, Ginsburg's granddaughter and a member of the Harvard Law School class of 2017, says, "My brother, cousins and I all call her bubbe," which she glosses for viewers as the "Yiddish word for grandmother." When discussing Ginsburg's nodding off at the State of the Union address, Spera admonishes her grandmother: "Bubbe, you can't do that!" And during the sequence on RBG's counterintuitive but enduring friendship with the politically and judicially conservative Justice Antonin Scalia, the odd couple nature of their relationship described by his son Eugene includes that "she's Jewish, he's Catholic." So, depending on whether you count "bubbe" as one or two instances, there are only three or four references to Ginsburg's Jewishness, none of which is terribly substantive in terms of content or screen time.

In addition to these explicit references to Jewishness, there are more coded moments that Jewishly literate viewers (whether Jewish or not) might notice. At one point, when "Bubbe" is sharing with her granddaughter glowing letters about Ruth that husband Marty Ginsburg saved in a binder, Clara can be seen wearing a *hamsa* (hand of Miriam) necklace. Much more significant are Ginsburg's memories of the McCarthy era, the government professor who lauded the lawyers defending the civil rights of those accused of being Communist, and the pivotal role such history played in her own desire to pursue a legal career and to "do something that could make your own society a little better." Archival footage of John Howard Lawson appearing before and castigating HUAC is part of this sequence. For those aware that Lawson was one of the six blacklisted Jews of the Hollywood Ten and that anti-Communism intertwined with antisemitism, this emphasis on the Red Scare as a motivating factor for Ginsburg (a point repeated toward the end of the doc) is a potent example of Jewish coding. More of a stretch but worth mentioning is Gloria Steinem describing Ginsburg as "the closest thing to a superhero I know." Given that the coded Jewishness of superheroes is part of popular culture studies—especially as a result of Michael Chabon's Pulitzer Prize–winning novel *The Amazing Adventures of Kavalier and Clay* as well as Israeli actress Gal Gadot's more recent rendition of *Wonder Woman*—this descriptor might be Jewishly resonant for some spectators. Personally, Ginsburg's calling then presumptive presidential nominee Donald Trump a "faker," an utterance that friend, journalist, and documentary talking head Nina Totenberg denounced in the film as inappropriate, was, to my Brooklyn Jewish ears, a dog whistle that gleefully conveyed Ginsburg's geographic, ethnic, and ethical origins.[18]

As fun as this Jewish detective work is, it does not at face value a Jewish movie make. Now one could argue that Ginsburg's Jewishness is so well known, to Jews and antisemites alike, that the "J word" need not speak its name more often than it does in the documentary. But the odd thing is that the "J word" is often used by Ginsburg herself, in film and in writing. In fact, Julie Cohen, codirector of *RBG*, first interviewed Ginsburg for her 2015 documentary *Sturgeon Queens*, about the Manhattan Lower East Side appetizing store Russ and Daughters. In that film, RBG is one of the eminent talking heads who remembers childhood trips to this store being part of her education about her roots. As Ginsburg tells it onscreen, Russ and Daughters represented "the best in the Jewish tradition" as well as her burgeoning feminist consciousness: "Even before I heard the word 'feminist,' it made me happy to see that this was an enterprise where the daughters counted just like sons counted; that was most uncommon in those days."

Ginsburg is even more assertively Jewish in David Grubin's PBS series *The Jewish Americans* (2008). In that series, she waxes poetic on the first Jewish justice of the Supreme Court, Louis Brandeis, and his "caring for the nation's most fundamental values" while enduring "with dignity" the antisemitism he experienced not only in the culture at large but also from one of his colleagues on the court. Ginsburg also reveals her own experiences with antisemitism, from encountering a sign at a roadside B&B that read "No Dogs or Jews Allowed" to the college quotas designed to restrict Jewish enrollment and her experience at Cornell, where all the Jewish women were housed together, as they still joke about it, "so we wouldn't contaminate the others."

In the collection of RBG's writings coedited with her authorized biographers, Ginsburg includes Jewish-themed pieces.[19] Irin Carmon and Shana Knizhnik's *Notorious RBG: The Life and Times of Ruth Bader Ginsburg*, which clearly informed the documentary, does not list the terms "Jew," "Jewish," or "Judaism" in the index; however, the writers indicate that RBG had difficulty accepting the sexism of Jewish tradition, especially when, as a woman, she could not be counted as part of the minyan when Kaddish was said for her mother, who died when RBG was seventeen. As Carmon and Knizhnik elegantly put it, "Jewish law taught Kiki about a commitment to justice, but after her mother died, it took her a long time to see herself in the faith."[20] Although Ginsburg was not an observant Jew, her affiliation with the tribe is a matter of public and private record. Upon receiving the Genesis Prize for Lifetime Achievement in Israel and attending a screening of *RBG* at the Jerusalem Cinematique in July 2018, she indicated that her room in the Supreme Court was the only one with a mezuzah and that a poster featuring a verse from Deuteronomy, "Justice, Justice, thou shalt pursue," hung on a wall in her chambers. According to her, this verse functioned as a daily reminder that "the demand for justice, peace and enlightenment runs through Jewish history and tradition."[21]

Notably, in interviews, director Julie Cohen is quite forthcoming about the foundational role that Jewishness played in key parts of RBG's story. According to Cohen, "Justice Ginsburg fits very neatly into the context of a long line of Jewish lawyers with a deep interest in social justice and fairness. Certainly, she thinks of Justice [Louis] Brandeis as having been a major influence in terms of his jurisprudence on the path that she took."[22] Cohen and West were hyperaware of RBG's parents' experience with antisemitism and "almost saw that as a launching pad for everything she fought for." They were also aware that antisemitism compounded the sexism she faced as she tried and failed to get a job at a legal firm after graduating from law school. Moreover, the great egalitarian love story between RBG and Marty, which is such a wonderful highlight of the documentary, also has a Jewish dimension. According to journalist Stephen Applebaum, Cohen identified "Marty's parents [as] progressive New York Jews who believed in equality and women's rights." As Cohen put it, "They imparted those values to Marty, and Ruth was the beneficiary."[23]

Although *RBG* does not portray Ginsburg as much of a Jew, the making of the film seems to have had an effect on Cohen's own Jewish consciousness. After indicating that she has been thinking "a lot about the importance of representation," she reflects on her own youthful infatuation with Carole King and the importance of "the cover image of this small, frizzy-haired Jewish woman—in other words, a woman who looked like me . . . it was a revelation that this, too, was a way to be beautiful."[24] Cohen freely admits that she relates to RBG as a "professional Jewish woman" and that, at times, talking with RBG was "like listening to one of my family members."[25] But Cohen's Jewish connections with the notorious RBG as well as the role that Jewishness played in the making of the great dissenter are at the margins or nonexistent onscreen. As West puts it, Judaism "seems to be an undercurrent in her life, [but it's] something that we didn't deal with overtly."[26] Early in the film, one of the talking heads says, "As much as people admire her, they don't know the half of it." Marginalizing the role that Jewishness played in RBG's judicial life and love story seems like an unfortunate irony in an otherwise stellar documentary. Like *Milk*, *RBG* can be and has been classified as a Jewish movie, but only by those in the know.

"They don't know the half of it" applies not only to *RBG* but also to American Jewish cinema more generally. Without in any way disparaging the holy trinity of Jewish movies cited by the Hebrew Hammer, the American Jewish cinematic tradition goes well beyond *Fiddler on the Roof*, *Yentl*, and *The Chosen*. This tradition has been shaped by antisemitism and its representation, by Shoah narratives that happened elsewhere but left an indelible mark on American Jewish consciousness, by assimilation narratives that bred discontent and assertive Jewy resistance, including by queer Jews, and by alliance narratives that show the world beyond black and white. This tradition includes fiction film as well as documentary, and its stories can be found onscreen as well as in production and reception histories. This tradition includes pawnbrokers and serious men, believers as well as those who do whatever works. It also features those who tremble before G-d, who commit crimes and misdemeanors, who declare "Hineini, here I am," who leave and then return to Delancey Street and Liberty Heights. For those who know where and how to look, this tradition has made and continues to make Jews, one moving image at a time.

Acknowledgments

Although I have always been very grateful for a room of my own in which to write, I am equally grateful to the village that helped bring *Movie-Made Jews* into being. The Jewish film area, organized by Laurie Baron, at the Film and History Conference was a welcoming scholarly venue in the early stages of this project. Formal presentations and informal conversations at annual meetings of the Association for Jewish Studies (AJS) provided much food for thought, and a wonderful dinner with Steven Carr at an AJS in Washington, DC, gave me the courage to pursue my vision for this book. And those ridiculously early AJS Women's Caucus breakfasts helped me to keep my Jewish feminist faith. I am grateful to the anonymous expert readers tapped by Rutgers University Press; they both confirmed some of my scholarly instincts and made this a better book. Elisabeth Maselli got me and this project from the outset; it has truly been a joy to work with her.

With gratitude, I acknowledge funding and time provided by Southwestern University's sabbatical fund and by the McManis University Chair that I hold. Dean Alisa Gaunder, Associate Dean Kendall Richards, and former president Ed Burger are administrators who continue to uphold the value and the values of the scholar-teacher; I will be forever grateful for their championing of academic freedom in an age of demagoguery. Laura Skandera Trombley assumed the presidency of Southwestern in the middle of a pandemic, yet she found time to express excitement about the project and to offer very kind words to a faculty member who was jubilant but also exhausted by the meeting of book deadlines. Kristen Paxson generously helped me with the images for the book. As a scholar-teacher, I have experienced great joy teaching and learning from several cohorts of Southwestern students enrolled in diverse Jewish film courses.

The library staff at Southwestern are top-notch. I especially want to thank Carol Fonken for remembering what databases were crucial to my research when pandemic budget cuts were in the offing! At Columbia University, my summer research home during nonpandemic times, Insaf M. Ali and Theodore C. White of Butler Library Media Services provided crucial assistance on numerous occasions, and my brief work at the Center for Jewish History toward the end of this project reinforced parts of my argument.

Parts of chapter 6 appeared originally in *Jewish Film and New Media*, a journal ably edited by Nathan Abrams and Nir Cohen. I am grateful to *Lilith Magazine*, the Jewish Women's Archive, and *Tablet Magazine* for giving me opportunities to write beyond the academy.

When in New York, I relish not only Jewish film culture but also Torah study at Rodeph Sholom. Rabbi Benjamin Spratt is an inspiring teacher, as is Rabbi Sari Laufer, who is now at Stephen Wise Temple in Los Angeles and a Twitter buddy. In Austin, members of my havurah—Lea Isgur, Del Garcia, Connie Haham, and Sandi Simon—keep me grounded, Jewishly and otherwise.

Whether in Austin or New York, I am blessed to make a home with Guy Raffa. More than three decades ago, we had our first fight—about how and how much movies matter. Although I never did or will apologize for viewing movies as very serious cultural business, I am very glad that we made up.

Filmography

Annie Hall (dir. Woody Allen, 1977)
Arranged (dir. Diane Crespo and Stefan C. Schaefer, 2007)
Avalon (dir. Barry Levinson, 1990)
Barton Fink (dir. Joel and Ethan Coen, 1991)
The Believer (dir. Henry Bean, 2001)
Bent (dir. Sean Mathias, 1997)
BlacKkKlansman (dir. Spike Lee, 2018)
Blacks and Jews (dir. Deborah Kaufman and Alan Snitow, 1997)
Body and Soul (dir. Robert Rossen, 1947)
The Celluloid Closet (dir. Rob Epstein and Jeffrey Friedman, 1995)
The Chosen (dir. Jeremy Kagan, 1981)
Crime after Crime (dir. Yoav Potash, 2011)
Crimes and Misdemeanors (dir. Woody Allen, 1989)
Crossfire (dir. Edward Dmytryk, 1947)
Crossing Delancey (dir. Joan Micklin Silver, 1988)
David (dir. Joel Fendelman and Patrick Daly, 2011)
Deconstructing Harry (dir. Woody Allen, 1997)
The Diary of Anne Frank (dir. George Stevens, 1959)
Enemies, A Love Story (dir. Paul Mazursky, 1989)
E.T. the Extra-Terrestrial (dir. Steven Spielberg, 1982)
Fading Gigolo (dir. John Turturro, 2013)
Fiddler on the Roof (dir. Norman Jewison, 1971)
Gentleman's Agreement (dir. Elia Kazan, 1947)
Get on the Bus (dir. Spike Lee, 1996)
The Golden Land on the Silver Screen (1987)
Heart of Stone (dir. Beth Toni Kruvant, 2009)
The Hebrew Hammer (dir. Jonathan Kesselman, 2003)
Hineini: Coming Out in a Jewish High School (dir. Irena Fayngold, 2005)
Hollywoodism: Jews, Movies, and the American Dream (dir. Simcha Jacobovici and Stuart Samuels, 1998)
I Now Pronounce You Chuck and Larry (dir. Dennis Dugan, 2007)

The Jazz Singer (dir. Alan Crosland, 1927)
The Jewish Americans (dir. David Grubin, 2008)
Judgment at Nuremberg (dir. Stanley Kramer, 1961)
Keeping Up with the Steins (dir. Scott Marshall, 2006)
Kissing Jessica Stein (dir. Charles Herman-Wurmfeld, 2001)
Liberty Heights (dir. Barry Levinson, 1999)
Maggie's Plan (dir. Rebecca Miller, 2015)
Menashe (dir. Joshua Z. Weinstein, 2017)
Milk (dir. Gus Van Sant, 2008)
The Mirror Has Two Faces (dir. Barbra Streisand, 1996)
Mo' Better Blues (dir. Spike Lee, 1990)
Next Stop, Greenwich Village (dir. Paul Mazursky, 1976)
93Queen (dir. Paula Eiselt, 2018)
The Pawnbroker (dir. Sidney Lumet, 1964)
Protocols of Zion (dir. Marc Levin, 2005)
RBG (dir. Julie Cohen and Betsy West, 2018)
Romeo and Juliet in Yiddish (dir. Eve Annenberg, 2010)
Saving Private Ryan (dir. Steven Spielberg, 1998)
Schindler's List (dir. Steven Spielberg, 1993)
School Ties (dir. Robert Mandel, 1992)
A Serious Man (dir. Ethan and Joel Coen, 2009)
Stardust Memories (dir. Woody Allen, 1980)
A Star Is Born (dir. Frank Pierson, 1976)
The Sturgeon Queens (dir. Julie Cohen, 2014)
The Times of Harvey Milk (dir. Rob Epstein, 1984)
Torch Song Trilogy (dir. Paul Bogart, 1988)
Trembling Before G-d (dir. Sandi Simcha Dubowski, 2001)
Treyf (dir. Alisa Lebow and Cynthia Madansky, 1998)
The Way We Were (dir. Sydney Pollack, 1973)
Whatever Works (dir. Woody Allen, 2009)
Wish I Was Here (dir. Zach Braff, 2014)
Yentl (dir. Barbra Streisand, 1983)
Zebrahead (dir. Anthony Drazan, 1992)

Notes

Chapter 1   Introduction

1   Laura Mulvey, "Visual Pleasure and Narrative Cinema," *Screen* 16, no. 3 (1975): 6–18.

2   Robert Sklar, *Movie-Made America: A Cultural History of American Movies*, revised and updated edition (New York: Vintage Books, 1994), x.

3   Sklar, 322.

4   Irena Fayngold, dir., *Hineini: Coming Out in a Jewish High School* (Keshet, 2005), Special Features: Stories. DVD.

5   Patricia Erens, *The Jew in American Cinema* (Bloomington: Indiana University Press, 1984), 179; Eric A. Goldman, *The American Jewish Story through Cinema* (Austin: University of Texas Press, 2013), 93.

6   Letty Cottin Pogrebin, *Deborah, Golda, and Me: Being Female and Jewish in America* (New York: Crown, 1991), 256–271.

7   Pogrebin, 257.

8   Pogrebin, 258.

9   Ilan Stavans, "I Found It at the Movies," in *Singer's Typewriter and Mine: Reflections on Jewish Culture* (Lincoln: University of Nebraska Press, 2012), 77–81.

10 Stavans, 80–81.

11 David E. Kaufman, *Jewhooing the Sixties: American Celebrity and Jewish Identity* (Waltham, MA: Brandeis University Press, 2012), 1.

12 Kaufman, 275.

13 Neal Gabler, *An Empire of Their Own: How the Jews Invented Hollywood* (New York: Anchor, 1988).

14 Deborah Kaufman, "American, Jewish, and Independent," in *Independent Jewish Film: A Resource Guide*, ed. Janis Plotkin et al., 4th ed. (San Francisco: San Francisco Jewish Film Festival, 2000), 17.

15 See Michael Rogin, *Blackface, White Noise: Jewish Immigrants in the Hollywood Melting Pot* (Berkeley: University of California Press, 1996), 73–120.

16 Henry Bial, *Acting Jewish: Negotiating Ethnicity on the American Stage and Screen* (Ann Arbor: University of Michigan Press, 2005).

17 See Thomas Doherty, *Hollywood and Hitler, 1933–39* (New York: Columbia University Press, 2013); Ben Urwand, *The Collaboration: Hollywood's Pact with Hitler* (Cambridge, MA: Harvard University Press, 2013); and Laura B. Rosenzweig, *Hollywood Spies: The Undercover Surveillance of Nazis in Los Angeles* (New York: New York University Press, 2017).

18 See Bial, *Acting Jewish*, esp. chap. 4, "How Jews Became Sexy, 1968–1983," 86–106; Nathan Abrams, *The New Jew in Film: Exploring Jewishness and Judaism in Contemporary Cinema* (New Brunswick, NJ: Rutgers University Press, 2012). In *The American Jewish Story through Cinema* , Eric Goldman also subscribes to this progressive normalizing narrative: "Over the last two decades, American Jewish screenwriters, directors, and producers have become increasingly comfortable with their heritage. As a result, we are seeing an unprecedented number of movies that spotlight Jewish protagonists, experiences, and challenges" (xi).

19 Abrams, *The New Jew in Film*, 12–13.

20 Vincent Brook, "Introduction: Seeing Isn't Believing," and Daniel Itzkovitz, "They All Are Jews," both in *You Should See Yourself: Jewish Identity in Postmodern American Culture*, ed. Vincent Brook (New Brunswick, NJ: Rutgers University Press, 2006), 1, 235.

21 Sarah Kozloff, "Empathy and the Cinema of Engagement: Reevaluating the Politics of Film," *Projections* 7, no. 2 (2013): 9.

22 Alan H. Feiler, "Directions Home: In His Newest Film, Barry Levinson Reaches the 'Heights' of His Baltimore Youth," *Baltimore Jewish Times*, 29 October 1999, Ethnic NewsWatch.

23 Warren Rosenberg, "Coming Out of the Ethnic Closet: Jewishness in the Films of Barry Levinson," *Shofar* 22, no. 1 (2003):38, 43, Ethnic NewsWatch.

24 Dylan Farrow, "An Open Letter from Dylan Farrow," *New York Times*, 1 February 2014, https://kristof.blogs.nytimes.com/2014/02/01/an-open-letter-from-dylan-farrow/.

25 Ezra Glinter, "I Can't Avoid Woody's Abuse Saga. Neither Can You," *Forward*, 14 February 2014, Ethnic NewsWatch.

26 Michael Elkin, "'Kiss' of Success: One Day She's a Lesbian, the Next She's Not—Is This the Jessica Stein Way?," *Jewish Exponent*, 21 March 2002, Ethnic NewsWatch.

27 Emily Nussbaum, *I Like to Watch: Arguing My Way through the TV Revolution* (New York: Random House, 2019), 110, 112.

28 Michael Renov, "Introduction: The Truth about Non-fiction," in *Theorizing Documentary*, ed. Michael Renov (New York: Routledge, 1993), 2–3.

29 Elkin, "'Kiss' of Success."

30 Karen Schoemer, "A Director Crosses the Line into a Reality of . . . More Lines," *New York Times*, 25 October 1992, https://www.nytimes.com/1992/10/25/movies/film-a-director-crosses-the-line-into-a-reality-of-more-lines.html.

31 Sam Wasson, *Paul on Mazursky* (Middletown, CT: Wesleyan University Press, 2011), 253.

32 Miriam Moster, "So, What's the Yiddish Word for Pimp? Hassids Help Hollywood Get It Right," *Jewish News Weekly of Northern California*, 22 August 2014, Ethnic NewsWatch.

33 "Introduction," in Plotkin, *Independent Jewish Film*, 6. In a 1999 Pilot Study of Jewish Film Festivals, prepared for the National Foundation for Jewish Culture, the San Francisco Jewish Film Festival was identified as "the model for all the rest."

34 "Film Festival Notes, Feb. 99," AJHS, I-527, Box 249, Folder 6, National Foundation for Jewish Culture Records, Center for Jewish History, New York.

35 Printed email about 2004 Conference of Film Festivals, 6 July 2004, AJHS, I-527, Box 249, Folder 8, National Foundation for Jewish Culture Records, Center for Jewish History, New York.

36 Larry Mark, "Mavericks and a Jewish Grand Dragon Reign Supreme at Annual Film Stampede: Is It Just Us, or Does the Sundance Logo Seem to Sport a Small Star of David This Year?," *Forward*, 9 February 2001, Ethnic NewsWatch.

37 Alan Spiegel, "The Vanishing Act: A Typology of the Jew in the Contemporary American Film," in *From Hester Street to Hollywood: The Jewish-American Stage and Screen*, ed. Sarah Blacher Cohen (Bloomington: Indiana University Press, 1983), 257–275.

38 Sanford Pinsker, "Mel Brooks and the Cinema of Exhaustion," in Cohen, *From Hester Street to Hollywood*, 245–256.

39 Sarah Blacher Cohen, "Yiddish Origins and Jewish-American Transformations," in Cohen, *From Hester Street to Hollywood*, 15–16.

40 Lester D. Friedman, *Hollywood's Image of the Jew* (New York: Frederick Ungar, 1982), 311; Erens, *The Jew in American Cinema*, 392 (my emphasis); David Desser and Lester D. Friedman, *American Jewish Filmmakers*, 2nd ed. (Urbana: University of Illinois Press, 2004), 320.

41 bell hooks, "The Oppositional Gaze: Black Female Spectators," in *Reel to Real: Race, Sex, and Class at the Movies* (New York: Routledge, 1996), 199.

42 As a reminder that what we look at impacts how we see Jews and American Jewish film history, Vincent Brook, focusing on Adam Sandler and Ben Stiller, views Jewish uncertainty rather than Jewish pluralism as a key trend: "More confident about being Jewish, but less sure about what being Jewish means, is the qualitatively new dilemma facing the assimilated multicultural Jew." Vincent Brook, "Boy-Man Schlemiels and Super-Nebishes," in *Hollywood's Chosen People: The Jewish Experience in American Cinema*, ed. Daniel Bernardi, Murray Pomerance, and Hava Tirosh-Samuelson (Detroit: Wayne State University Press, 2013), 174.

43 Judy Wilson, "*Protocols* Redux; Native New Jersey Filmmaker Explores Virulent Persistence of Historic Forgery," *Jewish News*, 3 November 2005, Ethnic NewsWatch.

Chapter 2   Looking at Antisemites and Jews

1 Steven Carr, *Hollywood and Anti-Semitism: A Cultural History up to World War II* (Cambridge: Cambridge University Press, 2001), 9.

2 Quoted in J. Hoberman and Jeffrey Shandler, "Hollywood's Jewish Question," in *Entertaining America: Jews, Movies, and Broadcasting*, J. Hoberman and Jeffrey Shandler (Princeton: Princeton University Press, 2003), 51–52.

3 Dennis Klein, "The Movies: Notes on the Ethnic Origins of an American Obsession," in *Jews and American Popular Culture*, vol. 1, *Movies, Radio and Television*, ed. Paul Buhle (Westport, CT: Praeger, 2007), 9.

4 Dan M. Bronstein, "Making a Scene: Jews, Stooges, and Censors in Pre-war Hollywood," in Buhle, *Jews and American Popular Culture*, 75.

5 Leonard Dinnerstein, *Anti-Semitism in America* (New York: Oxford University Press, 1994), 128–149.

6 See Joseph Litvak, *The Un-Americans: Jews, the Blacklist, and Stoolpigeon Culture* (Durham, NC: Duke University Press, 2009).

7 Vincent Brook, "Still an Empire of Their Own: How Jews Remain Atop a Reinvented Hollywood," in *From Shtetl to Stardom: Jews and Hollywood*, ed. Michael Renov and Vincent Brook (West Lafayette, IN: Purdue University Press, 2017), 13, 16.

8 Josh Grossberg, "Seth MacFarlane's Jews-Run-Hollywood Joke Draws Fire from Jewish Groups," *E-News*, 25 February 2013, https://www.eonline.com/news/391872/seth-macfarlane-s-jews-run-hollywood-joke-draws-fire-from-jewish-groups.

9 Sarah Kozloff, "Empathy and the Cinema of Engagement: Reevaluating the Politics of Film," *Projections* 7, no. 2 (2013): 2.

10 Laura Z. Hobson, *Laura Z: A Life* (New York: Arbor House, 1983), 56–58, 322.

11 David Desser and Lester D. Friedman, *American Jewish Filmmakers*, 2nd ed. (Urbana: University of Illinois Press, 2004), 1.

12 Patricia Erens, *The Jew in American Cinema* (Bloomington: Indiana University Press, 1984), 178.

13 Quoted in Lawrence Baron, "Picturing Prejudice in Hollywood's First Films about Anti-Semitism," in *American Judaism in Popular Culture*, ed. Leonard J. Greenspoon and Ronald A. Simkins (Omaha: Creighton University Press, 2006), 29. On the other hand, Litvak, in *The Un-Americans*, reads such distinctions as a lack of appropriate connections: "The film . . . fails to make the obvious connection between anti-Semitism 'over in Europe' and anti-Semitism over here" (101).

14 Erens, *The Jew in American Cinema*, 179; Eric A. Goldman. *The American Jewish Story through Cinema* (Austin: University of Texas Press, 2013), 93.

15 For complementary readings of *Gentleman's Agreement*, see Erens, *The Jew in American Cinema*, 177, and Henry Bial, *Acting Jewish: Negotiating Ethnicity on the American Stage and Screen* (Ann Arbor: University of Michigan Press, 2005), 36–37.

16 Bernard Weinraub, "The Talk of Hollywood; Anti-Semitism Film Strikes a Chord with Its Producers," *New York Times*, 14 September 1992, https://www.nytimes.com/1992/09/14/movies/the-talk-of-hollywood-anti-semitism-film-strikes-a-chord-with-its-producers.html.

17 Omer Bartov, *The "Jew" in Cinema: From "The Golem" to "Don't Touch My Holocaust"* (Bloomington: Indiana University Press, 2005), 40.

18 Daniel Schifrin, "Identity Crisis: With the New Film 'School Ties,' a Hollywood Producer-Director Team Explores Anti-Semitism and the Need to Fit In," *Baltimore Jewish Times*, 18 September 1992, Ethnic NewsWatch.

19 Kenneth Chanko, "Good Roles Hunting," *Entertainment Weekly*, 23 January 1998, Academic Search Complete.

20 Weinraub, "The Talk of Hollywood."

21 Weinraub.

22 Michael Elkin, "'School Ties': Hate Unraveled," *Jewish Exponent* 18 September 1992, Ethnic NewsWatch.

23 Benjamin Weiser, "Pine Bush School District Settles Anti-Semitism Suit for $4.48 Million," *New York Times*, 29 June 2015, https://www.nytimes.com/2015/06/30/nyregion/pine-bush-school-district-anti-semitism-suit.html.

24 Benjamin Weiser and Nate Schweber, "Swastika on a Bathroom Wall: Anti-Semitism Still Plagues Upstate School District," *New York Times*, 1 March 2019, https://www.nytimes.com/2019/03/01/nyregion/pine-bush-ny-schools-anti-semitism.html.

25 Liz Sawyer, "Minnetonka Schools, Jewish Community Denounce Photo of Nazi Salute, Sign," *Star Tribune*, 18 January 2019, http://www.startribune.com /minnetonka-schools-jewish-community-denounce-nazi-salute-photo/504523832/; Jennifer Amatulli, "Tennessee School Stops Teaching Kids to Do Nazi Salute after Student Pushes Back," *HuffPost*, 14 May 2019, https://www.huffpost.com /entry/tennessee-nazi-salute-elementary-school_n_5cdb0889e4b061f59bf88edf; Marcy Oster, "Jewish Student Union Sign Vandalized with Swastika in Boston-Area High School," *Jewish Telegraphic Agency*, 19 May 2019, https://www.jta.org /quick-reads/jewish-student-union-sign-vandalized-with-swastika-at-boston-area -high-school; Marcy Oster, "Nazi Posters Hung at School Whose Students Played Swastika Beer Game," *Jewish Telegraphic Agency*, 12 March 2019, https://www.jta .org/quick-reads/nazi-posters-hung-at-school-whose-students-played-swastika -beer-game.

26 Interview with Henry Bean, *The Believer* (Palm Pictures, 2003), DVD.

27 Henry Bean, "Introduction," in *The Believer: Confronting Jewish Self-Hatred* (New York: Thunder's Mouth Press, 2002), 17–18.

28 Leslie Camhi, "In a Skinhead's Tale, a Picture of Both Hate and Love," *New York Times*, 17 March 2002, https://www.nytimes.com/2002/03/17/arts/television -radio-in-a- skinhead-s-tale-a-picture-of-both-hate-and-love.html.

29 Ami Eden, "*Believer* Director Refuses to Lose Faith in His Movie," *Forward*, 5 October 2001, Ethnic NewsWatch.

30 Harriette Yahr, "A Jewish Nazi?," *Tikkun*, July/Aug 2002, Ethnic NewsWatch.

31 Jean Oppenheimer, "Identity Crisis," *American Cinematographer*, 24–28 March 2002, 24, 26, 28.

32 Sander Gilman views *The Believer* as an outgrowth of a Holocaust-based identity for Jewish Americans. Although I agree that this is an important part of what makes Balint and his bomb tick (pun intended), I think that locating Balint's identity crisis in history gives short shrift to the theological questions and obsessions also foundational to this narrative. See Sander Gilman, "*The Believer* II," in Bean, *The Believer: Confronting Jewish Self Hatred*, 238–242.

33 Camhi, "In a Skinhead's Tale"; see also Bean, "Introduction," 17–18.

34 Eden, "*Believer* Director Refuses to Lose Faith."

35 Yahr, "A Jewish Nazi?"

36 Larry Mark, "Mavericks and a Jewish Grand Dragon Reign Supreme at Annual Film Stampede: Is It Just Us, or Does the Sundance Logo Seem to Sport a Small Star of David This Year?," *Forward*, 9 February 2001, Ethnic NewsWatch.

37 Yahr, "A Jewish Nazi?"

38 Daniel Steinhart, "The Believer," *Film Journal International*, April 2002, MasterFILE Complete; Beth Pinsker expresses a similar sentiment in "The Believer in the Cultural Marketplace," an essay adapted from *The Independent* that appears in Bean, *The Believer: Confronting Jewish Self-Hatred*.

39 J. Hoberman, "Blind Faith," *Village Voice*, 21 May 2002, 123; Sanford Pinsker, "Showtime Finally Airs Controversial Film," *Jewish News*, 14 March 2002, Ethnic NewsWatch; Kirk Honeycutt, "Bean Film a 'Believer' in Contradiction," *Hollywood Reporter—International Edition*, 23 January 2001, MasterFILE Complete.

40 Michael Elkin, "Sundancer: Elkins Park Native Wins Top Festival Prize with Controversial New Film about Jewish Neo-Nazi," *Jewish Exponent*, 22 February 2001, Ethnic NewsWatch.

41 Yahr, "A Jewish Nazi?"

42 Camhi, "In a Skinhead's Tale."

43 Camhi.

44 For a brief discussion of Gosling as a non-Jew performing Jewishness, see Murray Pomerance, "Who Was Buddy Love? Screen Performance and Jewish Experience," in *Hollywood's Chosen People: The Jewish Experience in American Cinema*, ed. Daniel Bernardi, Murray Pomerance, and Hava Tirosh-Samuelson (Detroit: Wayne State University Press, 2013), 202.

45 Jason Nielsen, "Self-Hating Jews and 'The Believer': Henry Bean Looks Through the Eyes of a Jewish Neo-Nazi," *Jewish Advocate*, 20 June 2002, Ethnic NewsWatch.

46 Mike Davies, "Face to Face with the Softer Side of a Monster," *Birmingham Post*, 7 December 2001, Nexis Uni.

47 Philippa Hawker, "Paradox of the Anti-Semitic Jew," *The Age*, 8 November 2001, Nexis Uni.

48 Michael Fox, "Jewish Neo-Nazi Film Offers Ample Heat but Little Light," *Jewish Bulletin of Northern California*, 8 March 2002, Ethnic NewsWatch.

49 Bean, "Introduction," 21.

50 Bean, 22.

51 Davies, "Face to Face with the Softer Side of a Monster" (my emphasis).

52 John Anderson, "Protocols of Zion," *Variety*, 25 January 2005, Performing Arts Periodicals.

53 Aaron Dobbs, "Marc Levin, Director Protocols of Zion," *Gothamist*, 19 October 2005, https://gothamist.com/arts-entertainment/marc-levin-director -iprotocols-of-zioni.

54 Michael Elkin, "Marc Levin Uses an Anti-Semitic Screed as a Jumping-Off Point to Examine Hatred," *Jewish Exponent*, 17 November 2005, Ethnic NewsWatch.

55 Dobbs, "Marc Levin."

56 Dobbs.

57 Dobbs.

58 Elkin, "Marc Levin Uses an Anti-Semitic Screed."

59 Lloyd Grove and Morgan Hudson, "*Zion* Guest List May Be Inviting Trouble," *New York Daily News*, 27 September 2005, https://www.nydailynews.com /archives/gossip/zion-guest-list-inviting-trouble-article-1.639939.

60 Anthony Kaufman, "Doc Week in NYC: *Birch Street, Inside the Bubble, Protocols of Zion*," *Indie Wire*, 3 October 2005, https://www.indiewire.com/2005/10/doc -week-in-nyc-birch-street-inside-the-bubble-protocols-of-zion-135161/; Saul Austerlitz, "Conspirators Convene," *Forward*, 7 October 2005, Ethnic NewsWatch.

61 Marc Levin, website, Blog 3: "Words Matter," 14 October 2005, https://thinkfilm .blogs.com/protocols_of_zion/2005/10/blog_3_words_ma.html.

62 Tom White, "Lyin' 'bout Zion: Marc Levin's *Protocols* Debunks Anti-Semitic Tract," *Documentary*, 30 November 2005, https://www.documentary.org/feature /lyin-bout-zion-marc-levins-protocols-debunks-anti-semitic-tract.

63 Marc Levin, "Director's Defense: 'Cause It's Good for the Jews," *Jewish News Weekly of Northern California*, 4 November 2005, Ethnic NewsWatch.

64 Kevin Crust, "Talking a Way Out of Anti-Semitism," *LA Times*, 21 October 2005, https://www.latimes.com/archives/la-xpm-2005-oct-21-et-protocol21-story.html.

65 Elkin, "Marc Levin Uses an Anti-Semitic Screed."

66 Judy Wilson, "*Protocols* Redux," *Jewish News*, 3 November 2005, Ethnic NewsWatch.

67 Ty Burr, "*Protocols* Puts Spotlight on Hate, but Lacks Focus," *Boston Globe*, 18 November 2005, http://archive.boston.com/ae/movies/articles/2005/11/18 /protocols_puts_spotlight_on_hate_but_lacks_focus/; Ed Gonzalez and Nick Schager, "Review: *Protocols of Zion*," *Slant*, 23 June 2006, https://www.slantmagazine .com/dvd/protocols-of-zion/.

68 Neal Schindler, "*Protocols of Zion*," *Seattle Weekly News*, 9 October 2006, https://www.seattleweekly.com/film/protocols-of-zion/; Steve Erickson, "Anti-Semitism Gets Tabloid Treatment," *Gay City News*, 20–26 October 2005, https://gaycitynews.nyc/stories/2005/22/antisemitism-gets-2005-10-26.html.

69 Wilson, "*Protocols* Redux."

Chapter 3   Looking at the Shoah from a Distance

1 Joseph McBride, *Steven Spielberg: A Biography*, 2nd ed. (London: Faber and Faber, 2011), 20, e-book.

2 McBride, 50–51.

3 McBride, 538.

4 McBride, 574.

5 McBride, 560.

6 For a critique of this scene as "pornographic," see Sara Horowitz, "But Is It Good for the Jews? Spielberg's Schindler and the Aesthetics of Atrocity," in *Spielberg's Holocaust: Critical Perspectives on "Schindler's List,"* ed. Yosefa Loshitzky (Bloomington: Indiana University Press, 2000), 128.

7 McBride, 540.

8 McBride.

9 Lawrence Baron, *Projecting the Holocaust into the Present* (Lanham, MD: Rowman and Littlefield, 2005), 35.

10 Alan Mintz, *Popular Culture and the Shaping of Holocaust Memory in America* (Seattle: University of Washington Press, 2001), 103.

11 Judith E. Doneson, *The Holocaust in American Film*, 2nd ed. (Syracuse, NY: Syracuse University Press, 2002), 70–76.

12 Mintz, *Popular Culture and the Shaping of Holocaust Memory*, 167.

13 Gary Weissman, *Fantasies of Witnessing: Postwar Efforts to Experience the Holocaust* (Ithaca, NY: Cornell University Press, 2004).

14 Ralph Rosenblum and Robert Karen, *When the Shooting Stops . . . The Cutting Begins: A Film Editor's Story* (New York: Da Capo Press, 1979), 149.

15 "Keep Them on the Hook," in *Sidney Lumet: Interview*, ed. Joanna E. Rapf (Jackson: University Press of Mississippi, 2006), 16.

16 "Keep Them on the Hook," 12.

17 See, for example, Ilan Avisa, *Screening the Holocaust: Cinema's Images of the Unimaginable* (Bloomington: Indiana University Press, 1988), esp. 125–131.

18 Maggie Astor, "Holocaust Is Fading from Memory, Survey Finds," *New York Times*, 12 April 2018, https://www.nytimes.com/2018/04/12/us/holocaust -education.html?searchResultPosition=1.

19 Frank R. Cunningham, *Sidney Lumet: Film and Literary Vision* (Lexington: University Press of Kentucky, 1991), 173.

20 In "Teach Me Gold: Pedagogy and Memory in *The Pawnbroker*" (*Prooftexts* 22, no. 1–2 [2002]), Alan Rosen notes that "there was . . . pressure in the early stages of

production for the film to end by consummating, in a fashion, the romance between social worker Birchfield and pawnbroker Nazerman, perhaps, as one of the production consultants put it, by having them 'touch hands in some manner.' But the film determinedly dismisses this option" (98).

21 Cunningham, *Sidney Lumet*, 16.

22 "Interview with Sidney Lumet," in Rapf, *Sidney Lumet: Interviews*, 184.

23 Sam Wasson, *Paul on Mazursky* (Middletown, CT: Wesleyan University Press, 2011), 254, e-book.

24 See, for example, David Desser and Lester D. Friedman, *American Jewish Filmmakers*, 2nd ed. (Urbana: University of Illinois Press, 2004), 280.

25 In "Jewish Experience on Film—An American Overview" (*American Jewish Yearbook*, vol. 96, 1996, http://www.ajcarchives.org/AJC_DATA/Files/1996_3 _SpecialArticles.pdf), Joel Rosenberg notes that the setting is "a Jewish New York that appeared, as if out of nowhere, in the late 40's, unique by its complicated blend of newly arrived refugees and long-settled homeborn" (36).

26 David E. Kaufman, *Jewhooing the Sixties: American Celebrity and Jewish Identity* (Waltham, MA: Brandeis University Press, 2012).

27 Omer Bartov, *The "Jew" in Cinema: From "The Golem" to "Don't Touch My Holocaust"* (Bloomington: Indiana University Press, 2005), 100.

28 Wasson, *Paul on Mazursky*, 253–254.

29 William Grimes, "Rita Karin, Actress and a Film Narrator for U.S., Dies at 73," *New York Times*, 14 September 1993, https://www.nytimes.com/1993/09/14 /obituaries/rita-karin-actress-and-a-film-narrator-for-us-dies-at-73.html.

30 Wasson, *Paul on Mazursky*, 248.

31 Wasson, 254. For a discussion of film noir and its Holocaust-related roots, see Vincent Brook, *Driven to Darkness: Jewish Émigré Directors and the Rise of Film Noir* (New Brunswick: Rutgers University Press, 2009).

32 Wasson, 247.

33 Michael Fox, "Film Is History Lesson on Shoah," *Washington Jewish Week*, 2 December 2004, Ethnic NewsWatch; Kenneth Turan, "Ten Great Jewish American Films," *Moment*, May/June 2010, Ethnic NewsWatch.

34 Ilan Stavans, "I Found It at the Movies," in *Singer's Typewriter and Mine: Reflections on Jewish Culture* (Lincoln: University of Nebraska Press, 2012), 80–81.

35 Desser and Friedman, *American Jewish Filmmakers*, 37. Allen's romantic involvement with Soon-Yi Previn, Mia Farrow's stepdaughter and now his wife, certainly multiplied the numbers who fall into the anti-Woody camp; Dylan Farrow's sexual assault allegations against her stepfather have exponentially increased disdain for him and his work.

36 See Henry Bial, *Acting Jewish: Negotiating Ethnicity on the American Stage and Screen* (Ann Arbor: University of Michigan Press, 2005), 86–106. Gornick is quoted in Lawrence J. Epstein's *The Haunted Smile: The Story of Jewish Comedians in America* (New York: Public Affairs, 2008), 190.

37 Woody Allen, "Random Reflections of a Second-Rate Mind," *Tikkun*, January–February 1990, Ethnic NewsWatch.

38 This idea of a movie as a secular form of Torah study is in keeping with Desser and Friedman's view that, for Allen, film functions as a secular substitute for Judaism. See Desser and Friedman, *American Jewish Filmmakers*, 34–112.

39 Naomi Pfefferman, "'The Majestic' Martin Landau: Veteran Actor Continues to Find His Place in Hollywood," *Jewish Advocate* 3 January 2002, Ethnic NewsWatch.

40 See Leon Weiseltier, "Browbeaten," *New Republic*, 27 November 1989, 43; Carol Iannone, "The Devil and Woody Allen," *Commentary*, June 2000, https://www .commentarymagazine.com/articles/the-devil-and-woody-allen/; and Mary P. Nichols, *Reconstructing Woody: Art, Love, and Life in the Films of Woody Allen* (Lanham, MD: Rowman & Littlefield, 1998), 154.

41 Hal Hinson, "Bloodlines," in *The Coen Brothers: Interviews*, ed. William Rodney Allen (Jackson: University Press of Mississippi, 2006), 15.

42 Quoted in Allen, "Introduction," in Allen, *The Coen Brothers: Interviews*, xii.

43 See Emanuel Levy, *Cinema of Outsiders: The Rise of American Independent Film* (New York: New York University Press, 1999), esp. "The Stylists—The Coen Brothers," 262; R. Barton Palmer, *Joel and Ethan Coen* (Urbana: University of Illinois Press, 2004), esp. 45, 50.

44 Jim Emerson, "That Barton Fink Feeling: An Interview with the Brothers Coen," in Allen, *The Coen Brothers: Interviews*, 59.

45 Palmer, *Joel and Ethan Coen*, 114.

46 Michel Ciment and Hubert Niogret, "A Rock on the Beach," in Allen, *The Coen Brothers: Interviews*, 46.

47 See Brook, *Driven to Darkness*.

48 See Thomas Doherty, *Hollywood and Hitler, 1933–1939*, (New York: Columbia University Press, 2013); Ben Urwand, *The Collaboration: Hollywood's Pact with Hitler* (Cambridge, MA: Harvard University Press, 2013). For critical discussion of these texts and the historical narratives they promote, see Lawrence Baron, Joel Rosenberg, and Vincent Brook, "The Ben Urwand Controversy: Exploring the Hollywood-Hitler Relationship," in *From Shtetl to Stardom: Jews and Hollywood*, ed. Michael Renov and Vincent Brook (West Lafayette, IN: Purdue University Press, 2017), 23–46.

49 Otto Friedrich, *City of Nets: A Portrait of Hollywood in the 1940's* (New York: Harper and Row, 1986), 154.

50 Alexander Stille, "Turning Primo Levi's Journey Home into a Picaresque Post-Holocaust Tale," *Forward*, 7 November, 1997, Ethnic NewsWatch.

51 "Becoming Serious," special feature. *A Serious Man*, Director: Joel and Ethan Coen, 2009, DVD.

52 Riv-Ellen Prell, "A Serious Man in Situ: 'Fear and Loathing in St. Louis Park,'" *AJS Review* 35, no. 2 (2011), Ethnic NewsWatch.

53 See, for example, Yehuda Reinharz, "Where Can We Find Funders to Brighten Future of Education?," *Jewish Exponent*, 19 November 2009, Ethic NewsWatch.

54 For a considerably more positive reading of Rabbi Marshak as an "artistically and scientifically inclined rabbi [who] seems willing to meet all Jews where they are," in the mold of "such rabbis as Shlomo Carlebach and Zalman Schachter Shalomi," see Wendy Zierler's *Movies and Midrash: Popular Film and Jewish Religious Conversation* (Albany: SUNY Press, 2017), 184–186.

55 Naomi Pfefferman, "The Brothers Grim," *Jewish News Weekly of Northern California*, 2 October 2009, Ethnic NewsWatch.

56 "Becoming Serious."

57 Stephen Whitfield, "A Funny Thing," *Jewish News of Greater Phoenix*, 28 September 2012, Ethnic NewsWatch.

58 Prell, "A Serious Man in Situ."

Chapter 4 Focusing on Assimilation and Its Discontents

1 Joel Rosenberg, "Jewish Experience on Film—An American Overview," *American Jewish Yearbook* 96 (1996): 3–5; Henry Bial, *Acting Jewish: Negotiating Ethnicity on the American Stage and Screen* (Ann Arbor: University of Michigan Press, 2005); Nathan Abrams, *The New Jew in Film: Exploring Jewishness and Judaism in Contemporary Cinema* (New Brunswick, NJ: Rutgers University Press, 2012). In his overview, Rosenberg uses "assimilation and its discontents" to describe the period from 1928 to 1942.

2 Neal Gabler, *An Empire of Their Own: How the Jews Invented Hollywood* (New York: Anchor, 1988).

3 J. Hoberman and Jeffrey Shandler, "Hollywood's Jewish Question," in *Entertaining America: Jews, Movies, and Broadcasting* (Princeton, NJ: Princeton University Press, 2003), 74.

4 Rosenberg, "Jewish Experience on Film," 39, 30.

5 Abrams, *The New Jew in Film*, 13, 8.

6 For a good discussion of these sketches, see David E. Kaufman, *Jewhooing the Sixties: American Celebrity and Jewish Identity* (Waltham, MA: Brandeis University Press, 2012), 256–259.

7 Letty Cottin Pogrebin, *Deborah, Golda, and Me: Being Female and Jewish in America* (New York: Crown, 1991), 260; Felicia Herman, "The Way She *Really* Is: Images of Jews and Women in the Films of Barbra Streisand," in *Talking Back: Images of Jewish Women in American Popular Culture*, ed. Joyce Antler (Hanover, NH: Brandeis University Press, 1998), 172.

8 Bial, *Acting Jewish*, 86–106; Kaufman, *Jewhooing the Sixties*, 27.

9 Vivian Sobchack, "Assimilating Streisand: When Too Much Is Not Enough," in *Hollywood's Chosen People: The Jewish Experience in American Cinema*, ed. Daniel Bernardi, Murray Pomerance, and Hava Tirosh-Samuelson (Detroit: Wayne State University Press, 2013), 211.

10 See Sobchack, 216–217; Kaufman, *Jewhooing the Sixties*, 253–254.

11 *Golden Land on the Silver Screen* (Ergo Media, 1987), VHS.

12 Arthur Laurents, *Original Story by Arthur Laurents: A Memoir of Broadway and Hollywood* (New York: Alfred A. Knopf, 2000), 263.

13 Quoted in Michael Feeney Callan, *Robert Redford: The Biography* (New York: Alfred A. Knopf, 2011), 191.

14 See Laurents, *Original Story*; Claus Tieber, "The Way He Wrote: Dalton Trumbo and Sixteen Unused Pages for *The Way We Were*," *Film International* 8, no. 4 (2010): 51–64.

15 Callan, *Robert Redford*, 191.

16 Laurents, *Original Story*, 296.

17 Laurents, 272.

18 Laurents, 275.

19 Pauline Kael, "Three" (15 October 1973), in Pauline Kael, *Reeling* (Boston: Little, Brown, 1976), 177.

20 Herman, "The Way She *Really* Is," 173, 179.

21 Jeanne Lynn Hall, "Opposites Attract: Politics and Romance in *The Way We Were* and *Speechless*," *Quarterly Review of Film and Video* 23, no. 2 (2006): 159.

22 Laurents, *Original Story*, 257. In *The Jew in America Cinema* (Bloomington: Indiana University Press, 1984), Patricia Erens declares that Katie is "the most

dignified and positive Jewish heroine (apart from the two Streisand imperson-
ations of Fanny Brice) of the decade" (323).

23 Laurents, *Original Story*, 7.

24 "Ex and the City," Season 2, Episode 18, of *Sex and the City* (1999).

25 Laurents, *Original Story*, 5.

26 Stanley Kauffmann, *Before My Eyes: Film Criticism and Comment* (New York:
Harper & Row, 1980), 196–197.

27 Gene Siskel, "Nostalgia Gets a New Life," *Chicago Tribune*, 16 April 1976,
ProQuest Historical Newspapers.

28 Pauline Kael, "The Artist as a Young Comedian," *New Yorker*, 9 February 1976, in
The Age of Movies: Selected Writings of Pauline Kael, ed. Sanford Schwartz (New
York: Library of America, 2011), 521.

29 Sam Wasson, *Paul on Mazursky* (Middletown, CT: Wesleyan University Press,
2011), 110.

30 David Desser and Lester D. Friedman, *American Jewish Filmmakers*, 2nd ed.
(Urbana: University of Illinois Press, 2004), 272.

31 Abigail Pogrebin, *Stars of David: Prominent Jews Talk about Being Jewish* (New
York: Broadway Books, 2005), 361–362.

32 Wasson, *Paul on Mazursky*, 158.

33 Wasson, 118.

34 Elvis Mitchell, "Critic's Notebook: Doing Justice to Mazursky, Long Bypassed,"
New York Times, 30 August 2001, https://www.nytimes.com/2001/08/30/movies
/critic-s-notebook-doing-justice-to-mazursky-long-bypassed.html; Wasson, *Paul
on Mazursky*, 17.

35 Quoted in Wasson, *Paul on Mazursky*, 21, 19.

36 John Podhoretz, "Mazursky's Time," *Weekly Standard*, 29 August 2011, https://
www.washingtonexaminer.com/weekly-standard/mazurskys-time.

37 Quoted in Ally Acker, *Reel Women: Pioneers of the Cinema: The First Hundred
Years*, vol. 2, *1960's–2010* (New York: Reel Women Media, 2011), 12.

38 Leo Adam Biga, "Joan Micklin Silver's Classic *Hester Street* Included in National
Film Registry," *Jewish Press*, 24 February 2012, Ethnic NewsWatch.

39 Acker, *Reel Women*, 12.

40 "Dialogue on Film: Joan Micklin Silver," interview, *American Film*, May 1989, 24.

41 Alvin Klein, "The Arts: Crossing Obstacles for *Delancey*," *New York Times*, 2
October 1988, https://www.nytimes.com/1988/10/02/nyregion/the-arts-crossing
-obstacles-for-delancey.html.

42 Emanuel Levy, *Cinema of Outsiders: The Rise of American Independent Film* (New
York: New York University Press, 1999), 410.

43 My reading of *Crossing Delancey* here is in keeping with Shonni Enelow's
observation in "Stronger Together" (*Film Comment*, September/October 2017)
that Micklin Silver has an "abiding interest in narratives of female self-
determination that don't require their subjects to reject all traditional values" (54).

44 David I. Grossvogel, "Jewish New York in *Crossing Delancey*," in *The Modern
Jewish Experience in World Cinema*, ed. Lawrence Baron (Waltham, MA:
Brandeis University Press, 2011), 387.

45 Richard Shepard, "Film: At 74, a (Movie) Star Is Born," *New York Times*, 21
August 1988, https://www.nytimes.com/1988/08/21/movies/film-at-74-a-movie
-star-is-born.html?searchResultPosition=3.

46 Shepard.

47 Lawrence Van Gelder, "At the Movies," *New York Times*, 19 August 1988, https://www.nytimes.com/1988/08/19/movies/at-the-movies.html?search ResultPosition=2.

48 Leo Biga, "Shattering Cinema's Glass Ceiling," *Jewish Press*, 14 April 2000, Ethnic NewsWatch; Enelow, "Stronger Together"; Maya Montañez Smukler, *Liberating Hollywood: Women Directors and the Feminist Reform of 1970s American Cinema* (New Brunswick, NJ: Rutgers University Press, 2019).

49 Susan Faludi, *Backlash: The Undeclared War against American Women* (New York: Crown, 1991), 128.

50 Caryn James, "Film View: Are Feminist Heroines an Endangered Species?," *New York Times,* 16 July 1989, https://www.nytimes.com/1989/07/16/movies/film-view -are-feminist-heroines-an-endangered-species.html; Micklin Silver refutes the marriage plot reading in Graham Fuller's "Interview/East Side Stories: Graham Fuller Meets Joan Micklin Silver, the Director of *Crossing Delancey,* in New York," *Independent*, 7 April 1989, Nexis Uni.

51 Caryn James, "Film View: Are Feminist Heroines an Endangered Species?"

52 Elayne Rapping, "Liberation in Chains: 'The Woman Question' in Hollywood," *Cinéaste* 17, no. 1 (1989), JStor.

53 "Opening Shots: Janeane Garofalo's Guilty Pleasures," *Film Comment*, 1 March 2003, Performing Arts Periodicals.

54 Barry Levinson, "Baltimore, My Baltimore," *New York Times*, 14 November 1999, https://archive.nytimes.com/www.nytimes.com/library/film/111499levinson-film .html.

55 Bernard Weintraub, "The Man Who Gathers the Means for Barry Levinson's Movies," *New York Times*, 18 December 1991, https://www.nytimes.com/1991/12 /18/movies/the-man-who-gathers-the-means-for-barry-levinson-s-movies.html ?searchResultPosition=1.

56 "Barry Levinson: The Journey," interview by Patrick McGilligan, in *Backstory 5: Interviews with Screenwriters of the 1990s*, ed. Patrick McGilligan (Berkeley: University of California Press, 2010), 120.

57 According to Eric A. Goldman, Michael "represents Levinson," whose "shtetl is Avalon, a place and time in America that no longer exists, but the memory of which he is committed to passing along through *his* vehicle for narrative, the motion picture." See Goldman, *The American Jewish Story through Cinema* (Austin: University of Texas Press, 2013), 156.

58 Robert Emery, dir., *The Directors: The Films of Barry Levinson* (Media Entertain-ment, 2000). Levinson reiterates this point in Emery's "The Films of Barry Levinson," in *The Directors: Take Three* (New York: Allworth Press, 2003): "In my mind, it [*Avalon*] had almost nothing to do with the immigrant experience" (209). However, in Mervin Rothstein's "Barry Levinson Reaches Out to a Lost America" (*New York Times*, 30 September 1990), Levinson indicates that thinking about his grandfather's story—"the immigrant experience"—was part of the mix in *Avalon*: "Immigration, assimilation and the effects of television on the family is a peculiar blending. But it made sense."

59 Philip French, "Self-Indulgent in Paradise—Barry Levinson Falling into a Familiar Trap," *Observer*, 3 March 1991, Nexis Uni.

60 Warren Rosenberg, "Coming Out of the Ethnic Closet: Jewishness in the Films of Barry Levinson," *Shofar* 22, no. 1 (2003): 29–43, Ethnic NewsWatch.

61   In "Making Fragmentation Familiar: Barry Levinson's *Avalon*" (*Studies in Contemporary Jewry*, vol. 14, *Coping with Life and Death: Jewish Families in the Twentieth Century*, ed. Peter Y. Medding. New York: Oxford University Press [1998]), Stephen Whitfield writes, "It is predictable that the two most important holidays shown in the film are not, say, the Sabbath or Passover. The absence of a seder should not pass unnoticed, however, since *Avalon* therefore loses a certain resonance and even poignancy" (52).

62   Whitfield, 63.

63   In *The American Jewish Story through Cinema*, Goldman comments, "Levinson purposefully does not provide subtitles for the dialogue, leaving those of us unable to understand ignorant about what is going on" (162).

64   For discussion of Sam's response to this naming and the significance of it, see Goldman, *The American Jewish Story through Cinema*, 168.

65   Lisa Schwarzbaum, "A World of Difference," *Entertainment Weekly*, 26 November 1999, Academic Search Complete.

66   Levinson, "Baltimore, My Baltimore."

67   Levinson.

68   "Back to Baltimore: This Time, It's Jewish, Says Levinson," *Forward*, 19 November 1999, Ethnic NewsWatch.

69   Michael Elkin, "Of 'Liberty Heights' They Do Sing: Barry Levinson Film Has a Dramatic Feel for the Triumph of Tolerance," *Jewish Exponent*, 9 December 1999, Ethnic NewsWatch.

70   See, for example, Jeffrey Melnick, *A Right to Sing the Blues: African Americans, Jews, and American Popular Song* (Cambridge, MA: Harvard University Press, 2001).

71   Rosenberg, "Coming Out of the Ethnic Closet."

72   Alan H. Feiler, "Directions Home: In His Newest Film, Barry Levinson Reaches the 'Heights' of His Baltimore Youth," *Baltimore Jewish Times*, 29 October 1999, Ethnic NewsWatch.

73   Alan H. Feiler, "Fit for the Big Screen: Barry Levinson's Newest Film Will Include Two Local Synagogue Grand Dames," *Baltimore Jewish Times*, 25 September 1998, Ethnic NewsWatch.

74   Todd McCarthy, "*Liberty Heights*," *Variety*, 9 November 1999, https://variety.com/1999/film/reviews/liberty-heights-1200459767/.

75   Rosenberg, "Coming Out of the Ethnic Closet."

76   Feiler, "Directions Home."

77   Elkin, "Of 'Liberty Heights,' They Do Sing."

78   Mitchell Fink, with Lauren Rubin, "Some Thumbs Way Up for Levinson's 'Heights,'" *Daily News*, 4 October 1999, Nexis Uni.

79   Stephen Hunter, "Blind Alleys of 'Liberty Heights': Unfocused Look Back at Baltimore," *Washington Post*, 10 December 1999, https://www.washingtonpost.com/archive/lifestyle/1999/12/10/blind-alleys-of-liberty-heights/7b3d500c-1d15-4d28-8025-1b51c6120f23/.

80   Schwarzbaum, "A World of Difference."

81   Quoted in Kay Bourne, "'Liberty Heights' Defies Racial Stereotypes," *Bay State Banner*, 23 December 1999, Ethnic NewsWatch.

82   Bourne.

83   Abrams, *The New Jew in Film*, 14–15.

Chapter 5 Assertively Jewish Onscreen

1 In "Jewish Experience on Film—An American Overview," *American Jewish Yearbook* 96 (1996), Joel Rosenberg refers to the phenomenon of "reverse assimilation, that of mainstream culture to its marginal components" (40).

2 Katey Rich, "Interview: Woody Allen and the Cast of *Whatever Works*," *CinemaBlend*, 17 June 2009, https://www.cinemablend.com/new/Interview -Woody-Allen-Cast-Whatever-Works-13604.html.

3 Gordon Haber, "What's Working for Woody?," *Forward*, 26 June 2009, Ethnic NewsWatch.

4 Anthony Lane, "Off the Rails," *New Yorker*, 15 June 2009, https://www.newyorker .com/magazine/2009/06/22/off-the-rails-3.

5 Haber, "What's Working for Woody?"

6 Ann Hornaday, "Woody's Dreadful *Whatever*—So Unfunny It Hurts," *Washington Post*, 3 July 2009, https://www.washingtonpost.com/wp-dyn/content/article /2009/07/02/AR2009070204008.html.

7 Frank Scheck, "*Whatever Works*," *Film Journal International* 112, no. 6 (2009): 43–44, MasterFILE Complete.

8 Rich, "Interview."

9 Rich.

10 Gregg Kilday, "Allen to Tribeca: Oh Well, 'Whatever,'" *Hollywood Reporter*, 3 March 2009, Nexis Uni.

11 Rich, "Interview."

12 Mark Harris, "Twilight of the Tummlers," *New York Magazine*, 24 May 2009, https://nymag.com/movies/features/56930/.

13 Miriam Moster, "So, What's the Yiddish Word for Pimp? Hassids Help Hollywood Get It Right," *Jewish News Weekly of Northern California*, 22 August 2014, Ethnic NewsWatch.

14 Zach Baron, "Sweet Tale of Friendship (Sex, Too)," *New York Times*, 13 April 2014, https://www.nytimes.com/2014/04/13/movies/woody-allen-joins -john-turturro-in-fading-gigolo.html?searchResultPosition=1.

15 Michael Fox, "Crossing Lines," *Baltimore Jewish Times*, 2 May 2014, Ethnic NewsWatch.

16 Fox.

17 Mark Jenkins, "John Turturro Gets Out of Character for His Lead Role in *Fading Gigolo*," *Washington Post*, 25 April 2014, https://www.washingtonpost.com /entertainment/john-turturro-gets-out-of-character-for-his-lead-role-in-fading -gigolo/2014/04/24/c4555c6c-c6d5-11e3-b708-471bae3cb10c_story.html.

18 Elliot Gertel, "John Turturro's Sensitivity to Jewish Culture," *Jewish Currents*, 6 March 2015, https://jewishcurrents.org/john-turturros-sensitivity-to-jewish -culture/.

19 Ezra Glinter, "What He Did for Love," *Forward*, 25 April 2014, Ethnic NewsWatch.

20 For a more extensive discussion of Yiddish cinema's response to *The Jazz Singer*, see Eric Goldman's *The American Jewish Story through Cinema* (Austin: University of Texas Press, 2013). For a discussion of *The Jazz Singer*'s use of blackface, see Michael Rogin's *Blackface, White Noise: Jewish Immigrants in the Hollywood Melting Pot* (Berkeley: University of California Press, 1996).

21 Rebecca Margolis, "New Yiddish Film and the Transvernacular." *In Geveb: A Journal of Jewish Studies*, 18 December 2016, https://ingeveb.org/articles/new -yiddish-film-and-the-transvernacular.

22 Interview with Eve Annenberg, New York, 1 August 2017.

23 Danielle Berrin, "Yiddish 'Romeo and Juliet' Bound for Controversy," *Jewish News Weekly of Northern California*, 25 May 2012, Ethnic NewsWatch. In keeping with Annenberg's prediction, other Yiddish films have come down the pike, and *Romeo and Juliet in Yiddish* certainly seems to be a touchstone for and precursor of the widely reviewed *Menashe* (2017). Like its predecessor, *Menashe* boasts a nonprofessional cast, blurs the boundary between documentary and fiction film, and focuses on the relationship between a man on the margins of the community and his offspring. However, the marginalized figure, Menashe, is not a Hasidic exile but rather a widower. For more on *Menashe*, see my brief essay "The Misogyny of Menashe," *Lilith Blog*, 28 July 2017, https://www.lilith.org/blog/2017/07 /the-misogyny-of-menashe/.

24 In "A Journey in Film; On the Go," *Forward*, 21 January 2011, Ethnic NewsWatch, Leon Masha cites Eric Goldman: "The Yiddish cinema transcends territorial, political, and aesthetic boundaries."

25 Miryam Kabakov, "*Romeo and Juliet in Yiddish*: An Interview with the Filmmaker," *TC Jewfolk*, 14 March 2011, https://tcjewfolk.com/romeo-juliet-yiddish -interview-filmmaker/.

26 Alexa Dvorson, "Orthodox and Secular Jewish Worlds Collide in Yiddish Romeo and Juliet," *DW* (*Deutsche Welle*), 15 November 2010, https://www.dw.com/en /orthodox-and-secular-jewish-worlds-collide-in-yiddish-romeo-and-juliet/a -6220536.

27 Jed Lipinski, "A Familiar Story of Boy Meets Girl, but in Yiddish," *New York Times*, 20 January 2011, https://cityroom.blogs.nytimes.com/2011/01/20/a -familiar-story-of-boy-meets-girl-but-in-yiddish/.

28 Sue Fishkoff, "O Romeo, Romeo: Vu bist du, Romeo?," *Jewish News Weekly of Northern California*, 29 November 2013, Ethnic NewsWatch.

29 Lipinski, "A Familiar Story."

30 Jon Kalish, "*Romeo and Juliet in Yiddish*: Hasidic Reworking Debuts at New York Jewish Film Festival," *New York Daily News*, 13 January 2011, https://www.nydailynews .com/entertainment/tv-movies/romeo-juliet-yiddish-hasidic-reworking-debuts -new-york-jewish-film-festival-article-1.153967.

31 Ezra Glinter, "The Best of 2011 in Jewish Arts and Culture," *Forward*, 30 December 2011, Ethnic NewsWatch.

32 "Catching Up with Garry Marshall," *Philadelphia Daily News*, 12 May 2006, Nexis Uni.

33 Michael Elkin, "Going a Round at the Bar," *Jewish Exponent*, 11 May 2006, Ethnic NewsWatch.

34 Here I disagree with Michael Fox, who emphasizes "the general irrelevance of women to the story. Only Roberts, as Ben's bubbe, is given anything substantial to do. Jamie Gertz is woefully underutilized as Ben's mom, while Daryl Hannah (as Irwin's girlfriend Sacred Feather, aka Sandy Frost) exists as standard-issue comic relief." See Michael Fox, "Hokey 'Steins' Lets Stereotypes Flow Like Manischewitz," *Jewish News Weekly of Northern California*, 19 May 2006, Ethnic News Watch.

35 Eleanor Ringel Gillespie, "Rivalry Kicks in When Boy's Family Does the Rite Thing," *Atlanta Journal-Constitution*, 26 May 2006, Nexis Uni.

36 Craig Rosen, "Diamond's Screen Gems," *Billboard*, 9 December 2006, Academic Search Complete.

37 Bob Strauss, "Today He Is a Man: Bar Mitzvah Saga Puts Jeremy Piven in Touch with His Inner Dad," *Daily News of LA*, 12 May 2006, Nexis Uni.

38 Josh Walfish, "Actress Jami Gertz Discusses Being Jewish in Entertainment Industry," *Daily Northwestern*, 9 May 2013, https://dailynorthwestern.com /2013/05/09/campus/jami-gertz-shares-about-being-jewish-in-entertainment -industry/.

39 Jacob Sugarman, "Keeping Up with Legend Doris Roberts," *Jewish Advocate*, 19 May 2006, Ethnic NewsWatch.

40 Ronnie Scheib, "Keeping Up with the Steins," *Variety*, 15–21 May 2006; "Pentateuch Envy, Anyone," *Jewish Exponent*, 11 May 2006, Ethnic NewsWatch.

41 Joyce Wadler, "Embracing Irony," *New York Times*, 7 May 2006, https://www .nytimes.com/2006/05/07/fashion/sundaystyles/07NITE.html.

42 Jordana Horn Marinoff, "Actor 'Hugs Out' His Jewish Side," *Forward*, 12 May 2006, Ethnic NewsWatch.

43 Emma Stefansky, "Three More Women Accuse Jeremy Piven of Sexual Misconduct," *Vanity Fair*, 28 January 2018, https://www.vanityfair.com/hollywood/2018 /01/jeremy-piven-three-more-women-sexual-misconduct.

44 Itay Stern, "Jeremy Piven in Israel: A Falling Star Jokes before a Half-Empty Auditorium," *Haaretz*, 15 January 2019, https://www.haaretz.com/israel-news /culture/.premium-jeremy-piven-in-israel-a-falling-star-jokes-before-of-a-half -empty-auditorium-1.6844238.

45 Nathan Rabin, "*Keeping Up with the Steins*," *A.V. Club*, 10 May 2006, https://film .avclub.com/keeping-up-with-the-steins-1798201719.

46 Stephen Hunter, "*The Steins*: X-Treme Bar Mitzvahs," *Washington Post*, 26 May 2006, https://www.washingtonpost.com/archive/lifestyle/2006/05/26/the -steins-x-treme-bar-mitzvahs/c96a9269-a72e-4c70-9b10-bdea6282cf0f/.

47 Peter Howell, "Less Schmaltz, More Whales in Yarmulkes," *Toronto Star*, 26 May 2006, Nexis Uni.

48 Stephen Holden, "The Bar Mitzvah Status Wars Go Nuclear, Hollywood Style," *New York Times*, 12 May 2006, https://www.nytimes.com/2006/05/12/movies /12stei.html.

49 Steven Zeitchik, "Tribeca Film Festival Offerings," *Forward*, 28 April 2006, Ethnic NewsWatch.

50 Fox, "Hokey 'Steins' Lets Stereotypes Flow."

51 See, for example, Alina Tugend, "Party Peer Pressure, and Why You Shouldn't Succumb to It," *New York Times*, 13 September 2008, https://www.nytimes.com /2008/09/13/business/13shortcuts.html.

52 Nolan Feeney, "Zach Braff: 'There Are No Great Roles in Film, They're All Dried Up,'" *Time*, 11 July 2014, https://time.com/2976322/zach-braff-interview-wish-i -was-here/.

53 Molly Tolsky, "Talking with Zach Braff, Kate Hudson and Mandy Patinkin of *Wish I Was Here*," *Kveller*, 24 July 2014, https://www.kveller.com/talking-with -zach-braff-kate-hudson-mandy-patinkin-of-wish-i-was-here/.

54 Daniel M. Kimmel, "Despite Doubters, Zach Braff's New Film Puts Judaism Front and Center," *Jewish Advocate*, 18 July 2014, Ethnic NewsWatch.

55 Michael Fox, "Braff Grapples with Spirituality, Family in *Wish I Was Here*," *Jewish News Weekly of Northern California*, 18 July 2014, Ethnic NewsWatch.

56 Ari Kappel, "Zach Braff on His Giant Kickstarter Experiment, *Wish I Was Here*," *FastCompany*, 20 July 2014, https://www.fastcompany.com/3033214/zach-braff-on-his-giant-kickstarter-experiment-wish-i-was-here.

57 Lucy Vernasco, "Why I Walked Out Halfway through the New Zach Braff Movie," *Bitch*, 28 July 2014, https://www.bitchmedia.org/post/wish-i-wasn%E2%80%99t-there-why-i-walked-out-halfway-through-the-zach-braff-movie.

58 Devin Faraci, "Why People Hate Zach Braff," *Birth. Movies. Death*, 18 July 2014, https://birthmoviesdeath.com/2014/07/18/why-people-hate-zach-braff.

59 Molly Tolsky, "An Interview with Olaf from *Frozen*," *Kveller*, 7 July 2014, https://www.kveller.com/kveller-exclusive-an-interview-with-olaf-from-frozen/.

60 Greg Salisbury, "To Have and Have Knot: Exploring Family Ties in *Wish I Was Here*," *Jewish Exponent*, 17 July 2014, Ethnic NewsWatch.

61 Fox, "Braff Grapples with Spirituality."

62 Tolsky, "Talking With Zach Braff."

63 Kimmel, "Despite Doubters."

64 Naomi Pfefferman, "*Wish I Was Here*: Zach Braff on Love, His New Movie and Being a Jew," *Jewish Journal*, 16 July 2014, Ethnic NewsWatch.

Chapter 6 Queering the Jewish Gaze

1 See, for example, Omer Bartov, *The "Jew" in Cinema: from "The Golem" to "Don't Touch My Holocaust"* (Bloomington: Indiana University Press, 2005), 38–47.

2 In *Identity Papers: Contemporary Narratives of American Jewishness* (Albany: SUNY Press, 2011), I wrote, "Although I recognize that historically incorrect and competing narratives of victimization can potentially be drawn from this emotionally harrowing moment—that is, it's worse to be gay than Jewish—I do not think that is the source of dramatic tension or the intention of this scene. Rather, this image insists that the particularity of gay victims of the Shoah needs to be recognized, that the Nazi persecution of homosexuals must become a distinct narrative" (74). For additional commentary on this final scene and its implications for queer Jews, see pp. 74–75. It is worth noting that in the directors' commentary to *Paragraph 175*, Epstein and Friedman indicate that *Bent* was part of their inadequate education about pink triangles and the persecution of gays that had caused them to "lump together" the experience of gays and Jews, an analogy they strove to disrupt in *Paragraph 175*.

3 Although it is beyond my scope here, an in-depth analysis of the relationship between Jacobovici's documentary and Gabler's argument, as well as the ethnoracial politics of the film, would be a worthy scholarly project.

4 Samantha Baskind uses this term in "The Fockerized Jew? Questioning Jewishness as Cool in American Popular Entertainment," *Shofar: An Interdisciplinary Journal of Jewish Studies* 25, no. 4 (2007): 3–17.

5 Henry Bial, *Acting Jewish: Negotiating Ethnicity on the American Stage and Screen* (Ann Arbor: University of Michigan Press, 2005).

6 Alisa Lebow, *First Person Jewish* (Minneapolis: University of Minnesota Press, 2008), xxiii.

7 In the directors' commentary on *The Celluloid Closet* DVD, Epstein and Friedman note that Frey went on to play Motel, the tailor, in the paradoxically

paradigmatic American Jewish film *Fiddler on the Roof*. They also report that, when their film *Paragraph 175* was shown at Sundance, some assumed that its emphasis on "gays and Jews" meant that it would "definitely . . . be nominated" for major awards.

8 See, for example, Daniel Boyarin, *Unheroic Conduct: The Rise of Heterosexuality and the Invention of the Jewish Man* (Berkeley: University of California Press, 1997); Daniel Boyarin, Daniel Itzkovitz, and Ann Pellegrini, eds., *Queer Theory and the Jewish Question* (New York: Columbia University Press, 2003), esp. "Strange Bedfellows, An Introduction," 1–18.

9 "Queer" is a coalitional term that strives to honor the diverse communities represented by each letter of the GLBT acronym. However, it is also a term that challenges gender and sexual identity politics as well as the normalizing of a binary sex/gender system. By using the term "Jewish queerness," I strive to liberate Jewishness from the stranglehold of assumed heteronormativity and historically overdetermined "respectability" (George Mosse's term), which has impacted the lives of all Jews and impoverished many, especially those self-identified as gay, lesbian, bisexual, transgender, feminist, or queer.

10 See, for example, Warren Hoffman, *The Passing Game: Queering Jewish American Culture* (Syracuse, NY: Syracuse University Press, 2009); Riv-Ellen Prell, *Fighting to Become Americans: Assimilation and the Trouble between Jewish Women and Jewish Men* (Boston: Beacon Press, 1999).

11 In *First Person Jewish*, Lebow devotes a chapter to "first person filmmakers" who "have difficulty even negotiating these two identities in the same frame, developing a rather puzzling circumspection with regard to queerness or Jewishness, or both" (111). She continues, "If one identity (queer, for instance) is loudly proclaimed, it may at times follow that the other is just as 'loudly' suppressed" (117).

12 Janet Jakobsen, "Queers Are Like Jews, Aren't They? Analogy and Alliance Politics," in Boyarin, Itzkovitz, and Pellegrini, *Queer Theory and the Jewish Question*, 67.

13 For a discussion of Adam Sandler's Jewish performances, see Vincent Brook, "Boy-Man Schlemiels and Super-Nebbishes: Adam Sandler and Ben Stiller," in *Hollywood's Chosen People: The Jewish Experience in American Cinema*, ed. Daniel Bernardi, Murray Pomerance, and Hava Tirosh-Samuelson (Detroit: Wayne State University Press, 2013), 173–191. Brook does not discuss *I Now Pronounce You Chuck and Larry* in this essay.

14 Jason Nielsen, "Kissing Jennifer Westfeldt: Actress Views Her Latest Role as an Escape from Typecasting," *Jewish Advocate*, 28 March 2002, Ethnic NewsWatch.

15 Lisa Key, "When a Dismal Love Life Leads a Lonely Woman Down an Uncharted Road: In *Kissing Jessica Stein*, Two Actress-Writers Take on Interfaith Dating, Same-Sex Romance and the Mysteries of Female Friendship," *Forward*, 8 March 2002, Ethnic NewsWatch.

16 Michael Elkin, "'Kiss' of Success: One Day She's a Lesbian, the Next She's Not—Is This the Jessica Stein Way?," *Jewish Exponent*, 21 March 2002, Ethnic NewsWatch.

17 Elkin, "'Kiss' of Success."

18 Stacie Stukin, "How the Other Half Laughs," *The Advocate*, 19 March 2002, Academic Search Complete.

19 Nathan Abrams, *The New Jew in Film: Exploring Jewishness and Judaism in Contemporary Cinema* (New Brunswick, NJ: Rutgers University Press, 2012), 76.

20 For an alternative view, see Ruth D. Johnston, "Joke-Work: The Construction of Jewish Postmodern Identity in Contemporary Theory and American Film," in *You Should See Yourself: Jewish Identity in Postmodern American Culture*, ed. Vincent Brook (New Brunswick, NJ: Rutgers University Press, 2006), 207–229. Johnston reads *Kissing Jessica Stein* as "neither a lesbian nor a straight film, for it escapes such definitive categorization and rather explores the characters' sexual fluidity" (221). Johnston views *Kissing Jessica Stein* as one of several women's films that have "resisted the Jewish woman's systematic exclusion from representation by reclaiming Woody Allen territory" (216). Although I recognize the theoretical and even practical desire to recognize "sexual fluidity," we need to also recognize that such seemingly progressive postmodern play may have the unintended consequence of reinforcing the systematic exclusion of Jewish lesbians from representation.

21 Elkin, "'Kiss' of Success." It's worth noting that *Kissing Jessica Stein* appeared amid Westfeldt's highly publicized—though now defunct—relationship with Jon Hamm.

22 Karla Mantilla and Jennie Ruby, "Crash Landing for a Promising Lesbian Film," *Off Our Backs*, July/August 2002, Academic Search Complete.

23 Tamar Jeffers McDonald, *Romantic Comedy: Boy Meets Girl Meets Genre* (London: Wallflower, 2007), 81.

24 David E. Kaufman, *Jewhooing the Sixties: American Celebrity and Jewish Identity* (Waltham, MA: Brandeis University Press, 2012), 1.

25 Kaufman, 275.

26 Thomas Waugh, "Walking on Tippy Toes: Lesbian and Gay Liberation Documentary of the Post-Stonewall Period 1969–1984," in *Between the Sheets, in the Streets: Queer, Lesbian, Gay Documentary*, ed. Chris Holmlund and Cynthia Fuchs (Minneapolis: University of Minnesota Press, 1997), 113, 109–110.

27 B. Ruby Rich, *New Queer Cinema: The Director's Cut* (Durham, NC: Duke University Press, 2013), 125.

28 Stacey Palevsky, "Never Forget the Legacy of Harvey Milk," *Jewish News Weekly of Northern California*, 5 December 2008, Ethnic NewsWatch.

29 Lesléa Newman, , *A Letter to Harvey Milk and Other Stories* (Ithaca, NY: Firebrand Books, 1988).

30 For an extended reading of this short story, see my "To Queer or Not to Queer: That's Not the Question," *College Literature* 24, no. 1 (1997): 179–180.

31 Kaufman, *Jewhooing the Sixties*, 390.

32 Mark Segal, "There Are No Gay Jews," *Windy City Times*, 18 January 2012, http://www.windycitymediagroup.com/gay/lesbian/news/ARTICLE.php?AID =35755.

33 Lesléa Newman is also part of this series.

34 Iris Mann, "'Milk' Captures Doomed Life of Gay Jewish Politician," *Jewish Journal*, 10 December 2008, http://www.jewishjournal.com/film/article/milk _captures_doomed_life_of_gay_jewish_politician_20081210/.

35 Mann.

36 Rebecca Spence, "Harvey Milk, in Life and on Film, Typified the Proud Jew as Outsider," *Forward*, 19 December 2008, Ethnic NewsWatch.

37 Spence.

38 Randy Shilts, *The Mayor of Castro Street: The Life and Times of Harvey Milk* (New York: St. Martin's Press, 1982), 374.

39 Lillian Faderman, *Harvey Milk: His Lives and Death* (New Haven, CT: Yale University Press, 2018), 22.

40 Faderman, 19.

41 Mann, "'Milk' Captures Doomed Life."

42 Quoted in Bial, *Acting Jewish*, 19.

43 Spence, "Harvey Milk, in Life and on Film."

44 Mann, "'Milk' Captures Doomed Life."

45 Mann.

46 Faderman, 80 (my emphasis).

47 Joshua Schuster, "Slain S.F. Supe Harvey Milk Eulogized at Sha'ar Zahav," *Jewish Bulletin of Northern California*, 27 November 1998, Ethnic NewsWatch.

48 Spence, "Harvey Milk, in Life and on Film."

49 This is especially evident in the scene in which Arnold Beckstein (played by Fierstein) says Kaddish for his non-Jewish lover who has been murdered by homophobes and is challenged by his mother (played by Anne Bancroft), who objects to the comparison between her son's lover and her husband. It is noteworthy that Fierstein is also a presence in *The Celluloid Closet*.

50 Jon Else, special edition features, *The Times of Harvey Milk*.

51 *The Times of Harvey Milk*, audio commentary on DVD.

52 Notably, Passover seders are often occasions for linking the Exodus story to other liberation and social justice movements. Such practices embody the coalition politics for which Harvey Milk was known.

53 Mann, "'Milk' Captures Doomed Life."

54 Shilts, *The Mayor of Castro Street*, 21.

55 Shilts, 231.

56 In "Director's Research Tapes," special edition features, *The Times of Harvey Milk*, Judge Lillian Sing of the San Francisco Superior Court recognized Milk as one of the earliest proponents of coalition politics and lauded him for recognizing the discrimination that Chinese Americans have endured. According to Judge Sing, he "was able to do so because he was not only gay but also Jewish. From that background, he had a sense of fighting against injustices."

57 At the time of Milk's death, Dianne Feinstein was president of the San Francisco Board of Supervisors. She succeeded George Moscone as mayor of San Francisco. Of course, she is now best known as a senator from California.

58 Other preproduction interviews included in "Director's Research Tapes" also indicate awareness of Milk's Jewishness. At one point, Scott Smith, Milk's lover (played by James Franco in *Milk*), suggests that the 17,000 votes Milk won in his first campaign were significant given that he was "a person with long hair, Jewish, gay." He also reminisces about the morning car trips they often made to the House of Bagels and then to a local shop that supplied the whitefish, pickled herring, and "big globs of cream cheese" that went on the bagels. Such food might reasonably be considered a marker of ethnic Jewishness, especially given that "Milk talked briefly about opening a Jewish delicatessen in San Francisco" (Shilts, *The Mayor of Castro Street*, 40). These preproduction interviews would likely have been among the materials that Epstein generously shared with Van Sant and Black. At the Twenty-Fifth Anniversary Candlelight Memorial marking Milk and Moscone's assassination (special features, *The Times of Harvey Milk*), Tom Ammiano follows Rebecca Moscone's remembrance of her father by stating, "As Harvey might say, I'm very *farmisht* [Yiddish for mixed up or befuddled]."

59 See Rich, *New Queer Cinema*, 240–241; "Two Films, One Legacy," special edition features, *The Times of Harvey Milk*.

60 "Two Films, One Legacy."

61 "Two Films, One Legacy"; "Remembering Harvey," bonus features, *Milk* ; Rich, *New Queer Cinema*, 259n12

62 Rich, *New Queer Cinema*, 259n12.

63 For a discussion of the ways that *Brokeback Mountain* "signal[ed] a new era" (185) and constructed gay cinema for a mainstream audience, see Rich, *New Queer Cinema*, 185–201.

64 Rich, *New Queer Cinema*, 248. Other critics found Penn more convincing as a Jewish New Yorker. For example, Peter Travers, in his review of *Milk* for *Rolling Stone* (26 November 1998), comments that "Penn uses makeup to lengthen his nose and look more like Harvey. He adopts a New York accent to get Harvey's inflections." http://www.rollingstone.com/movies/reviews/milk -20081126#ixzz3eeYuQ6QA.

65 It is worth noting that in *Milk: A Pictorial History of Harvey Milk* (New York: Newmarket Press, 2009), released in conjunction with the film and including an introduction and interview extracts by screenwriter Dustin Lance Black, there is no mention of Milk's Jewish heritage, including and especially in the timeline devoted to his "East Coast Life pre-1972." This sharply contrasts with the narration in *The Times of Harvey Milk* that, at the outset, identifies Milk as the product of Jewish parents.

66 Notably, while *Milk* dramatizes the "pooper scooper law" archival sequence from the documentary, it leaves out Harvey Milk's citing New York as a model.

67 Quoted in Ari Karpel, "Forty under 40: Dustin Lance Black," *The Advocate*, 6 May 2009, http://www.advocate.com/arts-entertainment/film/2009/05/06/forty -under-40-dustin-lance-black?page=0,0.

68 Karpel.

69 Dustin Lance Black, *Milk: The Shooting Script* (New York: Newmarket Press, 2008), 109.

70 Schuster, "Slain S.F. Supe Harvey Milk."

71 Schuster.

72 The San Francisco Film Festival has been the prototype for Jewish film festivals nationally and internationally.

73 Palevsky, "Never Forget the Legacy of Harvey Milk."

74 Palevsky.

75 Palevsky.

76 Rich, *New Queer Cinema*, xxvi.

77 Following Bial, I emphasize literacy rather than identity to avoid the specter of essentialist spectatorship.

78 For a discussion of the history and politics of biopics, see George F. Custen, *Bio/Pics: How Hollywood Constructed Public History* (New Brunswick, NJ: Rutgers University Press, 1992). *The Life of Emile Zola* (1937) was directed by William Dieterle. For discussions of the erasure of Jewishness in Dieterle's film in particular and the whitewashing in biographies more generally, see, for example, Patricia Erens, *The Jew in American Cinema* (Bloomington: Indiana University Press, 1984) and Lester D. Friedman, *Hollywood's Image of the Jew* (New York: Frederick Ungar, 1982).

79 See Bial, *Acting Jewish*, 87–92, for the role that this film played in changing reception of the Jewish woman.

80 *Triumph of the Will*, directed by Leni Riefenstahl, 1935. See J. Hoberman's "'Triumph of the Will': Fascist Rants and the Hollywood Response," *New York Times*, 3 March 2016, for an example of the continued wrestling with the identity and cinematic impact of this film.

81 See Eric Goldman, *The American Jewish Story through Cinema* (Austin: University of Texas Press, 2013).

82 Bial, *Acting Jewish*, 19.

83 Anne Stockwell, "A Festival in Your Living Room," *The Advocate*, 25 May 1999, Academic Search Complete.

84 Alisa S. Lebow, *First Person Jewish* (Minneapolis: University of Minnesota Press, 2008), 109–110.

85 Caryn Aviv, "Treyf," *Lilith*, 31 March 1999, Ethnic NewsWatch.

86 Stockwell, "A Festival in Your Living Room."

87 Noma Faingold, "S.F. Film Festival Courts Controversy: In 18th Year, Director Focuses on Israeli Flicks," *Jewish Bulletin of Northern California*, 10 July 1998, Ethnic NewsWatch.

88 See, for example, Emily Shire, "We Were Kicked Off Chicago's Dyke March for Not Being 'the Right Kind of Jew,'" *Daily Beast*, 2 July 2017, https://www.thedailybeast.com/we-were-kicked-off-chicagos-dyke-march-for-not-being-the-right-kind-of-jew.

89 For Lebow, spending time in an Orthodox synagogue on the Lower East Side is part ethnography, part nostalgia, part drag show. Even and especially on the women's side of the *mehitzah* at Purim, she thinks of herself as playing with gender and wishes that she could don the clothes and the position of a yeshiva bocher. One might say she experiences Yentl envy!

90 Rebecca Spence, "Trembling toward Icon Status," *Forward*, 7 September 2007, Ethnic NewsWatch.

91 "The Forward 50: Making a Difference in a Difficult Year," *Forward*, 9 November 2001, Ethnic NewsWatch; "Sandi Dubowski," *Video Data Bank*, http://www.vdb.org/artists/sandi-dubowski.

92 Sandi Simcha Dubowski, "Trembling Before G-d," *Conscience*, Spring 2003, http://www.catholicsforchoice.org/wp-content/uploads/2014/01/CONSRelAndArt.pdf.

93 Michael Giltz, "For the Love of G-d," *The Advocate*, 23 October 2001, Academic Search Complete.

94 In *Women of Valor: Orthodox Jewish Troll Fighters, Crime Writers, and Rock Stars in Contemporary Literature and Culture* (New Brunswick, NJ: Rutgers University Press, 2018), Karen Skinazi writes, "I remember seeing [*Trembling*] at the Film Forum in New York City . . . thinking it was brilliant and so important but also not likely to be interesting to the general public. I was wrong" (65).

95 Larry Mark, "Mavericks and a Jewish Grand Dragon Reign Supreme at Annual Film Stampede: Is It Just Us, or Does the Sundance Logo Seem to Sport a Small Star of David This Year?," *Forward*, 9 February 2001, Ethnic NewsWatch; Sandi Simcha Dubowski, "Trembling on the Road: A Simcha Diary," in *Queer Jews*, ed. David Schneer and Caryn Aviv (New York: Routledge, 2002), 216.

96 Dubowski, "Trembling on the Road," 223; A. J. Wall, "Chabad Rabbi, Gay Man Work on Healing Wounds at Filmfest," *Jewish Bulletin of Northern California*, 3 August 2001, Ethnic NewsWatch.

97 Dubowski, "Trembling Before G-d"; *Trembling on the Road*.

98 Deborah Walike, "Chill in the Air: Protesters Braved a Cold Winter Night to Rally Against the *Trembling Before G-d* Documentary," *Baltimore Jewish Times*, 8 February 2002, Ethnic NewsWatch.

99 D. Walike, "*Trembling* All Over: A Film about Gay Orthodox Jews That Raised Controversy Earlier This Year Will Be Shown in a Local Orthodox Synagogue," *Baltimore Jewish Times*, 25 October 2002, Ethnic NewsWatch.

100 Spence, "Trembling toward Icon Status."

101 Debra Nussbaum Cohen, "Reunion Row Redux," *New York Jewish Week*, 18 January 2008, Ethnic NewsWatch.

102 Lisa Schwarzbaum, "Devouted," *Entertainment Weekly*, 16 November 2001,. Academic Search Complete; Mara Benjamin, "*Trembling Before G-d*," *Lilith*, Winter 2001, Ethnic NewsWatch.

103 Ellen Elgart, "Scene on the Screen; Trembling Before Ourselves," *In the Family*, Winter 2002, Gender Watch.

104 Jules Becker, "New Film Causes a Big Stir at the Box Office: *Trembling Before G-d* Look at Homosexuality and the Orthodoxy," *Jewish Advocate*, 27 December 2001, Ethnic NewsWatch.

105 Matthew M. Ross, "Pix Finding Niche under the Radar," *Variety*, 5 November 2001, Performing Arts Periodicals.

106 Special feature: "Behind the Scenes with the Producer and Director," *Hineini*, DVD.

107 Ann Jackman, "Out-Spoken," NEWENGLANDFILM.COM, 1 January 2006, https://newenglandfilm.com/magazine/2006/01/out-spoken.

108 Irene Sege, "Minds Wide Open: One Girl's Push to Form a Gay Group Forced a School to Search Its Soul," *Boston Globe*, 8 November 2005, http://archive.boston.com/news/education/higher/articles/2005/11/08/minds_wide_open/; "Behind the Scenes with the Producer and Director."

109 Judy Bolton-Fasman, "Coming Out in the Classroom," *Tablet*, 12 January 2016, https://www.tabletmag.com/jewish-life-and-religion/196468/coming-out-in-the-classroom.

110 E. Silverman, "Striking a Balance," *Jewish News*, 16 March 2006, Ethnic NewsWatch; "Behind the Scenes with the Producer and Director."

111 Lisa Traiger, "Coming Out in High School; Film Aims to Help Give Voice to Religious Gay Students," *Washington Jewish Week*, 15 December 2005. Ethnic NewsWatch.

112 "Behind the Scenes with the Producer and Director."

113 Ted Siefer, "Film on Gay Jewish Student Shown at State House Event," *Jewish Advocate*, 31 May 2006, Ethnic NewsWatch.

Chapter 7   Cinematic Alliances

1 I specify Gentile Blacks and white Jews here so that my language does not equate Jews with whites and Blacks with Gentiles; such equations erase Jews of color in general and Black Jews in particular.

2 Michael Rogin, *Blackface, White Noise: Jewish Immigrants in the Hollywood Melting Pot* (Berkeley: University of California Press, 1996).

3 Naomi Pfefferman, "Spike Lee: The Jewish Character in *BlacKkKlansman* Added a Lot of 'Complexity' to the Film," *Jewish Telegraphic Agency*, 12 February 2019 https://www.jta.org/2019/02/12/culture/spike-lee-the-jewish-character-in-blackkklansman-added-a-lot-of-complexity-to-the-film.

4 Jonathan Mahler, "A 'Disorienting' Look at Blacks and Jews: Film Zooms In on Crown Heights, Farrakhan, *Schindler's List*," *Forward*, 25 July 1997, Ethnic NewsWatch.

5 For a useful discussion of Black and Jewish spectatorship, see Dennis Hanlon, "Does Anyone Have the Right to Say, 'I Don't Care'? Resistance and Reverence at *Schindler's List*," *Film and History* 39, no. 1 (2009): 53–65. Hanlon uses Kaufman and Snitow's documentary as one of his sources.

6 Hanlon, 57.

7 Mahler, "A 'Disorienting' Look."

8 Suzy Hansen, "Amiri Baraka Stands by His Words," *Salon*, 18 October 2002, https://www.salon.com/2002/10/17/baraka_2/.

9 Lisa Acerbo, "A Single Person Can Make a Difference: Producer Reveals 'Heart of Stone,'" *Hollywood Scriptwriter*, March 2009, Film and Television Literature Index.

10 Ron Kaplan, "High Hopes," *Jewish News*, 21 January 2010, Ethnic NewsWatch.

11 Michael Fox, "Front Row," *Chicago Jewish Star*, 28 October–10 November 2011, Ethnic NewsWatch.

12 Fox.

13 Fox.

14 John Anderson, "*Crime after Crime*," *Variety*, 23 January 2011, Performing Arts Periodicals.

15 Karen Schoemer, "A Director Crosses the Line into a Reality of . . . More Lines," *New York Times*, 25 October 1992, https://www.nytimes.com/1992/10/25/movies /film-a-director-crosses-the-line-into-a-reality-of-more-lines.html.

16 Schoemer.

17 Janet Maslin, "Review/Film Festival: *Zebrahead*; A Racial Chameleon in a Hidebound World," *New York Times*, 8 October 1992, https://www.nytimes.com /1992/10/08/movies/review-film-festival-zebrahead-a-racial-chameleon-in-a -hidebound-world.html.

18 Askhari Johnson, "AFRO Talks to Star of *Zebrahead*," *Afro-American Red Star*, 31 October 1992, Ethnic NewsWatch.

19 Craig V. Smith, "Darkness Visible: The Politics of Being Seen from Ellison to *Zebrahead*," *Canadian Review of American Studies* 26, no. 1 (1996), Academic Search Complete.

20 Lawrence King, "The Return of Blaxploitation within the American Film Industry," *Philadelphia Tribune*, 27 January 1995, Ethnic NewsWatch.

21 Robin Wood, "The Spectres Emerge in Daylight," *Cineaction* 43 (1997), Performing Arts Periodicals.

22 Gregory Stephens, "*Zebrahead*," *Interrace*, 31 July 1994, Ethnic NewsWatch.

23 Marsha Mitchell, "*Zebrahead*, a Cinemagraphic Horse of a Different Color," *Los Angeles Sentinel*, 22 October 1992, Ethnic NewsWatch.

24 Michael Elkin, "On the Scene: *Zebrahead*: A Hip-Hop 'Romeo and Juliet' Debuts," *Jewish Exponent*, 23 October 1992, Ethnic NewsWatch.

25 Elicia Brown, "Yuta Goes to Hollywood," *Jewish Week*, 13 July 2007, Ethnic NewsWatch; Scott Weinberg, "SXSW '07 Interview: *Arranged* Directors Stefan Schaefer & Diane Crespo," February 27, 2007, updated March 27, 2007, https:// www.efilmcritic.com/feature.php?feature=2087.

26 Michael Rowin, "Review: Match Point: Stefan Schaefer and Diane Crespo's *Arranged*," *Indiewire*, 11 December 2007, https://www.indiewire.com/2007/12 /review-match-point-stefan-schaefer-and-diane-crespos-arranged-73361/.

27 Debra Nussbaum Cohen, "The Sheitel and the Hijab," *New York Jewish Week*, 7 December 2007, Ethnic NewsWatch.

28 "A Jew and a Muslim, United by Tradition," *Jewish News*, 29 November 2007, Ethnic NewsWatch.

29 Cohen, "The Sheitel and the Hijab."

30 Cohen.

31 Cohen.

32 Cohen.

33 Jeannette Catsoulis, "Teachers United," *New York Times*, 14 December 2007, https://www.nytimes.com/2007/12/14/movies/14arra.html.

34 Cate Marquis, "*David* Is Highlight of Annual Film Festival," *STL Jewish Light*, 9 November 2011, https://www.stljewishlight.com/features/entertainment/article_470f4e72-0ae7-11e1-b488-001cc4c002e0.html.

35 Lee J. Green, "Muslim/Jewish Film Featured at Sidewalk," *Southern Jewish Life*, August 2011, Ethnic NewsWatch; "Award-Winning *David* Opens Jewish Arts and Film Festival in Stamford," *Connecticut Jewish Ledger*, 11 October 2011, http://www.jewishledger.com/2011/10/award-winning-david-opens-jewish-arts-film-festival-in-stamford/.

36 Peter Fox, "*David*, One Boy, Two Faiths," *Venü Magazine*, January/February 2012, 84–85, https://static1.squarespace.com/static/5d1263eccd19f900016aad86/t/5d23808f59005400017a9f5f/1562607759921.

37 Chris Mautner, "Jewish Film Festival to Close by Bridging a Divide," *Penn Live*, 18 May 2012, https://www.pennlive.com/go/2012/05/jewish_film_festival_to_close.html.

38 Anna Faktorovich, "Interview with Joel Fendelman," *Pennsylvania Literary Journal*, June 2011, Academic Search Complete.

39 "*David*: The Casting Process," Yumpu, https://www.yumpu.com/en/document/read/51706954/jobrani-shtaynberger-mishal-david-the-movie.

40 Ella Goldblum, "New Movie Deals with Arab, Jewish Divide," *Washington Jewish Week*, 15 March 2012, Ethnic NewsWatch.

41 "Award-Winning *David* Opens Jewish Arts and Film Festival."

42 "Interview: Joel Fendelman and Patrick Daly about *David*," 2011, https://www.david-themovie.com/#press-section.

43 Dennis Harvey, "*David*," *Variety*, 29 August 2011, Performing Arts Periodicals; Sarah Cohen, "*David*," *Time Out*, 8 November 2012, https://www.timeout.com/london/film/david.

44 "Interview: Joel Fendelman and Patrick Daly."

45 "Interview: Joel Fendelman and Patrick Daly."

46 Green, "Muslim/Jewish Film"; Goldblum, "New Movie Deals."

47 Brendan Kelly, "Montreal World Film Festival 2011: A Path across the Cultural Gap," *Montreal Gazette*, 18 August 2011, Nexis Uni.

48 Mautner, "Jewish Film Festival."

49 "Director Joel Fendelman Discusses *David* at the Va. Film Festival," YouTube, 6 November 2011. https://www.youtube.com/watch?reload=9&v=ogFB7frCho8.

Chapter 8   Epilogue

1 Laura E. Adkins, "Ruchie Freier's Fight Exemplifies Orthodox Feminism: Is That a Good Thing?," *Forward*, 2 August 2018, https://forward.com/culture

/film-tv/407203/93-queen-ruchie-freier-documentary-shows-need-for-religious
-feminism/.

2 Jean Bentley, "Paula Eiselt Reveals How She Gained the Trust of Brooklyn's
Hasidic Community in *93Queen*," *IndieWire*, 23 October 2018, https://www
.indiewire.com/2018/10/93-queen-documentary-paula-eiselt-1202011503/.

3 Zainab Iqbal, "She May Not Call Herself a Feminist, but Ruchie Freier Is
Smashing the Patriarchy in Hasidic Brooklyn," *BKLYNER*, 10 October 2018,
https://bklyner.com/she-may-not-call-herself-a-feminist-but-ruchie-freier-is
-smashing-the-patriarchy-in-hasidic-brooklyn/.

4 Avital Chizhik-Goldschmidt, "It Is Incumbent upon Us Orthodox Jews to Tell
Our Stories," *Forward*, 22 June 2019, https://forward.com/life/426137/paula
-eiselt/.

5 Matt Prigge, "'Nobody Wanted This Story': Paula Eiselt and Heidi Reinberg on
Making *93Queen* at IFP Week 2018," *Filmmaker Magazine*, 19 September 2018,
https://filmmakermagazine.com/106022-nobody-wanted-this-story-paula-eiselt
-and-heidi-reinberg-on-making-93queen-at-ifp-week-2018/#.Xjb92Bd7n-Z.

6 Shira Lankin Sheps, "Paula's Story—the Behind the Scenes Journey to *93Queen*,"
Layers Project Magazine, 25 July 2018, https://thelayersprojectmagazine.com
/paulas-story-the-behind-the-scenes-journey-to-93queen/.

7 Chizhik-Goldschmidt, "It Is Incumbent upon Us Orthodox Jews."

8 For a discussion of texts that both represent and challenge the idea that feminism/
women's agency and Orthodoxy are incompatible, see "Feminism and Orthodoxy:
Not an Oxymoron," chapter 2 of my book *Identity Papers: Contemporary
Narratives of American Jewishness* (Albany: SUNY Press, 2011). In *Women of
Valor: Orthodox Jewish Troll Fighters, Crime Writers, and Rock Stars in Contemporary Literature and Culture* (New Brunswick, NJ: Rutgers University Press,
2018), Karen Skinazi counts Freier among contemporary Orthodox women of
valor (137), whom she argues represent "an empowered model of contemporary
womanhood" (221).

9 Verne Gay, "LI filmmaker's *93Queen* Showcases the First All-Female EMT Corps
in a Largely Hasidic Community," *Newsday*, 15 September 2018, https://www
.newsday.com/entertainment/tv/93-queen-documentary-1.21007977.

10 Paula Eiselt, "Paula Eiselt on Birthing Her Hasidic EMS Documentary
93QUEEN at the IFP Documentary Lab," *Filmmaker Magazine*, 25 May 2016,
https://filmmakermagazine.com/98599-paula-eiselt-birthing-her-hasidic-ems
-documentary-93queen-at-the-ifp-documentary-lab/#.Xjc4Zhd7n-Z.

11 Lauren Wissot, "Doc Star of the Month: Judge Ruchie Freier, Paula Eiselt's
93Queen," *Documentary Magazine*, 14 September 2018, https://www.documentary
.org/column/doc-star-month-judge-ruchie-freier-paula-eiselts-93queen.

12 Chizhik-Goldschmidt, "It Is Incumbent upon Us Orthodox Jews."

13 Quoted in Adkins, "Ruchie Freier's Fight Exemplifies Orthodox Feminism."

14 Wissot, "Doc Star of the Month."

15 Josefin Dolsten, "*RBG* Filmmakers Hope to Inspire Ruth Bader Ginsburg's
Millennial Fans," *Jewish Telegraphic Agency*, 30 April 2018, https://www.jta.org
/2018/04/30/culture/rbg-filmmakers-hope-inspire-ruth-bader-ginsburgs
-millennial-fans-new-documentary.

16 Sergio Carmona, "Film Festival Offering Free Screening," *Florida Jewish Journal*,
16 October 2018, https://www.sun-sentinel.com/florida-jewish-journal/news
/miami-dade/fl-jj-miami-jewish-film-festial-rgb-screening-20181024-story.html.

17 Emily Burack, "The RBG Documentary Is Coming to TV," *Kveller*, 13 August 2018, https://www.kveller.com/the-rbg-documentary-is-coming-to-tv/; A. O. Scott, "Review: In *RBG*, the Life and Times of a Beloved and Controversial Supreme Court Justice," *New York Times*, 3 May 2018, https://www.nytimes.com /2018/05/03/movies/rbg-review-documentary.html.

18 Ginsburg regretted her remarks, calling them "ill-advised." See Michael D. Shear, "Ruth Bader Ginsburg Expresses Regret for Criticizing Donald Trump," *New York Times*, 14 July, 2016, https://www.nytimes.com/2016/07/15/us/politics/ruth -bader-ginsburg-donald-trump.html.

19 See, for example, "From Benjamin to Brandeis to Breyer: Is There a Jewish Seat on the United States Supreme Court?" and "Three Brave Jewish Women," in Ruth Bader Ginsburg, with Mary Hartnett and Wendy W. Williams, *My Own Words* (New York: Simon and Schuster, 2016).

20 Irin Carmon and Shana Knizhnik, *Notorious RBG: The Life and Times of Ruth Bader Ginsburg* (New York: HarperCollins, 2015), 28.

21 Sam Sokol, "RBG: Judaism Shaped My Life," *Jewish Star*, 11 July 2018, https:// www.thejewishstar.com/stories/rbg-judaism-shaped-my-life,15776.

22 Alison Kaplan Sommer, "Female Empowerment and Pickled Herring: How Ruth Bader Ginsburg Became the Notorious RBG," *Haaretz*, 24 February 2019, https://www.haaretz.com/world-news/.premium-behind-the-scenes-on-the -making-of-the-oscar-nominated-rbg-1.6937494.

23 Stephen Applebaum, "Celebrating the 'Notorious' Ruth Bader Ginsburg," *Jewish Chronicle*, 20 December 2018, https://www.thejc.com/culture/film/ruth-bader -ginsburg-new-documentary-1.474156.

24 "Interview with Betsy West and Julie Cohen," *Intellects*, https://www.intellects.co /betsy-west-and-julie-cohen.

25 Sommer, "Female Empowerment and Pickled Herring."

26 Quoted in Dolsten, "*RBG* Filmmakers Hope to Inspire."

Selected Bibliography

Abrams, Nathan. *The New Jew in Film: Exploring Jewishness and Judaism in Contemporary Cinema*. New Brunswick, NJ: Rutgers University Press, 2012.

Adkins, Laura E. "Ruchie Freier's Fight Exemplifies Orthodox Feminism: Is That a
Good Thing?" *Forward*, 2 August 2018. https://forward.com/culture/film-tv
/407203/93-queen-ruchie-freier-documentary-shows-need-for-religious-feminism/.

Allen, William Rodney, ed. *The Coen Brothers: Interviews*. Jackson: University Press of
Mississippi, 2006.

Avisa, Ilan. *Screening the Holocaust: Cinema's Images of the Unimaginable*. Bloomington: Indiana University Press, 1988.

Aviv, Caryn. "Treyf." *Lilith*, 31 March 1999. Ethnic NewsWatch.

Baron, Lawrence, ed. *The Modern Jewish Experience in World Cinema*. Waltham, MA:
Brandeis University Press, 2011.

Baron, Lawrence. *Projecting the Holocaust into the Present*. Lanham, MD: Rowman
and Littlefield, 2005.

"Barry Levinson: The Journey." Interview by Patrick McGilligan. In *Backstory 5:
Interviews with Screenwriters of the 1990s*, Patrick McGilligan, ed., 113–133.
Berkeley: University of California Press, 2010.

Bartov, Omer. *The "Jew" in Cinema: From "The Golem" to "Don't Touch My Holocaust."*
Bloomington: Indiana University Press, 2005.

Baskind, Samantha. "The Fockerized Jew? Questioning Jewishness as Cool in
American Popular Entertainment." *Shofar: An Interdisciplinary Journal of Jewish
Studies* 25, no. 4 (2007): 3–17.

Bean, Henry. *The Believer: Confronting Jewish Self-Hatred*. New York: Thunder's
Mouth Press, 2002.

Bernardi, Daniel, Murray Pomerance, and Hava Tirosh-Samuelson, eds. *Hollywood's
Chosen People: The Jewish Experience in American Cinema*. Detroit: Wayne State
University Press, 2013.

Bial, Henry. *Acting Jewish: Negotiating Ethnicity on the American Stage and Screen*.
Ann Arbor: University of Michigan Press, 2005.

Black, Dustin Lance. *Milk: The Shooting Script*. New York: Newmarket Press,
2008.

Bolton-Fasman, Judy. "Coming Out in the Classroom." *Tablet*, 12 January 2016, https://www.tabletmag.com/jewish-life-and-religion/196468/coming-out-in-the -classroom.

Boyarin, Daniel. *Unheroic Conduct: The Rise of Heterosexuality and the Invention of the Jewish Man*. Berkeley: University of California Press, 1997.

Boyarin, Daniel, Daniel Itzkovitz, and Ann Pellegrini, eds., *Queer Theory and the Jewish Question*. New York: Columbia University Press, 2003.

Brook, Vincent. *Driven to Darkness: Jewish Émigré Directors and the Rise of Film Noir*. New Brunswick, NJ: Rutgers University Press, 2009.

————, ed. *You Should See Yourself: Jewish Identity in Postmodern American Culture*. New Brunswick, NJ: Rutgers University Press, 2006.

Buhle, Paul, ed. *Jews and American Popular Culture*. Vol. 1, *Movies, Radio and Television*. Westport, CT: Praeger, 2007.

Burr, Ty. "*Protocols* Puts Spotlight on Hate, but Lacks Focus." *Boston Globe*, 18 November 2005. http://archive.boston.com/ae/movies/articles/2005/11/18 /protocols_puts_spotlight_on_hate_but_lacks_focus/.

Carmon, Irin, and Shana Knizhnik. *Notorious RBG: The Life and Times of Ruth Bader Ginsburg*. New York: HarperCollins, 2015.

Carr, Steven. *Hollywood and Anti-Semitism: A Cultural History up to World War II*. Cambridge: Cambridge University Press, 2001.

Catsoulis, Jeannette. "Teachers United." *New York Times*, 14 December 2007. https://www.nytimes.com/2007/12/14/movies/14arra.html.

Chizhik-Goldschmidt, Avital. "It Is Incumbent upon Us Orthodox Jews to Tell Our Stories." *Forward*, 22 June 2019. https://forward.com/life/426137/paula-eiselt/.

Cohen, Debra Nussbaum. "The Sheitel and the Hijab." *New York Jewish Week*, 7 December 2007. Ethnic NewsWatch.

Cohen, Sarah Blacher, ed. *From Hester Street to Hollywood: The Jewish-American Stage and Screen*. Bloomington: Indiana University Press, 1983.

Cunningham, Frank R. *Sidney Lumet: Film and Literary Vision*. Lexington: University Press of Kentucky, 1991.

Desser, David, and Lester D. Friedman. *American Jewish Filmmakers*. 2nd ed. Urbana: University of Illinois Press, 2004.

"Dialogue on Film: Joan Micklin Silver." Interview. *American Film*, May 1989, 22–27.

Dinnerstein, Leonard. *Anti-Semitism in America*. New York: Oxford University Press, 1994.

Doherty, Thomas. *Hollywood and Hitler, 1933–1939*. New York: Columbia University Press, 2013.

Doneson, Judith E. *The Holocaust in American Film*. 2nd ed. Syracuse, NY: Syracuse University Press, 2002.

Dubowski, Sandi Simcha. "Trembling Before G-d." *Conscience*, Spring 2003. http://www.catholicsforchoice.org/wp-content/uploads/2014/01/CONSRelAndArt.pdf.

————. "Trembling on the Road: A Simcha Diary." In *Queer Jews*, edited by David Schneer and Caryn Aviv, 215–223. New York: Routledge, 2002.

Eiselt, Paula. "Paula Eiselt on Birthing Her Hasidic EMS Documentary *93QUEEN* at the IFP Documentary Lab." *Filmmaker*, 25 May 2016. https://filmmakermagazine .com/98599-paula-eiselt-birthing-her-hasidic-ems-documentary-93queen-at-the-ifp -documentary-lab/#.Xjc4Zhd7n-Z.

Emery, Robert, dir. *The Directors: The Films of Barry Levinson*. Media Entertainment, 2000.

Erens, Patricia. *The Jew in American Cinema*. Bloomington: Indiana University Press, 1984.

Faderman, Lillian. *Harvey Milk: His Lives and Death*. New Haven, CT: Yale University Press, 2018.

Faktorovich, Anna. "Interview with Joel Fendelman." *Pennsylvania Literary Journal*, June 2011. Academic Search Complete.

Faludi, Susan. *Backlash: The Undeclared War against American Women*. New York: Crown, 1991.

Farrow, Dylan. "An Open Letter from Dylan Farrow." *New York Times*, 1 February 2014. https://kristof.blogs.nytimes.com/2014/02/01/an-open-letter-from -dylan-farrow/.

Friedman, Lester D. *Hollywood's Image of the Jew*. New York: Frederick Ungar, 1982.

Gabler, Neal. *An Empire of Their Own: How the Jews Invented Hollywood*. New York: Anchor, 1988.

Gertel, Elliot. "John Turturro's Sensitivity to Jewish Culture." *Jewish Currents*, 6 March 2015. https://jewishcurrents.org/john-turturros-sensitivity-to-jewish -culture/.

Ginsburg, Ruth Bader, with Mary Hartnett and Wendy W. Williams. *My Own Words*. New York: Simon and Schuster, 2016.

Glinter, Ezra. "I Can't Avoid Woody's Abuse Saga. Neither Can You." *Forward*, 14 February 2014. Ethnic NewsWatch.

Goldman, Eric A. *The American Jewish Story through Cinema*. Austin: University of Texas Press, 2013.

Hall, Jeanne Lynn. "Opposites Attract: Politics and Romance in *The Way We Were* and *Speechless*." *Quarterly Review of Film and Video* 23, no. 2 (2006): 155–169.

Hanlon, Dennis. "Does Anyone Have the Right to Say, 'I Don't Care'? Resistance and Reverence at *Schindler's List*." *Film and History* 39, no. 1 (2009): 53–65.

Harris, Mark. "Twilight of the Tummlers." *New York Magazine*, 24 May 2009, https://nymag.com/movies/features/56930/.

Harvey, Dennis. "*David*." *Variety*, 29 August 2011.

Herman, Felicia. "The Way She *Really* Is: Images of Jews and Women in the Films of Barbra Streisand." In *Talking Back: Images of Jewish Women in American Popular Culture*, edited by Joyce Antler, 171–190. Hanover, NH: Brandeis University Press, 1998.

Hoberman, J., and Jeffrey Shandler. *Entertaining America: Jews, Movies, and Broadcasting*. Princeton, NJ: Princeton University Press, 2003.

Hoffman, Warren. *The Passing Game: Queering Jewish American Culture*. Syracuse, NY: Syracuse University Press, 2009.

hooks, bell. "The Oppositional Gaze: Black Female Spectators." In *Reel to Real: Race, Sex, and Class at the Movies*, 197–213. New York: Routledge, 1996.

"Interview: Joel Fendelman and Patrick Daly about *David*." 2011 https://www.david -themovie.com/#press-section.

"Interview with Betsy West and Julie Cohen." *Intellects*. https://www.intellects.co /betsy-west-and-julie-cohen.

Kabakov, Miryam. *"Romeo and Juliet in Yiddish*: An Interview with the Filmmaker."
TC Jewfolk, 14 March 2011. https://tcjewfolk.com/romeo-juliet-yiddish-interview
-filmmaker/.

Kael, Pauline. "The Artist as a Young Comedian," *New Yorker*, 9 February 1976. In *The Age of Movies: Selected Writings of Pauline Kael*, edited by Sanford Schwartz, 520–524. New York: Library of America, 2011.

Kaufman, David E. *Jewhooing the Sixties: American Celebrity and Jewish Identity.* Waltham, MA: Brandeis University Press, 2012.

Kozloff, Sarah, "Empathy and the Cinema of Engagement: Reevaluating the Politics of Film." *Projections* 7, no. 2 (2013): 1–40.

Laurents, Arthur. *Original Story by Arthur Laurents: A Memoir of Broadway and Hollywood.* New York: Alfred A. Knopf, 2000.

Lebow, Alisa S. *First Person Jewish.* Minneapolis: University of Minnesota Press, 2008.

Levin, Marc. Website. Blog 3: "Words Matter." 14 October 2005. https://thinkfilm
.blogs.com/protocols_of_zion/2005/10/blog_3_words_ma.html.

Levinson, Barry. "Baltimore, My Baltimore." *New York Times*, 14 November 1999. https://archive.nytimes.com/www.nytimes.com/library/film/111499levinson-film
.html.

Levy, Emanuel. *Cinema of Outsiders: The Rise of American Independent Film.* New York: New York University Press, 1999.

Litvak, Joseph. *The Un-Americans: Jews, the Blacklist, and Stoolpigeon Culture.* Durham, NC: Duke University Press, 2009.

Loshitzsky, Yosefa, ed. *Spielberg's Holocaust: Critical Perspectives on "Schindler's List."* Bloomington: Indiana University Press, 2000.

Margolis, Rebecca. "New Yiddish Film and the Transvernacular." *In Geveb: A Journal of Jewish Studies*, 18 December 2016. https://ingeveb.org/articles/new-yiddish-film
-and-the-transvernacular.

McBride, Joseph. *Steven Spielberg: A Biography.* 2nd ed. London: Faber and Faber, 2011. E-book.

McDonald, Tamar Jeffers. *Romantic Comedy: Boy Meets Girl Meets Genre.* London: Wallflower, 2007.

Meyers, Helene. *Identity Papers: Contemporary Narratives of American Jewishness.* Albany: SUNY Press, 2011.

Mintz, Alan. *Popular Culture and the Shaping of Holocaust Memory in America.* Seattle: University of Washington Press, 2001.

Montañez Smukler, Maya. *Liberating Hollywood: Women Directors and the Feminist Reform of 1970s American Cinema.* New Brunswick, NJ: Rutgers University Press, 2019.

Mulvey, Laura. "Visual Pleasure and Narrative Cinema." *Screen* 16, no. 3 (1975): 6–18.

Nichols, Mary. P. *Reconstructing Woody: Art, Love, and Life in the Films of Woody Allen.* Lanham, MD: Rowman and Littlefield, 1998.

Nussbaum, Emily. *I Like to Watch: Arguing My Way through the TV Revolution.* New York: Random House, 2019.

"Opening Shots: Janeane Garofalo's Guilty Pleasures." *Film Comment*, 1 March 2003. Performing Arts Periodicals.

Palmer, R. Barton. *Joel and Ethan Coen.* Urbana: University of Illinois Press, 2004.

Pfefferman, Naomi. "Spike Lee: The Jewish Character in *BlacKkKlansman* Added a Lot of 'Complexity' to the Film." *Jewish Telegraphic Agency*, 12 February 2019. https://www.jta.org/2019/02/12/culture/spike-lee-the-jewish-character-in -blackkklansman-added-a-lot-of-complexity-to-the-film.

Plotkin, Janis, Deborah Kaufman, Sam Ball, Peter Jacobson, and Caroline Libresco, eds. *Independent Jewish Film: A Resource Guide*. 4th ed. San Francisco: San Francisco Jewish Film Festival, 2000.

Pogrebin, Letty Cottin. *Deborah, Golda, and Me: Being Female and Jewish in America*. New York: Crown, 1991.

Prell, Riv-Ellen. "A Serious Man in Situ: 'Fear and Loathing in St. Louis Park.'" *AJS Review* 35, no. 2 (2011). Ethnic NewsWatch.

Prell, Riv-Ellen. *Fighting to Become Americans: Assimilation and the Trouble between Jewish Women and Jewish Men*. Boston: Beacon Press, 1999.

Prigge, Matt, "'Nobody Wanted This Story': Paula Eiselt and Heidi Reinberg on Making *93Queen* at IFP Week 2018." *Filmmaker Magazine*, 19 September 2018. https://filmmakermagazine.com/106022-nobody-wanted-this -story-paula-eiselt-and-heidi-reinberg-on-making-93queen-at-ifp-week-2018/# .Xjb92Bd7n-Z.

Rapf, Joanna E., ed. *Sidney Lumet: Interviews*. Jackson: University Press of Mississippi, 2006.

Rapping, Elayne. "Liberation in Chains: 'The Woman Question' in Hollywood." *Cinéaste* 17, no. 1 (1989). JStor.

Renov, Michael. "Introduction: The Truth about Non-fiction." In *Theorizing Documentary*, edited by Michael Renov, 1–11. New York: Routledge, 1993.

Renov, Michael, and Vincent Brook, eds. *From Shtetl to Stardom: Jews and Hollywood*. West Lafayette, IN: Purdue University Press, 2017.

Rich, B. Ruby. *New Queer Cinema: The Director's Cut*. Durham, NC: Duke University Press, 2013.

Rich, Katey. "Interview: Woody Allen and the Cast of *Whatever Works*." *Cinema-Blend*, 17 June 2009. https://www.cinemablend.com/new/Interview-Woody-Allen -Cast-Whatever-Works-13604.html.

Rogin, Michael. *Blackface, White Noise: Jewish Immigrants in the Hollywood Melting Pot*. Berkeley: University of California Press, 1996.

Rosen, Alan. "Teach Me Gold: Pedagogy and Memory in *The Pawnbroker*." *Prooftexts* 22, no. 1–2 (2002): 77–117.

Rosenberg, Joel. "Jewish Experience on Film—An American Overview." *American Jewish Yearbook* 96 (1996): 3–50. http://www.ajcarchives.org/AJC_DATA/Files /1996_3_SpecialArticles.pdf.

Rosenberg, Warren. "Coming Out of the Ethnic Closet: Jewishness in the Films of Barry Levinson." *Shofar* 22, no. 1 (2003): 29–43. Ethnic NewsWatch.

Rosenzweig, Laura B. *Hollywood Spies: The Undercover Surveillance of Nazis in Los Angeles*. New York: New York University Press, 2017.

Rowin, Michael. "Review: Match Point: Stefan Schaefer and Diane Crespo's *Arranged*." *Indiewire*, 11 December 2007. https://www.indiewire.com/2007/12 /review-match-point-stefan-schaefer-and-diane-crespos-arranged-73361/.

Schifrin, Daniel. "Identity Crisis: With the New Film 'School Ties,' a Hollywood Producer-Director Team Explores Anti-Semitism and the Need to Fit In." *Baltimore Jewish Times*, 18 September 1992. Ethnic NewsWatch.

Schwarzbaum, Lisa. "A World of Difference." *Entertainment Weekly*, 26 November 1999. Academic Search Complete.

Shilts, Randy. *The Mayor of Castro Street: The Life and Times of Harvey Milk*. New York: St. Martin's Press, 1982.

Skinazi, Karen. *Women of Valor: Orthodox Jewish Troll Fighters, Crime Writers, and Rock Stars in Contemporary Literature and Culture*. New Brunswick, NJ: Rutgers University Press, 2018.

Sklar, Robert. *Movie-Made America: A Cultural History of American Movies*. Revised and updated edition. New York: Vintage Books, 1994.

Smith, Craig V. "Darkness Visible: The Politics of Being Seen from Ellison to *Zebrahead*." *Canadian Review of American Studies* 26, no. 1 (1996). Academic Search Complete.

Sommer, Alison Kaplan. "Female Empowerment and Pickled Herring: How Ruth Bader Ginsburg Became the Notorious RBG." *Haaretz*, 24 February 2019. https://www.haaretz.com/world-news/.premium-behind-the-scenes-on-the -making-of-the-oscar-nominated-rbg-1.6937494.

Stavans, Ilan. "I Found It at the Movies." In *Singer's Typewriter and Mine: Reflections on Jewish Culture*, 77–81. Lincoln: University of Nebraska Press, 2012.

Stephens, Gregory. "*Zebrahead*." *Interrace*, 31 July 1994. Ethnic NewsWatch.

Tieber, Claus. "The Way He Wrote: Dalton Trumbo and Sixteen Unused Pages for *The Way We Were*." *Film International* 8, no. 4 (2010): 51–64.

Tolsky, Molly. "Talking with Zach Braff, Kate Hudson and Mandy Patinkin of *Wish I Was Here*." *Kveller*, 24 July 2014. https://www.kveller.com/talking-with-zach-braff -kate-hudson-mandy-patinkin-of-wish-i-was-here/.

Turan, Kenneth. "Ten Great Jewish American Films." *Moment*, May/June 2010. Ethnic NewsWatch.

Urwand, Ben. *The Collaboration: Hollywood's Pact with Hitler*. Cambridge, MA: Harvard University Press, 2013.

Vernasco, Lucy. "Why I Walked Out Halfway through the New Zach Braff Movie." *Bitch*, 28 July 2014. https://www.bitchmedia.org/post/wish-i-wasn%E2%80%99t -there-why-i-walked-out-halfway-through-the-zach-braff-movie.

Wasson, Sam. *Paul on Mazursky*. Middletown, CT: Wesleyan University Press, 2011. E-book.

Waugh, Thomas. "Walking on Tippy Toes: Lesbian and Gay Liberation Documentary of the Post-Stonewall Period 1969–1984." In *Between the Sheets, in the Streets: Queer, Lesbian, Gay Documentary*. edited by Chris Holmlund and Cynthia Fuchs. Minneapolis: University of Minnesota Press, 1997.

Weinraub, Bernard. "The Talk of Hollywood; Anti-Semitism Film Strikes a Chord with Its Producers." *New York Times*, 14 September 1992. https://www.nytimes .com/1992/09/14/movies/the-talk-of-hollywood-anti-semitism-film-strikes-a -chord-with-its-producers.html.

Weiser, Benjamin. "Pine Bush School District Settles Anti-Semitism Suit for $4.48 Million." *New York Times*, 29 June 2015. https://www.nytimes.com/2015/06/30 /nyregion/pine-bush-school-district-anti-semitism-suit.html.

Weiser, Benjamin, and Nate Schweber. "Swastika on a Bathroom Wall: Anti-Semitism Still Plagues Upstate School District." *New York Times*, 1 March 2019. https://www .nytimes.com/2019/03/01/nyregion/pine-bush-ny-schools-anti-semitism.html.

Weissman, Gary. *Fantasies of Witnessing: Postwar Efforts to Experience the Holocaust*. Ithaca, NY: Cornell University Press, 2004.

Whitfield, Stephen. "Making Fragmentation Familiar: Barry Levinson's *Avalon*." In *Studies in Contemporary Jewry*. Vol. 14, *Coping with Life and Death: Jewish Families in the Twentieth Century*, edited by Peter Y. Medding, 49–64. New York: Oxford University Press, 1998.

Wissot, Lauren. "Doc Star of the Month: Judge Ruchie Freier, Paula Eiselt's *93Queen*." *Documentary Magazine*, 14 September 2018. https://www.documentary.org /column/doc-star-month-judge-ruchie-freier-paula-eiselts-93queen.

Wood, Robin. "The Spectres Emerge in Daylight." *Cineaction* 43 (1997). Performing Arts Periodicals.

Zierler, Wendy. *Movies and Midrash: Popular Film and Jewish Religious Conversation*. Albany: SUNY Press, 2017.

Index

About the Author

HELENE MEYERS is a professor of English and McManis University Chair at Southwestern University. She is the author of *Femicidal Fears: Narratives of the Female Gothic Experience* (2001), *Reading Michael Chabon* (2010), and *Identity Papers: Contemporary Narratives of American Jewishness* (2011).